GAUTAMA BUDDHA
AND
ORIGIN OF BUDDHISM

Encyclopaedic History of India Series

GAUTAMA BUDDHA AND ORIGIN OF BUDDHISM

Dr. Mahesh Vikram Singh
Professor, Deptt. of History
Mahatma Gandhi Kashi Vidyapeeth
Varanasi (UP)

Dr. Brij Bhushan Shrivastava
Head of Deptt., Ancient History, Archeology & Culture
SMMTPG College, Ballia (UP)

CENTRUM PRESS
NEW DELHI-110002 (INDIA)

CENTRUM PRESS
H.O.: 4360/4, Ansari Road, Daryaganj,
New Delhi-110002 (India)
Tel: 23278000, 23261597, 23255577, 23286875
B.O.: No. 1015, Ist Main Road, BSK IIIrd Stage,
IIIrd Phase, IIIrd Block, Bangalore-560085 (INDIA)
Tel: 080-41723429
Email: centrumpress@gmail.com
Visit us at: www.centrumpress.com

Gautama Buddha and Origin of Buddhism

First Edition, 2011

ISBN 978-93-80836-58-4

PRINTED IN INDIA

Printed at Mehra Offset Press, Delhi

प्रो. विपिन चंद्रा
अध्यक्ष
Prof. Bipan Chandra
Chairman

नेशनल बुक ट्रस्ट, इंडिया
नेहरू भवन
5 इंस्टीट्यूशनल एरिया, फेज़-II, वसंत कुंज, नई दिल्ली-110 070
फोन/ Phone: 011-26121880 फैक्स/ Fax: 011-26121883

NATIONAL BOOK TRUST, INDIA
Nehru Bhawan
5 Institutional Area, Phase II, Vasant Kunj, New Delhi-110 070
ई-मेल / E-mail: chairman@nbtindia.org.in
वेबसाइट / Website: www.nbtindia.org.in

FOREWORD

The term 'history' is derived from the Greek word 'historia' that means knowledge acquired through investigation. Obviously, this knowledge can be correct if the method of investigation is objective and not vitiated by any kind of bias. In other words, if the study of human past is comprehensive and obtained through scientific inquiry, it can provide perspective on the present day problems and help one plan for the future.

A true historian has to identify the sources that can be most useful in a given context. Documents, coins, archaeology, anthropology, geography, travel accounts, oral traditions, mythology and so on can be useful but they can be used only after their veracity is tested and they are critically examined. They should be checked and counter-checked.

Over the centuries, one finds the study and writing of history vitiated by biases. There are numerous instances in which historical data have been distorted to support or oppose certain preconceived ideas and purposes. Strictly speaking such history is just like fiction to accord with preconceived notions and serve some ulterior purposes.

The study of the past has never been static. Conclusions go on changing because of the discovery of new materials and tools of investigation. To give a concrete example, the carbon 14 or radiocarbon dating test has revolutionized the study of civilizations and settlements, especially of prehistoric times, for which written documents, coins, etc. are seldom available. This method has enabled historians to determine more accurately than before the time period of a particular civilization or settlement. This method was discovered only 70 years ago by American scientists.

In our country, excavations brought to light the Indus Valley Civilization and its various features, hitherto unknown. Similarly, no complete text of Kautilya's Arthashastra was available before it was discovered by Shamasastry, the chief of the Mysore Government Oriental Library in the first decade of the last century. Likewise, people's knowledge of the history of the Buddhist period got extended after excavations at Sarnath and the ruins of the Asokan period at Patna. In the future, if the Harappan inscriptions are deciphered, our knowledge of the Indus Valley Civilization will increase enormously. All these instances underline the fact that our knowledge of history is never static and its frontiers go on extending.

In the light of what has been said above the encyclopedic history is going to be of great help to students interested in Indian history. It is comprehensive and as far as possible free from biases. It includes the latest materials, and objective conclusions.

Prof . Bipan Chandra
Professor Emeritus, JNU
Chairman, National Book Trust, India

Contents

Preface

The people of India have had a continuous civilization since 2500 B.C., when the inhabitants of the Indus River valley developed an urban culture based on commerce and sustained by agricultural trade. This civilization declined around 1500 B.C., probably due to ecological changes. During the second millennium B.C., pastoral, Aryan-speaking tribes migrated from the northwest into the subcontinent. As they settled in the middle Ganges River valley, they adapted to antecedent cultures.

The political map of ancient and medieval India was made up of myriad kingdoms with fluctuating boundaries. In the 4th and 5th centuries A.D., northern India was unified under the Gupta Dynasty. During this period, known as India's Golden Age, Hindu culture and political administration reached new heights. Islam spread across the Indian subcontinent over a period of 500 years. In the 10th and 11th centuries, Turks and Afghans invaded India and established sultanates in Delhi. In the early 16th century, descendants of Genghis Khan swept across the Khyber Pass and established the Mughal (Mogul) Dynasty, which lasted for 200 years. From the 11th to the 15th centuries, southern India was dominated by Hindu Chola and Vijayanagar Dynasties. During this time, the two systems—the prevailing Hindu and Muslim—mingled, leaving lasting cultural influences on each other.

The first British outpost in South Asia was established in 1619 at Surat on the northwestern coast. Later in the century, the East India Company opened permanent trading stations at Madras, Bombay, and Calcutta, each under the protection of native rulers. The British expanded their influence from these footholds until, by the 1850s, they controlled most of present-day India, Pakistan, and Bangladesh. In 1857, a rebellion in north India led by mutinous Indian soldiers caused the British Parliament to transfer all political power from the East India Company to the Crown. Great Britain began administering most of India directly while controlling the rest through treaties with local rulers.

In the late 1800s, the first steps were taken toward self-government in British India with the appointment of Indian councillors to advise the British viceroy and the establishment of provincial councils with Indian members; the British subsequently widened participation in legislative councils. Beginning in 1920, Indian leader Mohandas K. Gandhi transformed the Indian National Congress political party into a mass movement to campaign against British colonial rule.

—Authors

1

Introduction

Buddhism was founded by Gautama Buddha who had been given the name Siddhartha by his parents. His father was Suddhodana, the chief of the Sakya clan and mother was Maya, princess of the Koliya clan. He was born in the Lumbini grove (modem Rumindei) in Nepal Tarai. We know this through an inscribed pillar of Asoka. The date of birth of Buddha is a matter of dispute but most of the scholars place it about 566 B.C. traditions describe it, he was deeply affected by the sight of an old man, a sick person, a dead body and an ascetic. The misery of the human life cast a deep spell on Gautama. In order to find a solution to the misery of-mankind, he left home at the age of 29. Gautama spent six years as a wandering ascetic. From a sage named Alara Kalama he learned the technique of meditation and the teachings of the upanishadas. Since these teachings did not lead Gautama to the final liberation, he left him with five Brahmana ascetics.

He practised rigid austerities and resorted to different kinds of self torture to find the truth. Ultimately abandoning this he went to Uruvela (near, modem Bodh Gaya on the banks of river) and sat under a pipal tree (Bodhi tree). Here he attained the supreme knowledge (Enlightenment) on the 49th day of his continuous meditation. Since then he was called the Buddha (the enlightened one). From here he proceeded to the Deer park at Sarnath near Varinasi and gave his first sermon which is known as 'Dharmachakra Pravartana' (setting in motion the wheel of Dharma).

Asvajit, Upali, Mogallana, Sari-putra and Anada were the first five disciples of Buddha. Buddha formed the foundations of the Buddhist Sangha. He preached most of his sermons at Sravasti.

Anathapindika the rich merchant of Sravasti became his follower and made liberal donations to the Buddhist order. Soon he started visiting various places to propagate his teachings. He visited Sarnath, Mathura, Rajgir, Gaya and Padiputra. Kings like Bimbisara, Ajatasatru (Magadha), Prasenajita (Kosala) and Udayana (Kausarnbi) accepted his doctrines and became his disciples. He also visited Kapilavastu and converted his foster mother and his son Rahula to his faith. At the age of 80 (486 B.C.) he died at Kusinagaraq Casia in Deoria district in Uttar Pradesh), the capital of the Mallas. Let us examine the teachings of Buddha which became popular and gave a new direction to the religious ideas of the time.

Gautama Buddha

Siddhartha Gautama was a spiritual teacher in the north eastern region of the Indian subcontinent who founded Buddhism. In most Buddhist traditions, he is regarded as the Supreme *Buddha* (Sammasambuddha) of our age, "Buddha" meaning "awakened one" or "the enlightened one.". In Hinduism, he is considered to be the ninth avatar of God Vishnu. The time of his birth and death are uncertain: most early 20th-century historians dated his lifetime as c. 563 BCE to 483 BCE; more recently, however, at a specialist symposium on this question, the majority of those scholars who presented definite opinions gave dates within 20 years either side of 400 BCE for the Buddha's death, with others supporting earlier or later dates. Gautama, also known as *Uakyamuni* or *Shakyamuni* ("sage of the Shakyas"), is the key figure in Buddhism, and accounts of his life, discourses, and monastic rules are believed by Buddhists to have been summarized after his death and memorized by his followers. Various collections of teachings attributed to Gautama were passed down by oral tradition, and first committed to writing about 400 years later. Early Western scholarship tended to accept the biography of the Buddha presented in the Buddhist scriptures as largely historical, but currently "scholars are increasingly reluctant to make unqualified claims about the historical facts of the Buddha's life and teachings."

Life

The primary sources of information regarding Siddhartha Gautama's life are the Buddhist texts. According to these, the

Buddha and his monks spent four months each year discussing and rehearsing his teachings, and after his death his monks set about preserving them. A council was held shortly after his death, and another was held a century later. At these councils the monks attempted to establish and authenticate the extant accounts of the life and teachings of the Buddha following systematic rules. They divided the teachings into distinct but overlapping bodies of material, and assigned specific monks to preserve each one. In some cases, essential aspects of teachings attributed to the Buddha were incorporated into stories and chants in an effort to preserve them accurately.

From then on, the teachings were transmitted orally. From internal evidence it seems clear that the oldest texts crystallized into their current form by the time of the second council or shortly after it. The scriptures were not written down until three or four hundred years after the Buddha's death. By this point, the monks had added or altered some material themselves, in particular magnifying the figure of the Buddha.

The ancient Indians were generally not concerned with chronologies, being more focused on philosophy. The Buddhist texts reflect this tendency, providing a clearer picture of what Shakyamuni may have taught than of the dates of the events in his life. These texts contain descriptions of the culture and daily life of ancient India which can be corroborated from the Jain scriptures, and make the Buddha's time the earliest period in Indian history for which significant accounts exist. According to Michael Carrithers, and scholars such as Karen Armstrong, there are good reasons to doubt the traditional account, though, according to Carrithers, the outline of "birth, maturity, renunciation, search, awakening and liberation, teaching, death" must be true.

Conception and Birth

Siddhartha was born in Lumbini and raised in the small kingdom or principality of Kalpasutra, both of which are in modern day Nepal. At the time, a multitude of small city-states existed in Ancient India, called Janapadas. Republics and chiefdoms with diffused political power and limited social stratification, were not uncommon amongst them, and were referred to as gana-sanghas. The Buddha's community does not seem to have had a caste system, and their society was not structured according to

Brahminical theory. It was not a monarchy, and seems to have been structured either as an oligarchy, or as a form of republic. The more egalitarian gana-sangha form of government, as a political alternative to the strongly hierarchical kingdoms, may have influenced the development of the Shramana type Jain and Buddhist sanghas, where monarchies tended toward Vedic Brahmanism.

According to the traditional biography, although not later writers such as Armstrong, his father was King Suddhodana, the leader of Shakya clan, whose capital was Kapilavastu, and who were later annexed by the growing Kingdom of Kosala during the Buddha's lifetime; Gautama was the family name. His mother, Queen Maha Maya (Mayadevi) and Suddhodana's wife, was a Koliyan princess. On the night Siddhartha was conceived, Queen Maya dreamt that a white elephant with six white tusks entered her right side, and ten months later Siddhartha was born. As was the Shakya tradition, when his mother Queen Maya became pregnant, she left Kalpasutra for her father's kingdom to give birth. However, she gave birth on the way, at Lumbini, in a garden beneath a sal tree.

The day of the Buddha's birth is widely celebrated in Theravada countries as Vesak. Various sources hold that the Buddha's mother died at his birth, a few days or seven days later. The infant was given the name Siddhartha (Pail: Siddhatta), meaning "he who achieves his aim". During the birth celebrations, the hermit seer Asita journeyed from his mountain abode and announced that the child would either become a great king (chakravartin) or a great holy man. This occurred after Siddhartha placed his feet in Asita's hair and Asita examined the birthmarks. Suddhodana held a naming ceremony on the fifth day, and invited eight brahmin scholars to read the future. All gave a dual prediction that the baby would either become a great king or a great holy man. Kaundinya (Pail: Kondanna), the youngest, and later to be the first arahant, was the only one who unequivocally predicted that Siddhartha would become a Buddha.

While later tradition and legend characterized Œuddhodana as a hereditary monarch, the descendant of the Solar Dynasty of Ikcvku (Pail: Okkaka), many scholars believe that Uuddhodana was the elected chief of a tribal confederacy.

Early Life and Marriage

Siddhartha, said to have been destined to a luxurious life as a prince, had three palaces (for seasonal occupation) especially built for him. His father, King Œuddhodana, wishing for Siddhartha to be a great king, shielded his son from religious teachings or knowledge of human suffering. Siddhartha was brought up by his mother's younger sister, Maha Pajapati.

As the boy reached the age of 16, his father arranged his marriage to Yauodhara (Pail: Yasodhara), a cousin of the same age. According to the traditional account, in time, she gave birth to a son, Rahula. Siddhartha spent 29 years as a Prince in Kapilavastu. Although his father ensured that Siddhartha was provided with everything he could want or need, Siddhartha felt that material wealth was not the ultimate goal of life.

Departure and Ascetic Life

At the age of 29, Siddhartha left his palace in order to meet his subjects. Despite his father's effort to remove the sick, aged and suffering from the public view, Siddhartha was said to have seen an old man. Disturbed by this, when told that all people would eventually grow old by his charioteer Channa, the prince went on further trips where he encountered, variously, a diseased man, a decaying corpse, and an ascetic. Deeply depressed by these sights, he sought to overcome old age, illness, and death by living the life of an ascetic.

Siddhartha escaped his palace, accompanied by Channa aboard his horse Kanthaka, leaving behind this royal life to become a mendicant. It is said that, "the horse's hooves were muffled by the gods" to prevent guards from knowing the Bodhisatta's departure. This event is traditionally called "The Great Departure". Siddhartha initially went to Rajagaha and began his ascetic life by begging for alms in the street. Having been recognised by the men of King Bimbisara, Bimbisara offered him the throne after hearing of Siddhartha's quest. Siddhartha rejected the offer, but promised to visit his kingdom of Magadha first, upon attaining enlightenment.

Siddhartha left Rajagaha and practised under two hermit teachers. After mastering the teachings of Alara Kalama (Skr. Ara a Kalama), Siddhartha was asked by Kalama to succeed him, but moved on after being unsatisfied with his practices. He then became a student of Udaka Ramaputta (Skr. Udraka Ramaputtra), but although he achieved high levels of meditative consciousness and was asked to succeed Ramaputtra, he was still not satisfied with his path, and moved on.

Siddhartha and a group of five companions led by Kaundinya then set out to take their austerities even further. They tried to find enlightenment through near total deprivation of worldly goods, including food, practising self-mortification. After nearly starving himself to death by restricting his food intake to around a leaf or nut per day, he collapsed in a river while bathing and almost drowned. Siddhartha began to reconsider his path. Then, he remembered a moment in childhood in which he had been watching his father start the season's slowing, and he had fallen into a naturally concentrated and focused state that was blissful and refreshing, the jhana.

Enlightenment

After asceticism and concentrating on meditation and Anapana-sati (awareness of breathing in and out), Siddhartha is said to have discovered what Buddhists call the Middle Way—a path of moderation away from the extremes of self-indulgence and self-mortification. He accepted a little milk and rice pudding from a village girl named Sujata, who wrongly believed him to be the spirit that had granted her a wish, such was his emaciated appearance. Then, sitting under a pipal tree, now known as the Bodhi tree in Bodh Gaya, India, he vowed never to arise until he had found the Truth. Kaundinya and the other four companions, believing that he had abandoned his search and become undisciplined, left. After 49 days meditating, at the age of 35, he attained Enlightenment; according to some traditions, this occurred approximately in the fifth lunar month, and according to others in the twelfth. Gautama, from then on, was known as the *Buddha* or "Awakened One." Buddha is also sometimes translated as "The Enlightened One." Often, he is referred to in Buddhism as Shakyamuni Buddha or "The Awakened One of the Shakya Clan."

At this point, he is believed to have realized complete awakening and insight into the nature and cause of human suffering which was ignorance, along with steps necessary to eliminate it. This was then categorized into 'Four Noble Truths'; the state of supreme liberation—possible for any being—was called Nirvana.

He then allegedly came to possess the Nine Characteristics, which are said to belong to every Buddha.

According to one of the stories in the *Ayacana Sutta* (Samyutta Nikaya VI.1), a scripture found in the Pail and other canons, immediately after his Enlightenment, the Buddha was wondering whether or not he should teach the *Dharma* to human beings. He was concerned that, as human beings were overpowered by greed, hatred and delusion, they would not be able to see the true *dharma*, which was subtle, deep and hard to understand. However, Brahma Sahampati, interceded and asked that he teach the *dharma* to the world, as "there will be those who will understand the *Dharma*". With his great compassion to all beings in the universe, the Buddha agreed to become a teacher.

Formation of the Sangha

After becoming enlightened, two merchants whom the Buddha met, named Tapussa and Bhallika became the first lay disciples. They are given some hairs from the Buddha's head, which are believed to now be enshrined in the Shwe Dagon Temple in Rangoon, Burma. The Buddha intended to visit Asita, and his former teachers, Alara Kalama and Uddaka Ramaputta to explain his findings, but they had already died.

The Buddha thus journeyed to Deer Park near Varanasi (Benares) in northern India, he set in motion the Wheel of Dharma by delivering his first sermon to the group of five companions with whom he had previously sought enlightenment. They, together with the Buddha, formed the first sough, the company of Buddhist monks, and hence, the first formation of Triple Gem (Buddha, Dharma and Sangha) was completed, with Kaundinya becoming the first stream-enterer. All five soon become arahants, and with the conversion of Yasa and fifty four of his friends, the number of arahants swelled to 60 within the first two months. The conversion of the three Kassapa brothers and their 200, 300 and 500 disciples swelled the sangha over 1000, and they were dispatched to explain the dharma to the populace.

It is unknown what the Buddha's mother tongue was, and no conclusive documentation has been made at this point. It is likely that he preached and his teachings were originally preserved in a variety of closely related Middle Indo-Aryan dialects, of which Pail may be a standardization.

Travels and Teaching

For the remaining 45 years of his life, the Buddha is said to have travelled in the Gangetic Plain, in what is now Uttar Pradesh, Bihar and southern Nepal, teaching his doctrine and discipline to an extremely diverse range of people— from nobles to outcaste street sweepers, mass murderers such as Angulimala and cannibals such as Alavaka. This extended to many adherents of rival philosophies and religions. The Buddha founded the community of Buddhist monks and nuns (the *Sangha*) to continue the dispensation after his *Parinirvana* (Pail: Parinibbana) or "complete Nirvana", and made thousands of converts. His religion was open to all races and classes and had no caste structure. He was also subject to attack from opposition religious groups, including attempted murders and framings.

The sangha travelled from place to place in India, expounding the dharma. This occurred throughout the year, except during the four months of the vassana rainy season. Due to the heavy amount of flooding, travelling was difficult, and ascetics of all religions in that time did not travel, since it was more difficult to do so without stepping on submerged animal life, unwittingly killing them. During this period, the sangha would retreat to a monastery, public park or a forest and people would come to them.

The first vassana was spent at Varanasi when the sangha was first formed. After this, he travelled to Rajagaha, the capital of Magadha to visit King Bimbisara, in accordance with his promise after enlightenment. It was during this visit that Sariputta and Mahamoggallana were converted by Assaji, one of the first five disciples; they were to become the Buddha's two foremost disciples. The Buddha then spent the next three seasons at Veluvana Bamboo Grove monastery in Rajagaha, the capital of Magadha. The monastery, which was of a moderate distance from the city centre was donated by Bimbisara.

Upon hearing of the enlightenment, Suddhodana dispatched royal delegations to ask the Buddha to return to Kapilavastu. Nine delegations were sent in all, but the delegates joined the sangha and became arahants. Neglecting worldly matters, they did not convey their message. The tenth delegation, led by Kaludayi, a childhood friend, resulted in the message being successfully conveyed as well as becoming an arahant. Since it was not the vassana, the Buddha agreed, and two years after his enlightenment, took a two month journey to Kapilavastu by foot, preaching the dharma along the way. Upon his return, the royal palace had prepared the midday meal, but since no specific invitation had come, the sangha went for an alms round in Kapilavastu. Hearing this, Suddhodana hastened to approach the Buddha, stating "Ours is the warrior lineage of Mahamassata, and not a single warrior has gone seeking alms", to which the Buddha replied

That is not the custom of your royal lineage. But it is the custom of my Buddha lineage. Several thousands of Buddhas have gone by seeking alms Suddhodana invited the sangha back to the royal palace for the meal, followed by a dharma talk, after which he became a sotapanna. During the visit, many members of the royal family joined the sangha. His cousins Ananda and Anuruddha were to become two of his five chief disciples. His son Rahula also joined the sangha at the age of seven, and was one of the ten chief disciples. His half-brother Nanda also joined the sangha and became an arahant. Another cousin Devadatta also became a monk although he later became an enemy and tried to kill the Buddha on multiple occasions.

Of his disciples, Sariputta, Mahamoggallana, Mahakasyapa, Ananda and Anuruddha comprised the five chief disciples. His ten foremost disciples were completed by the quintet of Upali, Subhoti, Rahula, Mahakaccana and Punna.

In the fifth vassana, the Buddha was staying at Mahavana near Vesali. Hearing of the impending death of Suddhodana, the Buddha went to his father and preached the dharma, and Suddhodana became an arahant prior to death. The death and cremation led to the creation of the order of nuns. Buddhist texts record that he was reluctant to ordain women as nuns. His foster mother Maha Pajapati approached him asking to join the sangha, but the Buddha refused, and began the journey from Kapilavastu back to Rajagaha. Maha Pajapati was so intent on renouncing the world that she led a group of royal Sakyan and Koliyan ladies, following the sangha to Rajagaha. The Buddha eventually accepted them five years after the formation of the Sangha on the grounds that their capacity for enlightenment was equal to that of men, but he gave them certain additional rules (Vinaya) to follow. This occurred after Ananda interceded on their behalf. Yasodhara also became a nun, with both becoming arahants.

During his ministry, Devadatta (who was not an arahant) frequently tried to undermine the Buddha. At one point Devadatta asked the Buddha to stand aside to let him lead the sangha. The Buddha declined, and stated that Devadatta's actions did not reflect on the Triple Gem, but on him alone. Devadatta conspired with Prince Ajatasattu, son of Bimbisara, so that they would kill and usurp the Buddha and Bimbisara respectively. Devadatta attempted three times to kill the Buddha. The first attempt involved the hiring of a group of archers, whom upon meeting the Buddha became disciples. A second attempt followed when Devadatta attempted to roll a large boulder down a hill. It hit another rock and splintered, only grazing the Buddha in the foot. A final attempt by plying an elephant with alcohol and setting it loose again failed. Failing this, Devadatta attempted to cause a schism in the sangha, by proposing extra restrictions on the vinaya. When the Buddha declined, Devadatta started a breakaway order, criticising the Buddha's laxity. At first, he managed to convert some of the bhikkhus, but Sariputta and Mahamoggallana expounded the dharma to them and succeeded in winning them back.

When the Buddha reached the age of 55, he made Ananda his chief attendant.

Death/Mahaparinirvana

According to the Mahaparinibbana Sutta of the Pail canon, at the age of 80, the Buddha announced that he would soon reach Parinirvana or the final deathless state abandoning the earthly body. After this, the Buddha ate his last meal, which he had received as an offering from a blacksmith named Cunda. Falling violently ill, Buddha instructed his attendant Ananda to convince Cunda that the meal eaten at his place had nothing to do with his passing and that his meal would be a source of the greatest merit as it provided the last meal for a Buddha. Mettanando and von Hinuber argue that the Buddha died of mesenteric infarction, a symptom of old age, rather than food poisoning. The precise contents of the Buddha's final meal are not clear, due to variant scriptural traditions and ambiguity over the translation of certain significant terms; the Theravada tradition generally believes that the Buddha was offered some kind of pork, while the Mahayana tradition believes that the Buddha consumed some sort of truffle or other mushroom.

The Mahayana Vimalakirti Sutra claims, in Chapter 3, that the Buddha doesn't really become ill or old but purposely presents such an appearance only to teach those born into samsara about the impermanence and pain of defiled worlds and to encourage them to strive for Nirvana.

"Reverend Ananda, the Tathagatas have the body of the Dharma—not a body that is sustained by material food. The Tathagatas have a transcendental body that has transcended all mundane qualities. There is no injury to the body of a Tathgata, as it is rid of all defilements. The body of a Tathagata is uncompounded and free of all formative activity. Reverend Ananda, to believe there can be illness in such a body is irrational and unseemly!' Nevertheless, since the Buddha has appeared during the time of the five corruptions, he disciplines living beings by acting lowly and humble."

Ananda protested Buddha's decision to enter Parinirvana in the abandoned jungles of Culinary (present-day Kushinagar, India) of the Malla kingdom. Buddha, however, reminded Ananda how Kushinara was a land once ruled by a righteous wheel-turning king that resounded with joy:

Kusavati, Ananda, resounded unceasingly day and night with ten sounds—the trumpeting of elephants, the neighing of horses, the rattling of chariots, the beating of drums and tabours, music and song, cheers, the clapping of hands, and cries of "Eat, drink, and be merry!"

Buddha then asked all the attendant Bhikshus to clarify any doubts or questions they had. They had none. He then finally entered Parinirvana. The Buddha's final words were, "All composite things pass away. Strive for your own liberation with diligence." The Buddha's body was cremated and the relics were placed in monuments or stupas, some of which are believed to have survived until the present. For example, The Temple of the Tooth or "Dalada Maligawa" in Sri Lanka is the place where the relic of the right tooth of Buddha is kept at present.

According to the Pail historical chronicles of Sri Lanka, the Dpavasa and Mahvacsa, the coronation of Ashoka (Pail: Ashoka) is 218 years after the death of Buddha. According to one Mahayana record in Chinese, the coronation of Hooka is 116 years after the death of Buddha. Therefore, the time of Buddha's passing is either

486 BCE according to The ravada record or 383 BCE according to Mahayana record. However, the actual date traditionally accepted as the date of the Buddha's death in The ravada countries is 544 or 543 BCE, because the reign of Hooka was traditionally reckoned to be about 60 years earlier than current estimates.

At his death, the Buddha told his disciples to follow no leader, but to follow his teachings (dharma). However, at the First Buddhist Council, Mahakasyapa was held by the sangha as their leader, with the two chief disciples Mahamoggallana and Sariputta having died before the Buddha.

Physical Characteristics

Buddha is perhaps one of the few sages for whom we have mention of his rather impressive physical characteristics. A kshatriya by birth, he had military training in his upbringing, and by Shakyan tradition was required to pass tests to demonstrate his worthiness as a warrior in order to marry. He had a strong enough body to be noticed by one of the kings and was asked to join his army as a general. He is also believed by Buddhists to have "the 32 Signs of the Great Man".

The Brahmin Sonadanda described him as "handsome, good-looking, and pleasing to the eye, with a most beautiful complexion. He has a godlike form and countenance, he is by no means unattractive."

"It is wonderful, truly marvellous, how serene is the good Gotama's appearance, how clear and radiant his complexion, just as the golden jujube in autumn is clear and radiant, just as a palm-tree fruit just loosened from the stalk is clear and radiant, just as an adornment of red gold wrought in a crucible by a skilled goldsmith, deftly beaten and laid on a yellow-cloth shines, blazes and glitters, even so, the good Gotama's senses are calmed, his complexion is clear and radiant."

A disciple named Vakkali, who later became an Arahant, was so obsessed by Buddha's physical presence that Buddha had to tell him to stop and reminded Vakkali to know Buddha through the Dhamma and not physical appearances.

Although the Buddha was not represented in human form until around the 1st century CE, the physical characteristics of fully-enlightened Buddhas are described by the Buddha in the

Digha Nikaya's *LakkhaGa Sutta*. In addition, the Buddha's physical appearance is described by Yasodhara to their son Rahula upon the Buddha's first post-Enlightenment return to his former princely palace in the non-canonical Pail devotional hymn, *Narasiha Geisha* ("The Lion of Men").

Many Westerners associate the name "Buddha" with figurine depictions of a certain fat, bald, smiling person. This is inaccurate, as the person in these figurines is not Buddha at all, but Budai, a Chinese Buddhist monk who lived in the 10th century CE.

Teachings

Some scholars believe that some portions of the Pail Canon and the Agamas could contain the actual substance of the historical teachings (and possibly even the words) of the Buddha. This is not the case for the later Mahayana Sutras. The scriptural works of Early Buddhism precede the Mahayana works chronologically, and are treated by many Western scholars as the main credible source for information regarding the actual historical teachings of Gautama Buddha. Some of the fundamentals of the teachings of Gautama Buddha are:

- The Four Noble Truths: that suffering is an inherent part of existence; that the origin of suffering is ignorance and the main symptoms of that ignorance are attachment and craving; that attachment and craving can be ceased; and that following the Noble Eightfold Path will lead to the cessation of attachment and craving and therefore suffering.
- The Noble Eightfold Path: right understanding, right thought, right speech, right action, right livelihood, right effort, right mindfulness, and right concentration.
- Dependent origination: that any phenomenon 'exists' only because of the 'existence' of other phenomena in a complex web of cause and effect covering time past, present and future. Because all things are thus conditioned and transient (anicca), they have no real independent identity (anatta).
- Rejection of the infallibility of accepted scripture: Teachings should not be accepted unless they are borne out by our experience and are praised by the wise.

- *Anicca* (Sanskrit: *anitya*): That all things are impermanent.
- *Dukkha* (Sanskrit: *dukha*): That all beings suffer from all situations due to unclear mind.
- *Anatta* (Sanskrit: *anatman*): That the perception of a constant "self" is an illusion.

However, in some Mahayana schools, these points have come to be regarded as more or less subsidiary. There is some disagreement amongst various schools of Buddhism over more esoteric aspects of Buddha's teachings, and also over some of the disciplinary rules for monks.

According to tradition, the Buddha emphasized ethics and correct understanding. He questioned the average person's notions of divinity and salvation. He stated that there is no intermediary between mankind and the divine; distant gods are subjected to karma themselves in decaying heavens; and the Buddha is solely a guide and teacher for the sentient beings who must tread the path of Nirvga (Pail: Nibbana) themselves to attain the spiritual awakening called *bodhi* and see truth and reality as it is. The Buddhist system of insight and meditation practice is not believed to have been revealed divinely, but by the understanding of the true nature of the mind, which must be discovered by personally treading a spiritual path guided by the Buddha's teachings.

2

Places where Buddha Lived

Four Main Pilgrimage Sites

Gautama Buddha is said to have identified four sites most worthy of pilgrimage for his followers, saying that they would produce a feeling of spiritual urgency. These are:

- Lumbini: birth place (in Nepal)
- Bodh Gaya: the place of his Enlightenment (in the current Mahabodhi Temple).
- Sarnath: (formally Isipathana) where he delivered his first teaching.
- Kusinara: (now Kusinagar, India) where he died (Parinirvana).

The Eight Great Places

In the later commentarial tradition, four other sites are also raised to a special status because Buddha had performed a certain miracle there. These four places, partly through the inclusion in this list of commentarial origin, became important Buddhist pilgrimage sites in ancient India, as the Attha-mahathanani (Pail for 'The Eight Great Places'). It is important to note, however, that some of these events do not occur in the Tipitaka and are thus purely commentarial. The first four of the Eight Great Places are identical to the places mentioned by Buddha:

Lumbini

Lumbinî ("the lovely") is a Buddhist pilgrimage site in the Kapilavastu district of Nepal, near the Indian border. It is the place where Queen Mayadevi is said to have given birth to Siddhartha Gautama, who in turn, as the Buddha Gautama, gave birth to the Buddhist tradition. The Buddha lived between roughly 563 and 483 BCE. Lumbini is one of four magnets for pilgrimage that sprang up in places pivotal to the life of the Buddha, the others being at Kushinagar, Bodh Gaya, and Sarnath.

Lumbini is in the foothills of the Himalaya, 25 km east of the municipality of Kapilavastu, where the Buddha is said to have lived till the age of 29. Kalpasutra is the name of the place in question as well as of the neighbouring district. Lumbini has a number of temples, including the Mayadevi temple, and others under construction. Also here is the Puskarini or Holy Pond-where the Buddha's mother took the ritual dip prior to his birth and where he, too, had his first bath-as well as the remains of Kalpasutra palace. At other sites near Lumbini, earlier Buddhas were, according to tradition, born, achieved ultimate awakening and finally relinquished earthly form.

In Buddha's Time

In the Buddha's time, Lumbini was a park situated between Kapilavastu and Devadaha. It was there that the Buddha was born. A pillar now marks the spot of Ashoka's visit to Lumbini. According to an inscription on the pillar, it was placed there by the people then in charge of the park to commemorate Ashoka's visit and gifts. The park was previously known as Rummindei, two miles north of Bhagavanpura.

In the Sutta Nipata (vs. 683) it is stated that the Buddha was born in a village of the Sakyans, in the Lumbineyya Janapada. The Buddha stayed in Lumbinivana during his visit to Devadaha and there preached the Devadaha Sutta.

Re-discovery

In 1896, Nepalese archaeologists (effort by Khadga Samsher Rana) discovered a great stone pillar at the site, attributed to Emperor Ashoka. Records made by the Chinese pilgrim Fa Xian were also used in the process of identifying this religiously acclaimed site.

Present-day

Lumbini, as of 1997, is an UNESCO World Heritage Site

specifically nominated for the international World Heritage program. The holy site of Lumbini is bordered by a large monastic zone, in which only monasteries can be built, no shops or hotels or restaurants. It is separated into an eastern and western monastic zone, the eastern having the Theravadin monasteries, the western having Mahayana and Vajrayana monasteries.

The holy site of Lumbini has ruins of ancient monasteries, a sacred Bodhi tree, an ancient bathing pond, the Asokan pillar and the Mayadevi temple, where the precise place of birth of Buddha is located. From early morning to early evening, pilgrims from various countries perform chanting and meditation at the site.

Bodh Gaya

Bodh Gaya or Bodhgaya is a city in Gaya district in the Indian state of Bihar. It is famous for being the place of Gautama Buddha's attainment of nirvana (Enlightenment).

Historically, it was known as the Bodhimanda (ground around the Bodhi-tree), Uruvela, Sambodhi, Vajrasana and Mahabodhi. The name Bodh Gaya did not come into use until the 18th century. The main monastery of Bodhgaya used to be called the Bodhimanda-vihara (Pail). Now it is called the Mahabodhi Temple.

For Buddhists, Bodh Gaya is the most important of the main four pilgrimage sites related to the life of Gautama Buddha, the other three being Kushinagar, Lumbini, and Sarnath. In 2002, Mahabodhi Temple, located in Bodh Gaya, became a UNESCO World Heritage Site.

The surrounding town, by contrast, is dusty, noisy and somewhat polluted, due in large part to the large numbers of pilgrims and tourists who visit there. A new development plan has been proposed to "ensure a sustainable and prosperous future" for Bodh Gaya, but has become controversial because such a plan may require the relocation of whole neighbourhoods.

History

Offerings found in Bodh Gaya under the "Enlightenment Throne of the Buddha", with a decorated coin of the Kushan emperor Huvishka, 3rd century CE.

According to Buddhist traditions, circa 500 BC Prince Gautama Siddhartha, wandering as an ascetic, reached the sylvan banks of

Falgu River, near the city of Gaya. There he sat in meditation under a bodhi tree (*Ficus religiosa*). After three days and three nights of meditation, Siddharta attained enlightenment and insight, and the answers that he had sought. He then spent seven weeks at seven different spots in the vicinity meditating and considering his experience. After seven weeks, he travelled to Sarnath, where he began teaching Buddhism.

Disciples of Gautama Siddhartha began to visit the place where he had gained enlightenment during the full moon in the month of Vaisakh (April-May), as per the Hindu calendar. Over time, the place became known as Bodh Gaya, the day of enlightenment as Buddha Purnima, and the tree as the Bodhi Tree.

The history of Bodh Gaya is documented by many inscriptions and pilgrimage accounts. Foremost among these are the accounts of the Chinese pilgrims Faxian in the 5th century and Xuanzang in the 7th century. The area was at the heart of a Buddhist civilization for centuries, until it was conquered by Turkish armies in the 13th century.

Mahabodhi Temple

The complex, located about 96 kilometres from Patna, at contains the Mahabodhi Temple with the diamond throne (called the *Vajrasana*) and the holy Bodhi tree. This tree was originally a sapling of the Sri Maha Bodhi tree in Sri Lanka, itself grown from a sapling of the original Bodhi tree.

It is believed that 250 years after the Enlightenment of the Buddha, Emperor Ashoka visited Bodh Gaya. He is considered to be the founder of the original Mahabodhi temple. It consisted of an elongated spire crowned by a miniature stupa and a *chhatravali* on a platform. A double flight of steps led up to the platform and the upper sanctum. The mouldings on the spire contained Buddha images in niches. Some historians believe that the temple was constructed or renovated in the 1st century during the Kushan period. With the decline of Buddhism in India, the temple was abandoned and forgotten, buried under layers of soil and sand.

The temple was later restored by Sir Alexander Cunningham as part of his work for the British Archaeological Society in the late 19th century. In 1883, Cunningham along with J. D. Beglar and Dr. Rajendralal Miitra painstakingly excavated the site. Extensive renovation work was carried out to restore Bodh Gaya to its former glory.

Other Buddhist Temples

Kittisirimegha of Sri Lanka, a contemporary of Samudragupta, erected with the permission of Samudragupta, a Sangharama near the Mahabodhi-vihara, chiefly for the use of the Singhalese monks who went to worship the Bodhi tree. The circumstances in connection with the Sangharama are given by Hiouen Thsang (Beal, op. cit., 133ff) who gives a description of it as seen by himself. It was probably here that Buddhaghosa met the Elder Revata who persuaded him to come to Ceylon.

Presently, several Buddhist temples and monasteries have been built by the people of Bhutan, China, Japan, Myanmar, Nepal, Sikkim, Sri Lanka, Thailand, Tibet and Vietnam in a wide area around the temple. These buildings reflect the architectural style, exterior and interior decoration of their respective countries. The statue of Buddha in the Chinese Temple is 200 years old and was brought from China. Japan's Nippon Temple is shaped like a pagoda. The Myanmar (Burmese) Temple is also pagoda shaped and is reminiscent of Bagan. The Thai Temple has a typical sloping, curved roof covered with golden tiles. Inside, the temple holds a massive and spectacular bronze statue of Buddha. Next to the Thai temple there is a recent 25 meter statue of Buddha located within a garden which has existed there for over 100 years. For Tibetan buddhism there are two temples.

Sarnath

Sarnath (also Mrigadava, Migadaya, Rishipattana, Isipatana) is the deer park where Gautama Buddha first taught the Dharma, and where the Buddhist Sangha came into existence through the enlightenment of Kondanna. Sarnath is located 13 kilometres north-east of Varanasi, in Uttar Pradesh, India. Singhpur, a village one km away from the site, was the birth place of Shreyansanath, the eleventh Jain Tirthankar of the present age (Avasarpini), and a temple dedicated to him, is an important Jain pilgrimage.

Isipatana is mentioned by the Buddha as one of the four places of pilgrimage which his devout followers should visit, if they wanted to visit a place for that reason.

Origin of Names

Mrigadava means "deer-park". Isipatana is the name used in the Pail Canon, and means the place where holy men (Pail: *isi*, Sanskrit: *rishi*) fell to earth.

The legend says that when the Buddha-to-be was born, some devas came down to announce it to 500 rishis. The rishis all rose into the air and disappeared and their relics fell to the ground. Another explanation for the name is that Isipatana was so called because sages, on their way through the air (from the Himalayas), alight here or start from here on their aerial flight (isayo ettha nipatanti uppatanti cati-Isipatanam). Pacceka Buddhas, having spent seven days in contemplation in the Gandhamadana, bathe in the Anotatta Lake and come to the habitations of men through the air, in search of alms. They descend to earth at Isipatana. Sometimes the Pacceka Buddhas come to Isipatana from Nandamulaka-puberal.

Xuanzang quotes the Nigrodhamiga Jataka to account for the origin of the Migadaya. According to him the Deer Park was the forest gifted by the king of Benares of the Jataka, where the deer might wander unmolested. The Migadaya was so-called because deer were allowed to roam about there unmolested.

Sarnath, from *Saranganath,* means "Lord of the Deer" and relates to another old Buddhist story in which the Bodhisattva is a deer and offers his life to a king instead of the doe the latter is planning to kill. The king is so moved that he creates the park as a sanctuary for deer. The park is still there today.

Gautama Buddha at Isipatana

The Buddha went from Bodhgaya to Sarnath about 5 weeks after his enlightenment. Before Gautama (the Buddha-to-be) attained enlightenment, he gave up his austere penances and his friends, the Pancavaggiya monks, left him and went to Isipatana.

After attaining Enlightenment the Buddha, leaving Uruvela, travelled to the Isipatana to join and teach them. He went to them because, using his spiritual powers, he had seen that his five former companions would be able to understand Dharma quickly. While travelling to Srimath, Gautama Buddha had to cross the Ganges. Having no money with which to pay the ferryman, he crossed the Ganges through the air. When King Bimbisara heard of this, he abolished the toll for ascetics. When Gautama Buddha found his five former companions, he taught them, they understood and as a result they also became enlightened. At that time the Sangha, the community of the enlightened ones, was founded. The sermon Buddha gave to the five monks was his first sermon, called the Dhammacakkappavattana Sutta.

It was given on the full-moon day of Asalha. Buddha subsequently also spent his first rainy season at Srimath at the *Mulagandhakuti*. The Sangha had grown to 60 in number (after Yasa and his fiends had become monks), and Buddha sent them out in all directions to travel alone and teach the Dharma. All 60 monks were Arahants.

Several other incidents connected with the Buddha, besides the preaching of the first sermon, are mentioned as having taken place in Isipatana. Here it was that one day at dawn Yasa came to the Buddha and became an Arahant. It was at Isipatana, too, that the rule was passed prohibiting the use of sandals made of talipot leaves. On another occasion when the Buddha was staying at Isipatana, having gone there from Rajagaha, he instituted rules forbidding the use of certain kinds of flesh, including human flesh. Twice, while the Buddha was at Isipatana, Mara visited him but had to go away discomfited.

Besides the Dhammacakkappavattana Sutta mentioned above, several other suttas were preached by the Buddha while staying at Isipatana, among them

- the Anattalakkhana Sutta,
- the Saccavibhanga Sutta,
- the Panca Sutta (S.iii.66f),
- the Rathakara or Pacetana Sutta (A.i.110f),
- the two Pasa Suttas (S.i.105f),
- the Samaya Sutta (A.iii.320ff),
- the Katuviya Sutta (A.i.279f.),
- a discourse on the Metteyyapanha of the Parayana (A.iii.399f), and
- the Dhammadinna Sutta (S.v.406f), preached to the distinguished layman Dhammadinna, who came to see the Buddha.

Some of the most eminent members of the Sangha seem to have resided at Isipatana from time to time; among recorded conversations at Isipatana are several between Sariputta and Mahakotthita, and one between Mahakotthita and Citta-Hatthisariputta. Mention is made, too, of a discourse in which several monks staying at Isipatana tried to help Channa in his difficulties.

According to the Udapana Jataka there was a very ancient well near Isipatana which, in the Buddha's time, was used by the monks living there.

Isipatana after the Buddha

According to the Mahavamsa, there was a large community of monks at Isipatana in the second century B.C. For, we are told that at the foundation ceremony of the Maha Thupa in Anuradhapura, twelve thousand monks were present from Isipatana led by the Elder Dhammasena.

Hiouen Thsang found, at Isipatana, fifteen hundred monks studying the Hinayana. In the enclosure of the Sangharama was a vihara about two hundred feet high, strongly built, its roof surmounted by a golden figure of the mango. In the centre of the vihara was a life-size statue of the Buddha turning the wheel of the Law. To the south-west were the remains of a stone stupa built by King Ashoka.

The Divy. (389-94) mentions Ashoka as intimating to Upagupta his desire to visit the places connected with the Buddha's activities, and to erect thupas there. Thus he visited Lumbinî, Bodhimûla, Isipatana, Migadaya and Kusinagara; this is confirmed by Ashoka's lithic records, e.g. Rock Edict, viii.

In front of it was a stone pillar to mark the spot where the Buddha preached his first sermon. Near by was another stupa on the site where the Pancavaggiya spent their time in meditation before the Buddha's arrival, and another where five hundred Pacceka Buddhas entered Nibbana. Close to it was another building where the future Buddha Metteyya received assurance of his becoming a Buddha.

Buddhism flourished in Srimath in part because of kings and wealthy merchants based in Varanasi. By the third century Srimath had become an important centre for the arts, which reached its zenith during the Gupta period (4th to 6th centuries CE). In the 7th century by the time Xuan Zang visited from China, he found 30 monasteries and 3000 monks living at Srimath.

Srimath became a major centre of the Sammatiya school of Buddhism, one of the early Buddhist schools. However, the presence of images of Heruka and Tara indicate that Vajrayana Buddhism was (at a later time) also practiced here. Also images of Brahminist gods as Shiva and Brahma were found at the site, and there is still a Jain temple (at Chandrapuri) located very close to the Dhamekh Stupa.

At the end of the 12th century Srimath was sacked by Turkish Muslims, and the site was subsequently plundered for building materials.

Discovery of Isipatana

Isipatana is identified with the modern Srimath, six miles from Benares. Alexander Cunningham found the Migadaya represented by a fine wood, covering an area of about half a mile, extending from the great tomb of Dhamekha on the north to the Chaukundi mound on the south.

Legendary Characteristics of Isipatana

According to the Buddhist commentarial scriptures, all the Buddhas preach their first sermon at the Migadaya in Isipatana. It is one of the four avijahitatthanani (unchanging spots), the others being the bodhi-pallanka, the spot at the gate of Sankassa, where the Buddha first touched the earth on his return from Tavatimsa, and the site of the bed in the Gandhakuti in Jetavana

In past ages Isipatana sometimes retained its own name, as it did in the time of Phussa Buddha , Dhammadassi (BuA.182) and Kassapa (BuA.218). Kassapa was born there (ibid., 217). But more often Isipatana was known by different names (for these names see under those of the different Buddhas).

Thus in Vipassi's time it was known as Khemauyyana. It is the custom for all Buddhas to go through the air to Isipatana to preach their first sermon. Gotama Buddha, however, walked all the way, eighteen leagues, because he knew that by so doing he would meet Upaka, the Ajivaka, to whom he could be of service.

Current Features of Isipatana

Most of the ancient buildings and structures at Srimath were damaged or destroyed by the Turks. However, amongst the ruins can be distinguished:

- The Dhamek Stupa; it is an impressive 128 feet high and 93 feet in diameter.
- The Dharmarajika Stupa is one of the few pre-Ashokan stupas remaining, although only the foundations remain. The rest of the Dharmarajika Stupa was removed to Varanasi to be used as building materials in the 18th century. At that time, also relics were found in the Dharmarajika Stupa. These relics were subsequently thrown in the Ganges river.
- The Chaukhandi Stupa commemorates the spot where the Buddha met his first disciples, dating back to the fifth century or earlier and later enhanced by the addition of an octagonal tower of Islamic origin. In recent years it is undergoing restoration.
- The ruins of the Mulagandhakuti vihara mark the place where the Buddha spent his first rainy season.
- The modern Mulagandhakuti Vihara is a monastery built in the 1930s by the Sri Lankan Mahabodhi Society, with beautiful wall paintings. Behind it is the Deer Park (where deer are still to be seen).
- The Ashoka Pillar erected here, originally surmounted by the "Lion Capital of Ashoka" (presently on display at the Srimath Museum), was broken during Turk invasions but the base still stands at the original location.
- The Srimath Archeological Museum houses the famous Ashokan lion capital, which miraculously survived its 45-foot drop to the ground (from the top of the Ashokan Pillar), and became the National Emblem of India and national symbol on the Indian flag. The museum also houses a famous and refined Buddha-image of the Buddha in Dharmachakra-posture.
- There is also a Bodhi tree planted by Anagarika Dharmapala which was grown from a cutting of the Bodhi Tree at Bodh Gaya.

Kushinagar

Kushinagar, Kusinagar or Kusinara is a town and a nagar panchayat in Kushinagar district in the Indian state of Uttar Pradesh. It is an important Buddhist pilgrimage site, where Gautama Buddha died.

Ancient History

In ancient times, it was known as Kushavati (Jatakas). It finds mention in epic Ramayana as the city of Kusha the son of Rama, the famous king of Ayodhya. Kushinagar was a celebrated centre of the Malla kingdom of ancient India. Later, it would be known as Kushinara, one of the most important four holy sites for Buddhists. At this location, near the Hiranyavati River, Gautama Buddha attained Parinirvana (or 'Final Nirvana') after falling ill from eating a meal of a species of mushroom.

Many of the ruined stupas and viharas here date back to 3rd century BCE-5th century CE when prosperity was at its peak. The Mauryan emperor Ashoka is known to have contributed to significant construction at this site.

Prior to its rediscovery in the 19th century, there was a silence of more than half a millennium at Kasia. Due to violent invasions, Kushinagar lost its vitality and eventually was neglected.

Visits by the Buddha to Kushinagar

At the time of the Buddha, Kushinagar was the capital of the Mallas, and the scene of the Buddha's death. It was twenty-five yojanas from Rajagaha (DA.ii.609; acc. to Fa Hsien, it was twenty-four yojanas from Kapilavatthu) and lay on the high road from Alaka to Rajagaha, the road taken by Bavari's disciples. At that time it was a small city, "a branch-township with wattle-and-daub houses in the midst of the jungle," and Ananda was, at first, disappointed that the Buddha should have chosen it for his Parinibbana. But the Buddha, by preaching the Maha-Sudassana Sutta, pointed out to him that in ancient times it had been Kusavati, the royal city of Maha-Sudassana.

It is said that the Buddha had three reasons for coming to Kusinara to die:

1. Because it was the proper venue for the preaching of the Maha-Sudassana Sutta;

2. Because Subhadda would visit him there and, after listening to his sermon, would develop meditation and become an arahant while the Buddha was still alive; and
3. Because the brahman Doha would be there, after the Buddha's death, to solve the problem of the distribution of his relics.

Between Kusinara and Pava, three gavutas away (DA.ii.573) from where the Buddha came to Kusinara on his last journey from Rajagaha, stopping at various places-lay the stream of Kakuttha on the banks of which was the Ambavana; beyond that was the Hiranavati river, and near the city, in a south-westerly direction, lay the Upavattana, the Sala-grove of the Mallas, which the Buddha made his last resting-place.

After the Buddha's death his body was carried into the city by the northern gate and out of the city by the eastern gate; to the east of the city was Makutabandhana, the shrine of the Mallas, and there the body was cremated. For seven days those assembled at the ceremony held a festival in honour of the relics.

As the scene of his death, Kusinara became one of the four holy places declared by the Buddha (in the Mahaparinibbana Sutta) to be fit places of pilgrimage for the pious, the other three being Kapilavatthu, Buddhagaya and Isipatana .

Mention is made of other visits paid to Kusinara by the Buddha, prior to that when his death took place. Thus, once he went there from Apana and having spent some time at Kusinara, proceeded to Atuma. The Mallas of Kusinara were always great admirers of the Buddha, even though not all of them were his followers, and on the occasion of this visit they decided that any inhabitant of Kusinara who failed to go and meet the Buddha and escort him to the city, would be fined five hundred. It was on this occasion that Roja the Mallan was converted and gave to the Buddha and the monks a supply of green vegetables and pastries. During some of these visits the Buddha stayed in a wood called Baliharana, and there he preached two of the Kusinara Suttas and the "Kinti" Sutta. A third Kusinara Sutta he preached while staying at Upavattana.

According to a late tradition, one-eighth of the Buddha's relics were deposited in a cairn in Kusinara and honoured by the Mallas.

In Hiouen Thsang's day there still existed towers and Sarigharamas erected to mark the spots connected with the Buddha's last days and obsequies at Kusinara. According to his account Kusinara was nineteen yojanas from Vessel. A copper plate belonging to the Thupa erected at the site of the Buddha's death has recently been discovered there are many pilgrims over out sides.

Rediscovery

The remains of the Parinirvana Stupa and Parinirvana Temple, when rediscovered, were covered in a 40 foot high mound of bricks surrounded by a dense thorny forest. After E. Buchanan, an officer of the East India Company, arrived in Kasia in the course of his survey-work, H. H. Wilson, in 1854, made the suggestion that ancient Kushinagar and Kasia were the same. Work resumed around 1861–1862 when General Alexander Cunningham, an archaeological surveyor, would prove the site to be that of Gautama Buddha's passing. A British officer named Mr. A.C.L. Carlleyle followed suit. Excavations began in the late 1800s and many important remnants of the main site such as the Matha Kuar and Ramabhar stupa were unveiled.

The last four are places where a certain miraculous event is reported to have occurred:

Sravasti

Uravasti or Sravasti, a city of ancient India, was one of the six largest cities in India during Gautama Buddha's lifetime. The city was located in the fertile Gangetic plains in the present day's Gonda district of Uttar Pradesh. Jetavana monastery was a famous monastery close to Sravasti.

Origin of Sravasti

According to the epic Ramayana, Sravasti was a new city created for Lava (the son of Raghava Rama). Rama divided his Kosala Kingdom into two parts and installed his son Lava at Sravasti and another son Kusha at Kushavati, another town in Kosala. According to the Mahabharata, the origin of Sravasti lies with the legendary king Shravasta. According to Buddhist tradition, the city was called Sravasti because the sage Savattha lived there. Another tradition says there was a caravanserai there, and people meeting there asked each other what they had ("Kim bhandam atthi?"), then replied "Sabbam atthi" (meaning "we have all things", as in everything). And the name of the city was based on the reply.

Sravasti in the Buddha's Time

Sravasti was located on the banks of the river Aciravati (now called the Rapti river). It was the capital city of the kingdom of Kosala, and its king was called Pasenadi, who was a disciple of Buddha. It is a beautiful city with vast amounts of agriculture and diversity. Buddhaghosa says that, in the Buddha's day, there were fifty seven thousand families in Sravasti, and that it was the chief city in the country of Kasi Kosala, which was three hundred leagues in extent and had eighty thousand villages. He stated the population of Sravasti to have been 180 million. The road from Rajagaha to Sravasti passed through Vesali, and the Parayanavagga gives as the resting places between the two cities: Setavya, Kapilavatthu, Kusinara, Pava and Bhoganagara. Further on, there was a road running southwards from Sravasti through Saketa to Kosambi. Between Saketa and Sravasti was located Toranavatthu.

The Buddha passed the greater part of his monastic life in Sravasti. His first visit to Sravasti was at the invitation of Anathapindika, whom he met in Rajagaha. The main monasteries in Sravasti were the Jetavana and the Pubbarama. Sravasti also contained the monastery of Rajakarama, built by Pasenadi, opposite Jetavana. Not far from the city was a dark forest called the Andhavana, where some monks and nun went to live. Outside the city gate of Sravasti was a fisherman's village of five hundred families.

The chief patrons of the Buddha in Sravasti were Anathapindika, Visakha, Suppavasa and Pasenadi. When Bandhula left Vesali he came to live in Sravasti.

Woodward states that, of the four Nikayas, 871 suttas are said to have been preached in Sravasti; 844 of which are in Jetavana, 23 in the Pubbarama, and 4 in the suburbs of Sravasti. These suttas are made up of 6 in the Digha Nikaya, 75 in the Majjhima Nikaya, 736 in the Samyutta Nikaya, and 54 in the Anguttara Nikaya. The Commentaries state that the Buddha spent twenty five rainy seasons in Sravasti, this leaving only twenty to be spent elsewhere. Of the 25 rainy seasons Buddha lived in Sravasti, he spent 19 in the monastery named Jetavana, and 6 in the monastery called

Pubbarama. Thus, Sravasti is the place where Buddha lived the longest amount of time, and it is the place where he gave the largest amount of discourses and instructions.

Sravasti is the place where the Twin Miracle (Pali: Yamaka Patihara) took place, in which Buddha made a demonstration of his supernatural powers for the purpose of silencing certain believers of other faiths who proclaimed that the Buddha was incapable of performing supernatural miracles. The Buddhist commentarial tradition says that Sravasti is the scene of each Buddha's Yamaka patihariya; Gotama Buddha performed this miracle under the Gandamba tree.

The Chinese Pilgrim Xuanzang found the old city in ruins, but recorded the sites of various buildings.

Current Sravasti

Of the ancient Sravasti the city walls are still standing. Within these, the remains of 3 ancient buildings can be visited: Angulimala's stupa, Anathapindika's stupa, and an old temple dedicated to a Jain Tirthankara. Outside of Sravasti is located the stupa where the Twin Miracle (Pali: Yamaka Patihara) took place. The site of Jetavana monastery is the main pilgrim destination, with meditation and chanting mainly done at the Gandhakuti (Buddha's hut) and the Anandabodhi tree. Buddhist monasteries from the following countries have been constructed at Sravasti: Thailand, South Korea, Sri Lanka, Myanmar, Tibet and China.

Rajgir

Rajgir is a city and a notified area in Nalanda district in the Indian state of Bihar. The city of Rajgir (ancient Rajagriha or Rajag was the first capital of the kingdom of Magadha, a state that would eventually evolve into the Mauryan Empire. Its date of origin is unknown, although ceramics dating to about 1000 BC have been found in the city.

One may visit Rajgir from Patna. Rajgir is connected to Patna via Bakhtiarpur by rail and road. Bakhtiarpur lies midway between Patna and Mokameh. One has to take NH 30A to Bakhtiarpur and NH 31 towards south to reach Bihar Sharif. From Mokameh, one can directly take NH 31 to Bihar Sharif. From there, NH 82 will lead you to Rajgir. Rajgir is around 100 KM from both Patna and Mokameh. It is located in a verdant valley surrounded by rocky hills. Indian Railways run trains directly from Rajgir to Kolkata and New Delhi.

History

Rajgir, which means 'house of the king', was the ancient capital city of the Magadha kings until the 5th century BC when Ajatashatru moved the capital to Pataliputra. In those days, it was called Rajgrih, which translates as 'the home of Royalty'.

The epic Mahabharata calls it Girivraja and recounts the story of its king, Jarasandha, and his battle with the Pandava brothers and their allies Krishna. Jarasandha who hailed from this place had been defeated by Krishna 17 times. The 18th time Krishna left the battlefield without fighting. Because of this Krishna is also called 'ranacora' (one who has left the battlefield). Mahabharata recounts a wrestling match between Bhima, one of the pandavas, and Jarasandha, the then king of Rajgir. Jarasandha was invincible as his body could rejoin any dismembered limbs. According to the legend, Bhim split Jarasandha into two and threw the two halves facing opposite to each other so that they could not join. There is a famous Jarasandha's Akhara (place where you practice martial arts).

It is also mentioned in Buddhist and Jain scriptures, which give a series of place-names, but without geographical context. The attempt to locate these places is based largely on reference to them and to other locations in the works of Chinese Buddhist pilgrims, particularly Faxian and Xuanzang. It is on the basis of Xuanzang in particular that the site is divided into Old and New Rajgir. The former lies within a valley and is surrounded by low-lying hills. It is defined by an earthen embankment (the Inner Fortification), with which is associated the Outer Fortification, a complex of cyclopean walls that runs (with large breaks) along the crest of the hills. New Rajgir is defined by another, larger, embankment outside the northern entrance of the valley and next to the modern town.

It is sacred to the memory of the founders of both the religions: Buddhism and Jainism and associated with both the historical Buddha and Mahavira.

It was here that Gautama Buddha spent several months meditating, and preaching at Griddhkuta, ('Hill of the Vultures').

He also delivered some of his famous sermons and converted King Bimbisara of Magadha and countless others to his religion. On one of the hills is the Saptparni cave where the First Buddhist Council was held under the leadership of Maha Kassapa. Lord Mahavira spent fourteen years of his life at Rajgir and Nalanda, spending *chaturmas* (i.e. 4 months of the rainy season) at a single place in Rajgir (Rajgruhi) and the rest in the places in the vicinity. It was the capital of his favourite *shishya* (follower) king Shrenik. Thus Rajgir is a very important religious place for Jains also.

Rajgir is also famous for its association with Shishunaga Kings Bimbisara and Ajatashatru. Ajatashatru kept his father Bimbsara in captivitiy here. The sources do not agree which of the Buddha's royal contemporaries, Bimbisara and Ajatashatru, was responsible for its construction. Ajatashatru is also credited with moving the capital to Pataliputra (modern Patna).

Sankassa

Sankassa (also Sankasia, Sankissa and Sankasya) was an ancient city in India. The city came into prominence at the time of Gautama Buddha. According to a Buddhist source, it was thirty leagues from Sravasti. Currently it has ruins of old monasteries and Buddhist monuments. It is rarely visited by pilgrims since it is difficult to go to, and there are not many facilities.

Sankassa is now identified with Sankissa Basantapura on the north bank of the Ikkhumati river (Kalinadi), between Atranji and Kannauj, twenty-three miles west of Fatehgarh and forty five north of Kannauj, in Farrukhabad district of Uttar Pradesh state of India.

Ancient Buddhist Events at Sankassa

Sankassa received its fame from statements and claims recorded in the ancient commentaries to the Tipitaka. However, in the Tipitaka itself the events that are supposed to have occurred at Sankassa are not mentioned at all.

It was at Sankassa that (according to the commentaries) the Buddha returned to earth, after preaching the Abhidhamma Pitaka in Tavatimsa, following the performance of the Twin Miracle under the Gandamba tree. As the time approached for the Buddha to leave Tavatimsa, Moggallana announced his coming return to the multitude, who had been waiting at Sravasti, fed by Culla Anathapindika, while Moggallana expounded the Dhamma. They then made their way to Sankassa. The descent of the Buddha took place on the day of the Mahapavarana festival. Sakka provides three ladders for the Buddha's descent from Sineru to the earth: on the right was a ladder of gold for the gods; on the left a silver ladder for Maha Brahma and his retinue; and in the middle a ladder of jewels for the Buddha. The assembled people covered the earth for thirty leagues round. There was a clear view of the nine Brahma worlds above and of Avici (a hell) below. The Buddha was accompanied by Pancaikha, Matali, Maha Brahma and Suyama. Sariputta was the first to welcome him (followed by Uppalavanna, and the Buddha preached the Law, starting with what was within the comprehension even of a puthujjana, and ending with what only a Buddha could understand.

On this occasion was preached the Parosahassa Jataka to proclaim to the multitude the unparalleled wisdom of Sariputta. It is said' that the Buddha's descent to Sankassa had provided opportunity for Moggallana to show his eminence in iddhi, Anuruddha in dibbacakkhu, and Punna in skill in preaching, and the Buddha wished to give Sariputta a chance of shining in his wisdom. He therefore asked of Sariputta questions which no one else could answer. The opening words of the Sariputta Sutta are supposed to refer to this descent from Tusita.

The site of the city gate of Sankassa is one of the "unchangeable" spots of the world. All Buddhas descend at that spot to the world of men after preaching the Abhidhamma. From Sankassa the Buddha went to Jetavana.

A shrine was erected on the spot where the Buddha's right foot first touched the ground at Sankassa. When the Chinese pilgrims, Hiouen Thsang and Fa Hien, visited the place, they found three ladders, which had been built of brick and stone by the ancients, to commemorate the Buddha's descent, but the ladders were nearly sunk in the earth.

There was, in the Buddha's time, a deer park at Sankassa where Suhemanta Thera heard the Buddha preach. During the Vajjiputta controversy, Revata Thera, on his way from Soreyya to Sahajati, went through Sankassa. The road he took passed through Sankassa, Kannakujja, Udumbara and Aggalapura

Vaishali (Ancient City)

Vaishali or Vesali (Pail) was the capital city of the Licchavi, one of world's first democratic republics, in the Vajjian Confederacy (Vrijji) *mahajanapada*, around the 6th century BC. It was here that Gautama Buddha preached his last sermon before his death ca 483 BCE, then in 383 BCE the Second Buddhist council was convened here by King Kalasoka. Also in 599 BCE the 24th Jain Tirthankara, Mahavira was born and brought up in Vaishali republic, making it an important place in both religions.

At the time of the Buddha, Vaishali, which he visited on many occasions, was a very large city, rich and prosperous, crowded with people and with abundant food. There were seven thousand seven hundred and seven pleasure grounds and an equal number of lotus ponds. Its courtesan, Ambapali, was famous for her beauty, and helped in large measure in making the city prosperous. The city had three walls, each one gavuta away from the other, and at three places in the walls were gates with watch towers. Outside the town, leading uninterruptedly up to the Himalaya, was the Mahavana, a large, natural forest. Nearby were other forests, such as Gosingalasala.

The city finds mention in the travel accounts of Chinese explorers, Fa Hian (4th century CE) and Xuanzang (Hiuen Tsang) (7th century CE), which were later used in 1861 by British archaeologist Alexander Cunningham to first identify Vaishali with the present village of Basrah in Vaishali District, Bihar.

Etymology

Vaishali derives its name from King Vishal of the Mahabharata age. The city was also called Visual. Buddhaghosa, the a 5th-century Indian Theravadin Buddhist commentator and scholar says, that Vesali was so called because it was extensive or *Vishal.*

History

Even before the advent of Buddhism and Jainism, Vaishali was the capital of the vibrant republican Licchavi state. In that period, Vaishali was an ancient metropolis and the capital city of the republic of the Vaishali state, which covered most of the Himalayan Gangetic region of present-day Bihar state, India. However, very little is known about the early history of Vaishali. The Vishnu Purana records 34 kings of Vaishali, the first being *Nabhaga,* who is believed to have abdicated his throne over a matter of human rights and believed to have declared: "I am now a free tiller of the soil, king over my acre." The last among the 34 was *Sumati*, who is considered a contemporary of Dasaratha, father of the Hindu god, Lord Rama.

Numerous references to Vaishali are found in texts pertaining to both Jainism and Buddhism, which have preserved much information on Vaishali and the other *Maha Janapadas*. Based on the information found in these texts, Vaishali was established as a republic by the 6th century BC, prior to the birth of Gautama Buddha in 563, making it the world's first republic.

In the republic of Vaishali, Lord Mahavira was born. Gautama Buddha delivered his last sermon at Vaishali and announced his Parinirvana there. Vaishali is also renowned as the land of Ambapali (also spelled as Amrapali), the great Indian courtesan, who appears in many folktales, as well as in Buddhist literature. Ambapali became a disciple of Buddha. A kilometre away is *Abhishek Pushkarini*, the coronation tank. The sacred waters of the tank anointed the elected representatives of Vaishali. Next to it stands the Japanese temple and the Vishwa Shanti Stupa (World Peace Pagoda) built by the Nipponzan Myohoji sect of Japan. A small part of the Buddha's relics found in Vaishali have been enshrined in the foundation and in the *chhatra* of the Stupa.

Near the coronation tank is Stupa 1 or the Relic Stupa. Here the Lichchavis reverentially encased one of the eight portions of the Master's relics, which they received after the Mahaparinirvana. After his last discourse the Awakened One set out for Kushinagar, but the Licchavis kept following him. Buddha gave them his alms bowl but they still refused to return. The Master created an illusion of a river in spate which compelled them to go back. This site can be identified with Deora in modern Kesariya village, where Ashoka later built a stupa. Ananda, the favourite disciple of the Buddha, attained Nirvana in the midst of the Ganga outside Vaishali.

Visits of the Buddha to Vaishali

The Buddha first visited Vaishali in the fifth year after his Enlightenment, and spent the rainy season there. The Buddhist Theravadin Commentaries give detailed descriptions of the circumstances of this visit. Vesaai was inhabited by seven thousand and seven rajas, each of whom had large retinues, many palaces and pleasure parks. There came a shortage in the food supply owing to drought, and people died in large numbers. The smell of decaying bodies attracted evil spirits, and many inhabitants were attacked by intestinal disease. The people complained to the ruling prince, and he convoked a general assembly, where it was decided, after much discussion, to invite the Buddha to their city. As the Buddha was then at Veluvana in Rajagaha, the Licchavi Mahali, friend of King Bimbisara and son of the chaplain of Vesali, was sent to Bimbisara with a request that he should persuade the Buddha to go to Vessel. Bimbisara referred him to the Buddha himself, who, after listening to Mahali's story, agreed to go.

The Buddha started on the journey with five hundred monks. Bimbisara decorated the route from Rajagaha to the Ganges, a distance of five leagues, and provided all comforts on the way. He accompanied the Buddha, and the Ganges was reached in five days. Boats, decked with great splendour, were ready for the Buddha and his monks, and we are told that Bimbisara followed the Buddha into the water up to his neck. The Buddha was received on the opposite bank by the Licchavis, with even greater honour than Bimbisara had shown him. As soon as the Buddha set foot in the Vajjian territory, there was a thunderstorm and rain fell in torrents.

The distance from the Ganges to Vessel was three leagues; as the Buddha approached Vessel, Sakka came to greet him, and, at the sight of the devas, all the evil spirits fled in fear. In the evening the Buddha taught Ananda the Ratana Sutta, and ordered that it should be recited within the three walls of the city, the round of the city being made with the Licchavi princes. This Ananda did during the three watches of the night, and all the pestilences of the citizens disappeared.

The Buddha himself recited the Ratana Sutta to the assembled people, and eighty four thousand beings were converted. After repeating this for seven consecutive days, the Buddha left Vessel. (According to the DhA. account the Buddha stayed only seven days in Vessel; KhA. says two weeks). The Licchavis accompanied him to the Ganges with redoubled honours, and, in the river itself, Devas and Nagas vied with each other in paying him honour. On the farther bank, Bimbisara awaited his arrival and conducted him back to Rajagaha. On his return there, the Buddha recited the Sankha Jataka.

It is not possible to know how many visits were paid by the Buddha to Vessel, but the books would lead us to infer that they were several. Various Vinaya rules are mentioned as having been laid down at Vessel.

The visit mentioned in the last context seems to have been a long one; it was on this occasion that the Buddha ordered the monks to turn their bowls upon the Licchavi Vaddha. Also other Vinaya rules were laid down at Vessel.

It was during a stay in Vessel, whither he had gone from Kapilavatthu, that Mahapajapati Gotami followed the Buddha with five hundred other Sakyan women, and, with the help of Ananda's intervention, obtained permission for women to enter the Order under certain conditions.

The books describe at some length the Buddha's last visit to Vesali on his way to Kusinara. On the last day of this visit, after his meal, he went with Ananda to Cabala cetiya for his siesta, and, in the course of their conversation, he spoke to Ananda of the beauties of Vessel: of the Udena cetiya, the Gotamaka cetiya, the Sattambaka cetiya, the Bahuputta cetiya, and the Sárandada cetiya, where a Kapinayha-cetiya is also mentioned.

All these were once shrines dedicated to various local deities, but after the Buddha's visit to Vessel, they were converted into places of Buddhist worship. Other monasteries are also mentioned, in or near Vessel (for example Patikarama, Válikarama).

The Buddha generally stayed at the Kutagarasala during his visits to Vessel, but it appears that he sometimes lived at these different shrines. During his last visit to the Cabala cetiya he decided to die within three months, and informed Mara and, later, Ananda, of his decision. The next day he left Vessel for Bhandagama, after taking one last look at the city, "turning his whole body round, like an elephant". The rainy season which preceded this, the Buddha spent at Beluvagama, a suburb of Vessel, while the monks stayed in and around Vessel. On the day before he entered into the vassa, Ambapali invited the Buddha and the monks to a meal, at the conclusion of which she gave her Ambavana for the use of the Order.

Among important suttas preached at Vessel are the Mahali, Mahasihanada, Cula Saccaka, Maha Saccaka. Tevijja, Vacchagotta,

Sunakkhatta and Ratana. After the Buddha's death a portion of his relics was enshrined in the City.

One hundred years later Vessel was again the scene of interest for Buddhists, on account of the "Ten Points" raised by the Vajjiputtaka, and the Second Buddhist Council held in connection with this dispute at the Válikarama.

Jain Religion at Vaishali

Vessel was a stronghold of the last jain Tirthankar Mahavira aka Niganthas, and it is said that of the forty two rainy seasons of the latter part of Mahavira's ascetic life, he passed twelve at Vessel. Vessel was also the residence of Kandaramasuka and Patikaputta. Among eminent followers of the Buddha who lived in Vessel, special mention is made of Ugga (chief of those who gave pleasant gifts), Pingiyani, Karanapali, Siha, Vasettha, and various Licchavis.

The Buddha's presence in Vessel was a source of discomfort to the Niganthas, and we find mention of various devices resorted to by them to prevent their followers from coming under the influence of the Buddha.

Important Structures in Vaishali

Relic Stupa

Near the coronation tank is Stupa 1 or the Relic Stupa. Here the Licchavis reverentially encased on of the eight portions of the Master's relics, which they received after the Mahaparinirvana. After his last discourse the Awakened One set out for Kushinagar, but the Licchavis kept following him. Buddha gave them his alms bowl but they still refused to return. The Master created an illusion of a river in spate which compelled them to go back. This site can be identified with Deora in modern Kesariya village, where Ashoka later built a stupa.

Kutagarasala Vihara

Kutagarasala Vihara is the monastery where Buddha most frequently stayed while visiting Vaishali. It is located 3 kilometres from the relic Stupa, and on its ground can be found the Ananda Stupa, with an Asokan pillar in very good condition (perhaps the only complete Asokan pillar left standing), and an ancient pond.

Coronation Tank

A few hundred metres from the Relic Stupa is Abhishek Pushkarini, the coronation tank. The sacred waters of the tank anointed the elected representatives of Vaishali.

World Peace Pagoda

Next to the coronation tank stands the Japanese temple and the *Viva Anti Stoup* (World Peace Pagoda) built by Japanese Nichiren Buddhist sect Nipponzan-Myohoji. A small part of the Buddha's relics found in Vaishali have been enshrined in the foundation and in the chhatra of the Stupa

Other Sites

Some other pilgrimage places in India and Nepal connected to the life of Gautama Buddha are: Pataliputta, Nalanda, Vikramshila, Gaya, Kapilavastu, Kosambi, Amaravati, Nagarjuna Konda, Sanchi, Varanasi, Kesariya, Devadaha, Pava and Mathura. Most of these places are located in the Gangetic plain.

3

Teachings of Buddha

The basic teachings of Buddha are contained in:

a) Four Noble Truths, and

b) Eight Fold Path.

The following are the Four Noble Truths:

i) The world is full of sufferings.

ii) All sufferings have a cause: desire, ignorance and attachment are the causes of sufferings.

iii) The suffering could be removed by destroying its cause.

iv) In order to end sufferings one must know the right path. This path is the Eight Fold Path (Ashtangika Marga).

The Eight Fold Path consists of the following principles:

i) Finding the right view. It is to understand that the world is filled with sorrow generated by desire. The ending of desire will lead to the liberation of the soul.

ii) Right aim. It seeks to avoid the enjoyment of the senses and luxury. It aims to love humanity and increase the happiness of others.

iii) Right speech, which seeks to emphasise the speaking of truth always.

iv) Right action, which is understood to be unselfish action.

v) Right livelihood. It instructs that a man should live by honest means.

vi) Right effort. It is the proper way of controlling one's senses so as to prevent bad thoughts. It is through correct mental exercises that one can destroy desire and attachment.

vii) Right mindfulness. It is the understanding of the idea that the body is impermanent and meditation is the means for the removal of worldly evils.

viii) Right concentration. The observation of it will lead to peace. Meditation will unravel the real truth.

Buddhism laid great emphasis on the law of 'karma'. According to this law present is determined by the past actions. The condition of a man in this life and the next depends upon his own actions.

Every individual is the maker of his own destiny. We are born again and again to reap the fruits of our 'karma'. If an individual has no sins, he is not born again. Thus the doctrine of k m a is the essential part of the teachings of Buddha.

Buddha preached 'nirvana', the ultimate goal in the life of a man. It means the shedding of all desires, and ending of sufferings, which finally leads to freedom from rebirth. By a process of elimination of desire, one can attain 'nirvana'. Therefore, Buddha preached that annihilation of desire is the real problem. Prayers and sacrifices will not end the desire. So unlike the emphasis on rituals and ceremonies in Vedic religion he laid emphasis on the moral life of an individual.

Buddha neither accepted nor rejected the existence of God. He was more concerned about the individual and his actions. Buddhism also did not believe in the existence of soul.

Besides these Buddha laid stress on certain other aspects:

Buddha emphasised on the spirit of love. Love could be expressed on all living beings by following 'ahimsa' (non-killing). Though the principle was well understood, it was not emphasised as much as in Jainism.

An individual should pursue the middle path and both severe asceticism as well as luxurious life are to be avoided.

Teachings of Buddha put forward a serious challenge to the existing Brahmanical ideas:

i) Buddha's liberal and democratic approach quickly attracted the people of all sections. His attack on the caste system and the supremacy of the Brahmins was welcomed by the people of the lower orders. Irrespective of caste and sex people were taken into the. Buddhist order. In

Buddhism salvation lay in one's good deals. So there was no need of a priest or middle man to achieve 'nirvana' the ultimate goal of life.

ii) Buddha rejected the authority of the Vedas and condernnccl animal sacrifices. He protested against the complicated and meaningless. He said that neither a sacrifice to gods can wash away sin, nor any prayer ol any priest do any good to a sinner.

Buddhism in a very short period emerged into an organised religion and Buddha's teachings were codified.

The Buddhist canons (collection of teachings) are divided into three sections namely:

i) The Sutta Pitaka consists of five sections (nikayas) of religious discourses and sayings of Buddha. The fifth section contains the Jataka tales (birth stories of Buddha).

ii) The Vinaya Pitaka contains the rules of monastic discipline.

iii) The Abhidhamma Pitaka contains the philosophical ideas of teachings of Buddha. It is written in the form of questions and answers.

Spread of Buddhism

Even during the life time of its founder, Buddhism was accepted by a large section of people. For example people of Magadha, Kosala and Kausambi had embraced Buddhism. The republics of Sakyas, Vajjis and Mallas also followed the process. Later on, Asoka and Kanishka made Buddhism state religion and it spread into central Asia, West Asia and Sri Lanka. This appeal of Buddhism to a large section of population was because of the following factors :

Emphasis on practical morality, an easily acceptable solution to the problems of mankind and a simple philosophy, attracted the masses towards Buddhism.

The ideas of social equality laid down in the codes of Buddhism made many lay followers accept Buddhism.

Merchants, like Anathirpindika, and courtesans, like Amrapali, accepted the faith because they got due respect in this religion.

The use of popular language (Pail) to explain the doctrines also helped in the spread of the religion. This was because the

Brahmanical religion had limited itself so the use of Sanskrit which was not the language of the masses.

The patronage extended by kings was another important reason for the rapid growth of Buddhism. For example according to tradition Asoka sent his son Mahendra and his daughter Sangamitra to Sri Lanka to preach Buddhism. He also established many monastries and contributed liberally to the Sangha. The institution of Sangha had helped to organise the spread of Buddhism effectively.

The Institution of the Sangha

The Sangha was the religious order of the Buddhists. It was a well organised and powerful institution which popularised Buddhism. Membership was open to all persons, irrespective of caste, above fifteen years of age. Criminals, lepers and persons affected by infectious diseases were not given admission into the Sangha. Initially Buddha was not in favour of admitting women in the Sangha. However he admitted them at the repeated requests of his chief disciple Ananda and his foster mother Mahapajapati Gotami.

On admission, the monks had to ceremonially shave their head and wear yellow or saffron robes. Monks were expected to go on a daily round in order to preach Buddhism and seek alms. During the four months of the rainy season they took up a fixed abode and meditated. This was called the retreat or 'vasa'. The Sanghas also promoted education among the people. Unlike Brahmanism people of different orders of the society had entry to education. Naturally the non-Brahmins who were deprived of education got access to education in Buddhism and thus education reached wider sections of the society.

The Sangha was governed by democratic principles and was empowered to enforce discipline amongst its members. There was a code of conduct for the monks and nuns and they were bound to obey it. The Sangha had the power to punish the erring members.

The Sangha of monks and the Sangha of nuns were originally established by Gautama Buddha in the 5th century BCE in order to provide a means for those who wish to practise the Dhamma full time, in a direct and highly disciplined way, free from the restrictions and responsibilities of the household life. The Sangha also fulfils the function of preserving the Buddha's original teachings and of providing spiritual support for the Buddhist lay-community.

The key feature of Buddhist monasticism is the adherence to the vinaya which contains an elaborate set of rules of conduct including complete chastity and eating only before noon. Between midday and the next day, a strict life of scripture study, chanting, meditation, and occasional cleaning forms most of the Sangha's duties. Transgression of rules carries penalties ranging from confession to permanent expulsion from the Sangha. The founder of Japanese Tendai sects took the decision to reduce the number of rules down to about 60 (Enkai). In Kamakura Era, many sects (Zen, Pureland and Nichiren) which originated from Tendai sect abolished vinaya entirely. Therefore Japanese Zen, Pureland and Nichiren, are led by priests (or minister) rather than by monks.

Monks and nuns may own only the barest minimum of possessions due to their samaya as renunciates (ideally, three robes, an alms bowl, a cloth belt, a needle and thread, a razor for shaving the head, and a water filter). In practice, they often have a few additional personal possessions.

Traditionally, Buddhist monastics eschew ordinary clothes and wear robes. Originally the robes were sewn together from rags and stained with earth. The idea that robes were dyed with saffron seems unlikely to be true since it was and still is a very expensive commodity, and monks were poor. The colour of modern robes varies from community to community (saffron is characteristic for southeast Asian Theravada and Mahayana groups, maroon in Tibet, gray in Korea, black in Japan etc.)

The word which is usually translated as monk is *bhikkhu* in Pail or *bhikshu* in Sanskrit. The feminine form is *bhikkhuni* or *bhikshuni*. These words literally mean "beggar", and it is traditional for bhikkhus to beg their food. In most places this has become an elaborate ritual, where lay people feed monastics in order to obtain merit which will ensure them a fortunate rebirth. Although monastics in India traditionally did not work for income, this changed when Buddhism moved to east Asia, so that in China and the surrounding countries monks often engage in agriculture.

The idea that all Buddhists, especially monks and nuns practice vegetarianism is a Western misperception. In some Sanskrit sutras meat eating is strongly discouraged whilst in Pail Sutras the Buddha specifically rejected a suggestion by a senior monk to impose vegetarianism on the Sangha. The Buddha himself is recorded as having consumed meat.

The Buddha allowed Sangha members to eat whatever food is donated to them by laypeople, except that they may not eat meat if they know or suspect the animal was killed specifically for them. Consequently, the Theravadan tradition (Sri Lanka, Thailand, Laos, Cambodia and Burma) which follows the Pail scriptures does not practice vegetarianism though an individual may do so at his or her personal choice.

On the other hand, the Mahayana and Vajrayana traditions accept both Theravada and Mahayana scriptures, and consequently the practice will vary depending on their interpretation of the sutras. In particualr, East Asian monastics take on the bodhisattva vows from the Brahma Net Sutra which has a vow of vegetarianism as part of the Triple Platform Ordination where they receive the sramanera/sramanerika, bhikshu/bhikshuni and bodhisattva vows, whereas the Tibetan lineages transmit the bodhisattva vows from Asanga's Yogacarabhumi, which doe not include a vow of vegetarianism. In some areas such as China, Korea and Vietnam one expects the Sangha to practice strict vegetarianism while in other areas such as Japan or Tibet one does not.

The lay community is responsible for the production of goods and services in society, and for the production and raising of children. According to Mahayana sutras, the Buddha always maintained that lay persons were capable of great wisdom in the Buddhadharma and of reaching enlightenment. In the west, there is a misconception that Theravada regards enlightenment to be an impossible goal outside the Sangha. This is incorrect. In Theravada suttas, it is clearly recorded that the Buddha's uncle—who was a lay follower—reached enlightenment by hearing the Buddha's discourse.

The distinction between Sangha and lay persons has always been important and forms the *Parisa*, Buddhist community. Here, monastics teach and counsel the laity at request while laymen and laywomen offer donations for their future support. This interconnectedness serves as a marriage and has sustained Buddhism to this day.

Women's Role in the Sangha

Although always maintaining that women were just as capable of attaining enlightenment as men, the canonical texts depict the Buddha as being reluctant to permit women to join the Sangha. After several entreaties from his aunt and foster-mother, Maha Pajapati Gotami, who wished to become ordained, and from his cousin and aide Ananda, who supported her cause, the Buddha relented and ordained Maha Pajapati and several others as nuns. It is interesting to note that this was one of the few issues about which the Buddha is recorded to have changed his mind. The Buddha later established the condition that each new ordination would be sanctioned by at least five bhikkhunis.

There have been several theories regarding the Buddha's reluctance to ordain women, including the possibility that it was due to fears that a community of women would not be safe in the society of his day. According to the scriptures the reason the Buddha himself gave was that the admission of women would weaken the Sangha and shorten its lifetime, and he laid down strict rules subordinating nuns to monks (The Eight Garudhammas).

Before the modern era, the Bhikkhuni Sangha spread to most Buddhist countries including Burma, with the notable exceptions being Tibet and Thailand. However, in Sri Lanka, it died out in the 11th century during a civil war and was not revived. Consequently, as Theravada Buddhism spread to Thailand, the Theravada Sangha consisted only of monks.

In recent decades, there has been a serious attempt to revive the Theravada Bhikkhuni Sangha with the assistance of Mahayana bhikkhunis from the Chinese lineage. These were introduced from Sri Lanka in 433 C. E., following the Dharmaguptaka Vinaya, and subsequently spread to Korea, Taiwan, Vietnam, and Japan. This has resulted in a small but thriving community of nuns in Sri Lanka, who in turn ordained the first Theravada Buddhist nun in the history of Thailand, Ven. Dhammananda. However, the validity of these ordinations is strongly disputed by some of the conservative Theravada establishment.

Meanwhile, a similar process has produced the first fully ordained bhikkhunis in Tibetan Buddhism, where only the novice ordination for bhikkhunis existed. In the west, where feminism has been a strong influence, there have been many remarkable Buddhist nuns: three notable examples are Pema Chodron, Ayya Khema and Tenzin Palmo.

The first bhikkhuni ordination in Australia in the Theravadin tradition was held in Perth on October 22nd at Bodhinyana Monastery. Venerable Ajahn Vayama together with Venerables Nirodha, Seri and Hasapanna were ordained as bhikkhunis by a dual sangha act of bhikkhus and bhikkhunis in full accordance with the pail vinaya.

Bhikkhu

A Bhikku (Pail), Bhikcu (Sanskrit) is a fully ordained male Buddhist monastic. Female monastic is called Bhikkhuni (Skt: Bhikcugi). Bhikkhus and Bhikkhunis keep many precepts: they live by the vinaya's framework of monastic discipline, the basic rules of which are called the patimokkha. Their lifestyle is shaped so as to support their spiritual practice, to live a simple and meditative life, and attain Nirvana.

Introduction

Bhiksu may be literally translated as "beggar" or more broadly as "one who lives by alms". It is philologically analysed in the Pail commentary of Buddhaghosa as "the person who sees danger (in samsara or cycle of rebirth)" (Pail = Bhayac ikkhatiti: bhikkhu). He therefore seeks ordination in order to release from it. The Dhammapada states:

- Not therefore is he a bhikkhu.
- Merely because he begs from others.
- Not by adopting the outward form.
- Does one truly become a bhikkhu.
- He who wholly subdues evil,
- Both small and great,
- Is called a monk (bhikkhu).
- Because he has overcome all evil. Dhp 266, 267.

A bhikkhu has taken a vow to enter the Sangha (Buddhist monastic community) and is expected to obey rules of conduct (typically around 227 for a male) as set out in the Vinaya, although there are considerable local variations in the interpretations of these rules. A novice monk or nun in the Tibetan tradition takes 36 vows of conduct. The minimum age to take bhikkhu vows is 21 years (although this varies from country to country).

In English literature prior to the mid-20th Century, Buddhist monks were often referred to by the term *bonze,* particularly when describing monks from East Asia and French Indo-China. This term is derived via Portuguese and French from the Japanese word *bonos* for a priest or monk, and has become less common in modern literature.

Vows and Ordination

Although the European concepts "monk" and "nun" are applied to Buddhism relatively unproblematically, the situation of 'ordination' is more complicated.

Becoming a Bhikkhu/Bhikkhuni

In Buddhism, monasticism is part of the system of "vows of individual liberation". These vows are taken by monks and nuns from the ordinary sangha, in order to develop personal ethical discipline. In Mahayana Buddhism, the term "sangha" is, in principle, often understood to refer particularly to the *Arya Sangha* the "community of the noble ones who have reached the first bhumi. These, however, need not be monks and nuns.

The vows of individual liberation are taken in four steps. A lay person may take the five upasaka (Pail and Sanskrit; feminine: *upasaka;* Tibetan *edge snyanedge snyan ma,* pronounced *genyen/ genyenma,* "approaching virtue") vows.

The next step is to enter the pabbajja, or monastic way of life, which includes wearing monk's or nun's robes. After that, one can become a samanera, or novice monk/nun. The last and final step is to take all the vows of a bhikkhu/bhukkhuni a "fully ordained monk/nun."

Monks and nuns take their vows for a lifetime, but they can "give them back" (up to three times in one life), a possibility which is actually used by many people. In this way, Buddhism keeps the vows "clean". It is possible to keep them or to leave this lifestyle, but it is considered extremely negative to break these vows.

In Tibet, rabjung, getshül, gelong ordinations are usually taken at ages six, fourteen and twenty-one or older, respectively.

Robes

The special dress of ordained people, the robes, comes from the idea of wearing cheap clothes just to protect the body from weather and climate. They shall not be made from one piece of cloth, but mended together from several pieces. Since dark red was the cheapest colour in Kashmir, the Tibetan tradition has red robes. In the south, yellow played the same role, though the colour of saffron also had cultural associations in India; in East Asia, robes are yellow, grey or black. The robes of getshül novices and gelong monks differ in various aspects, especially in the application of "holes" in the gelong dress. Some monks tear their robes into pieces and then mend these pieces together again. The rabjung novices shall not wear the "chogo", the yellow tissue worn during Buddhist teachings by both getshuls and gelongs.

In observance of the Kathina Puja, a special Kathina robe is made in 24 hours from donations by lay supporters of a temple. The robe is donated to the temple or monastery, and the resident monks then select from their own number a single monk to receive this special robe.

Additional Vows in the Mahayana and Vajrayana Traditions

In Mahayana traditions, a Bhikcu may take additional vows not related to ordination, including the bodhisattva vow, samaya vows, and others, which are also open to laypersons in most instances.

In addition, in some traditions there are forms of non-vinaya ordinations, the holders of which are not considered Bhikcus. These included ordination into the "White Sangha" lineage of Tibetan yogis and all of the ordination lineages of the various Japanese traditions.

Conclusion

"Ordination" in Buddhism is a cluster of methods of self-discipline according to the needs, possibilities and capabilities of individuals. According to the spiritual development of his followers, the Buddha gave different levels of vows. The most advanced method is the state of a bikshu (ni), a fully ordained follower of the Buddha's teachings. The goal of the bhikku (ni) in all traditions is to achieve liberation from suffering.

Bhikkhuni

A bhikkhuni is a fully ordained female Buddhist monastic. Male monastics are called bhikkhus. Both bhikkhunis and bhikkhus live by the vinaya. Bhikkhuni lineages enjoy a broad basis in Mahayana countries like Korea, Vietnam, China and Taiwan.

According to Buddhist scriptures, the order of bhikkhunis was first created by the Buddha at the specific request of his foster-mother Mahapajapati Gotami, who became the first ordained bhikkhuni, relayed via his attendant Ananda (who also urged for the Buddha's acceptance of it). The bhikkhuni order spread to many countries.

For a country or nation to be considered as truly Buddhist, the majority of the nation must be Buddhist and include at least a fourfold sangha of bhikkhus, bhikkhunis, upasakas and, upasikas..

History

According to Theravada tradition, the bhikkhuni order of nuns came to be 5 years after the bhikkhu order of monks.

Buddhism is unique among Dharmic Religions in that Buddha, as founder of a spiritual tradition, explicitly states in canonical literature that a woman is as capable of nirvana (enlightenment) as a man, and can fully attain all four stages of enlightenment in the Dhamma and Vinaya of the Buddha Sasana. There is no equivalent, in other traditions, of the Therigatha or Apadanas which record the high levels of spiritual attainment by women..

In a similar vein, major canonical Mahayana sutras such as the Lotus Sutra, chapter 12, records 6000 bhikkhuni Arahants as receiving predictions of Bodhisatvahood and future Buddhahood by Sakyamuni Buddha. In Buddhism, women can openly aspire to and practice for the highest level of spiritual attainment.

The Eight Precepts

According to the available canon, Buddha was initially quite reluctant to ordain women into the Sangha. His stepmother and aunt, Mahaprajapati Gotami, made repeated requests on behalf of herself and five hundred other ladies of the court. These women had only known lives of comfort. Eventually, his attendant and half-brother Ananda (Mahaprajapati Gotami's son) relayed a final request, which was granted—but only on condition that the women accept eight garudhammas, or eight heavy rules. The Buddha is quoted by Thannisaro Bhikkhu as saying: *Ananda, if Mahaprajapati Gotami accepts eight vows of respect, that will be her full ordination (upasampada).* Modern scholars have shown that this story abounds in textual problems, and cannot possibly be a factual account.

According to the scriptural accounts, the reason the Buddha gave for his actions was that admission of women to the sangha would weaken it and shorten its lifetime to 500 years. This prophecy occurs only once in the Canon and is the only prophecy involving time in the Canon, leading some to suspect that it is a late addition.

Some modern Buddhist scholars explain the Buddha's reluctance by noting that these women (many who were mothers, daughters, wives, sisters, cousins of many of the bhikkhus) might be subjected to rape, assault, sexual harassment and being termed "prostitutes and thieves", which in fact, did later occur as recorded in the Vinaya. One example as told in the Vinaya in which a Brahmin calling the bhikkhunis "strumpets" (i.e., prostitutes), tries to set fire to the bhikkhunis' dwelling:

Then that Brahmin... spread it about, saying:

These shaven headed strumpets are not true recluses. How can they

let a pot fall on my head? I will set fire to their dwelling, and having taken up a fire brand, he entered the dwelling.

In Young Chung noticed that society as recorded in the Vinaya always criticized the bhikkhunis more harshly using "shaven headed strumpets or whores", whereas the bhikkhus were simply called "shaven headed". This harsher treatment (which also included rape and assault) of bhikkhunis by society required greater protection. Within these social conditions, Gautama Buddha opened up new horizons for women by founding the bhikkhuni sangha. This social and spiritual advancement for women was ahead of the times and, therefore, drew many objections from men, including bhikkhus. He was probably well aware of the controversy that would be caused by the harassment of his female disciples."

Early Buddhism did not have monasteries and it was a requirement of the bhikkhus and early bhikkhunis to spend a lot of time in the forests alone, but due to the consequent rape and assault of some of the bhikkhunis by outsiders recorded in the Vinaya— Buddha eventually forbade women from wandering in forests away from society. Bhikkhunis eventually resided in more fixed residences near populated areas than the bhikkhus.

According to some modern Buddhist apologists, most of the rules (including the more controversial 8 Garudhammas) of the Bhikkhuni Vinaya are more for the protection of the bhikkhunis by association with the more senior Sangha of the male bhikkhus and thus the homage for protection and teaching the newer Bhikkhuni Sangha and not "sexual discrimination". Dr. Chatsumarn Kabilsingh writes, "Nuns at the time of the Buddha had equal rights and an equal share in everything. In one case, eight robes were offered to both sanghas at a place where there was only one nun and four monks. The Buddha divided the robes in half, giving four to the nun and four to the monks, because the robes were for both sanghas and had to be divided equally however many were in each group. Because the nuns tended to receive fewer invitations to laypeople's homes, the Buddha had all offerings brought to the monastery and equally divided between the two sanghas. He protected the nuns and was fair to both parties. They are subordinate in the sense of being younger sisters and elder brothers, not in the sense of being masters and slaves." The Vinaya does not allow for any power-based relationship between the monks and nuns.

Many of the more controversial rules were clarified or amended, implying that these rules were not unalterable:

1) A nun who has been ordained even for a hundred years must greet respectfully, rise up from her seat, salute with joined palms, do proper homage to a monk ordained but that day.
   - clarification: The Vinaya recounts the story of six monks who lifted up their robes to show their thighs to the nuns. When the Buddha learned about this, he made an exception to that rule and told the nuns not to pay respect to these monks. A nun, then, does not have to bow to every monk, but only to a monk who is worthy of respect.
   - Pajapati's later request: "I would ask one thing of the Blessed One, Ananda. It would be good if the Blessed

One would allow making salutations, standing up in the presence of another, paying reverence and the proper performance of duties, to take place equally between both bhikkhus and bhikkhunis according to seniority."

2) A nun must not spend the rains in a residence where there are no monks.

3) Every half month a nun should desire two things from the Order of Monks : the asking as to the date of the Observance [uposatha] day, and the coming for the exhortation [bhikkhunovada].

4) After the rains a nun must 'invite' [pavarana] before both orders in respect of three matters, namely what was seen, what was heard, what was suspected.

    - amended: However, practical considerations soon necessitated amendments to these and we see in the revised version of these conditions the sanction given to the bhikkhunis to perform these acts, in the first instance, by themselves.

5) A nun, offending against an important rule, must undergo manatta discipline for half a month before both orders.

    - another translation: "(5) A bhikkhuni who has broken any of the vows of respect must undergo penance for half a month under both Sanghas... (by Thanissaro Bhikkhu)

6) When, as a probationer, she has trained in the six rules [cha dhamma] for two years, she should seek higher ordination from both orders.

    - note contradiction: One of the gurudhamma mentions sikkhamanas, probationary nuns who train for two years in preparation to become bhikkhunis. It says that after a probationary nun has trained with a bhikkhuni for two years, that bhikkhuni preceptor has the responsibility to fully ordain her. However, when the Buddha ordained Mahapajapati, there were no probationary nuns. He ordained her directly as a bhikkhuni. So how do we explain that within the eight important rules, one of them states that before becoming a bhikkhuni, a woman must be a probationary nun? "

7) A monk must not be abused or reviled in any way by a nun.

8) From today, admonition of monks by nuns is forbidden.

- note Buddhist lay-women can: This is in contrast to the rules for Buddhist lay-women who can single-handedly accuse a bad monk:

"Equality of bhikuni and bhikuu, men and women, can be inferred in several of the rules groupings. The penalties for offences against those aniyata dharmas written only for bhikuus, for example, point up a landmark of female-male equality. Here, in a gesture of trust in women most unusual for the time, a trustworthy female lay follower can bring a charge against a bhikuu based only on her personal eyewitness testimony, in order to force an investigation of that bhikuus conduct. Additionally, equal abilities of men and women are presumed in the regulations for settlement of disciplinary matters in the seven Adhikaraoa–amatha Dharmas, which are exactly the same, in both numbers and contents, for both the Bhikuu and the Bhikuni Sanghas."

Nuns were also given the right to select the monk who would be allowed to give counsel to the order of nuns (he had to be acceptable to all the nuns) and the selection criteria was quite stringent:

There seems to be little doubt about his anxiety and his foresight regarding the safety and well-being of the female members of his Order.

These eight qualities were: the teacher of nuns must be virtuous; second, have comprehensive knowledge of the Dhamma; third he must be well acquainted with the Vinaya, especially the rules for nuns; fourth, he must be a good speaker with a pleasant and fluent delivery, faultless in pronunciation, and intelligibly convey the meaning; fifth, he should be able to teach Dhamma to the nuns in an elevating, stimulating, and encouraging way; sixth, he must always be welcome to the nuns and liked by them — that is, they must be able to respect and esteem him not only when he praises them but especially when there is an occasion for reproach; seventh, he must never have committed sexual misconduct with a nun;

eighth, he must have been a fully ordained Buddhist monk for at least 20 years (AN 8.52).

Some scholars argue that these 8 rules were added later since:

1) there is a discrepancy between the Pail bhikkhuni Vinaya
2) the fact that these same rules are treated only as a minor offence (requiring only confession as expiation) in the bhikkhuni Payantika Dharmas.

In Young Chung clarifies, "Haeju Chun, a bhikuni and assistant professor at Tongguk University in Seoul, Korea, argues that six of the Eight Rules belong to the Bhikuni Payantika Dharmas, as they are the same as or similar to rules found there. We may compare the differences in the punishment for any offence of the Eight Rules with that for an offence of the payantika dharmas. Violation of any of the Eight Rules means that women cannot be ordained. The Eight Rules must be observed throughout the bhikuus lives. However, the pàyantika dharmas require only confession, as there offences of bhikunis are considered to be violations of minor rules. Based on the differences in the gravity of offences between the Eight Rules and the pàyantika dharmas, she also asserts the probability that the Eight Rules might have been added later. The first of the Eight Rules does not appear in the Pail Bhikuni Vinaya.

Most of these rules are also found in the Bhikkhuni Payantika Dharmas as minor rules since they only require confession:

Theriya tradition, which at some stage, seems to have accommodated the idea that the Buddha conceded the abrogation of the minor rules.

Other scholars argue that questioning canonical sources is a slippery slope. Buddha's main concern was about the rest of society, which was the main supporter of the Sangha, and how they would view the ordination of women—something quite revolutionary at the time. There were many men who even after the apparent success of the Bhikkhuni Sangha, were opposed to its formation. However, we have Buddha himself admit that the social factors were foremost in his mind when making these rules:

the Theriya tradition attempts to make out that in the organization of the Sasana social considerations, as much as moral and ethical values, loomed large in the mind of the Master. In the

Cullavagga he is reported as saying: ' Not even the Titthiyas who propound imperfect doctrines sanction such homage of men towards women. How could the Tathagata do so?' .

This agrees with the fact that rival sects such as the Jains also had the first rule according to the Svetambara rules.

Ian Astley argues that under the conditions of society where there is such great discrimination and threat to women, Buddha could not be blamed for the steps he took in trying to secure the Sangha from negative public opinion:

In those days (and this still applies to much of present Indian society) a woman who had left the life of the household would otherwise have been regarded more or less as a harlot and subjected to the appropriate harassment. By being formally associated with the monks, the nuns were able to enjoy the benefits of leaving the household life without incurring immediate

harm. Whilst it is one thing to abhor, as any civilized person must do, the attitudes and behaviour towards women which underlie the necessity for such protection, it is surely misplaced to criticize the Buddha and his community for adopting this particular policy.

The so-called Eight rules of respect (which are vows) are still in force, they are part of the process of full ordination.

Becoming a Bhikkhuni

The progression to ordination as a Bhikkhuni is taken in four steps. A lay person may take the five upasaka (Pail and Sanskrit; masculine: *upasaka;* Tibetan *edge snyan ma,* pronounced *genyenma,* "approaching virtue") vows. The next step is to enter the pabbajja (Srt: *pravrajya,* Tib. *cab byung* pronounced *rabjung*), or monastic way of life, which includes wearing monk's or nun's robes. After that, one can become a samaneri a "fully ordained nun."

Nuns take their vows for a lifetime, but they can "give them back" (up to three times in one life), a possibility which is actually used by many people. In this way, Buddhism keeps the vows "clean". It is possible to keep them or to leave this lifestyle, but it is considered extremely negative to break these vows.

The Fourteen Precepts of Thich Nhat Hanh

In Buddhist Order of Interbeing established in 1964 there are fourteen precepts to be observed by nuns and monks equally. They are written by Vietnamese monk and Zen Master Thich Nhat Hanh giving words to what he felt carried the deepest teachings of the Buddha and would be fit for our time.

In an interview, a Vietnamese nun named Chan Khong described Nhat Hanh's approach:

In Plum Village, the Eight Observations of Respect that nuns have to observe towards Buddhist monks are not observed, as Nhat Hanh claims they were invented only to help the stepmother of the Buddha, and that one need only keep Nhat Hanh's 14 precepts properly. That's all. But of course he doesn't despise the traditional precepts. And I can accept them just to give joy to the monks who practice in the traditional way. If I can give them joy, I will have a chance to share my insights about women with them, and then they will be unblocked in their understanding.

Bhikkhunis in Theravada

The traditional appearance of Theravadan bhikkhunis is nearly identical to that of male monks, including a shaved head and saffron robes. White or pink robes are worn by Theravadan nuns who are not fully ordained, in some counties nuns wear dark chocolate robes or sometimes the same colour as monks. These nuns are known as dasa sila mata in Sri Lanka, silashin in Myanmar (Burma) and the siladharas of Amaravati monastery in the United Kingdom and its branch monasteries. In the Theravada tradition, some scholars believe that the bhikkhuni lineage became extinct in the 11th to 13th centuries, after which no new bhikkhunis could be ordained since there were no bhikkhunis left to give ordination. For this reason, the leadership of the Theravada bhikkhu Sangha in Burma and Thailand deem fully ordained bhikkhunis as "untrue." Other members support the ordination of woman as bhikkhunis.

Dr.Chatsumarn Kabilsingh, now known as Dhammananda Bhikkhuni, is a Thai scholar who took bhikkhuni ordination in Sri Lanka and returned to Thailand, where bhikkhuni ordination is forbidden and can result in arrest or imprisonment for a woman. She is considered a pioneer by many in Thailand and a "devil" by others.

The first bhikkhuni ordination in Australia in the Theravadin tradition was held in Perth on October 22nd at Bodhinyana Monastery. Venerable Ajahn Vayama together with Venerables Nirodha, Seri and Hasapanna were ordained as bhikkhunis by a dual sangha act of bhikkhus and bhikkhunis in full accordance with the pail vinaya.

Indo-China

In Indo-China Theravada tradition, many women who are not allowed to ordain, continue as dedicated practitioners, following the spirit and often the letter of the bhikkhuni vows. They are considered mae jis, laywomen or "semi-ordained," since they are not officially recognized by the Theravada Sangha. These women attempt to lead a life following the teachings of the Buddha. They observe 8–10 precepts, but do not follow exactly the same codes as ordained Buddhist monks. They receive popular recognition for their role. But they are not granted official endorsement or the educational support offered to men. They spend most of their time as temple maids and cooks for monks.

Samanera

In Buddhist context, a samanera can be translated as novice monk. It literally means 'small samana', or small renunciate, where 'small' has the meaning of boy or girl. In the Vinaya (monastic discipline), a man under the age of 20 cannot ordain as a bhikkhu, but can ordain as a samanera. The female counterpart of the samanera is the samaneri. Samaneras and samaneris keep the ten precepts as their code of behaviour, and are devoted to the Buddhist religious life.

After a year or at the age of 20, a samanera will be considered for the higher Bhikkhu or Bhikkhuni ordination (Pail: upasampada). Some monasteries will require people who want to ordain as a monk to be a novice for a set period of time, as a period of preparation and familiarization.

The issue of ordination is different for samaneras and samaneris; the rules governing higher ordination are different for samaneras and samaneris.

The female form of the samanera is the samaneri.

According to Swami Satyananda the sanskrit word Shramanera can also be translated as "labourer" and is related to the sanskrit word Ashram (a place of work). The Buddha is said to have called his first followers "Shramaneras" or labourers.

Samaneri

A samaneri (Pail language) is a novice Buddhist nun, who lives according to the ten precepts. Male novices are called samaneras. A woman is to be ordained, according to Theravada tradition, by both a monk and a nun, first as a samaneri. After a year or at the age of 20, she will be ordained as a full bhikkhuni. The Theravada vinaya has 311 rules of discipline for bhikkhunis. Within Chinese society, as an example, members of the Sangha are expected to renounce family connections and accept the Sangha as their family.

Sikkhamana

In Buddhism, a Sikkhamana is a female novice (Pail: *samaneri*) training to become a nun (Pail: *bhikkhuni*). In the Vinaya Pitaka's Cullavagga X.1.4, the Buddha prescribed that this training period is to be two years long, supervised by both a monk and a nun.

A young woman should be ordained, according to Theravada tradition, by both a monk and a nun, first as a samaneri. Then, after a year or at the age of 20, she will be ordained as a full bhikkhuni. The Theravada vinaya has 311 rules of discipline for bhikkhunis. Within Chinese society, as an example, members of the Sangha are expected to renounce family connections and accept the Sangha as their family.

Thus, according to Vinaya Pitaka, the ordination order for women is: samaneri-> Sikkhamana-> bhikkhuni.

4

Buddhist Councils

Lists and numbering of Buddhist councils vary between and even within schools. The numbering here is normal in Western writings.

First Buddhist Council (C. 400 BCE)

The First Buddhist council was convened in the year following the Buddha's Parinibbana, which would be 499/8 BCE according to Theravada tradition, at various earlier dates according to various Mahayana traditions, and various later dates according to various Western estimates. According to late commentarial accounts, King Ajatashatru sponsored the council. Tradition holds that the Council was held in a hall erected by Ajatasattu outside the Sattaparnaguha Cave (Pail: Sattapanniguha) in Rajgir, three months after the Buddha had died. Detailed accounts of the council can be found in the Khandhaka sections of the canonical Vinayas.

According to this record the incident which prompted the Elder Mahakassapa to call this meeting was his hearing a disparaging remark about the strict rule of life for monks. This is what allegedly happened. The monk Subhadda, who had ordained late in life, upon hearing that the Buddha had expired, voiced his resentment at having to abide by all the rules for monks laid down by the Buddha. Many monks lamented the passing of the Buddha and were deeply grieved. However, the Elder Mahakassapa heard Subhadda say: "Enough your Reverences, do not grieve, do not lament. We are well rid of this great recluse (the Buddha). We were tormented when he said, 'this is allowable to you, this is not allowable to you' but now we will be able to do as we like and we will not have to do what we do not like."

Mahakassapa was alarmed by his remark and feared that the Dhamma and the Vinaya might be corrupted and not survive intact if other monks were to behave like Subhadda and interpret the Dhamma and the Vinaya rules as they pleased. To avoid this he decided that the Dhamma must be preserved and protected. To this end after gaining the Sangha's approval he called to council five hundred Arahants. Ananda was to be included in this provided he attained Arahanthood by the time the council convened.

With the Elder Mahakassapa presiding, the five-hundred Arahant monks met in council during the rainy season. The first thing Mahakassapa did was to question the foremost expert on the Vinaya of the day, Venerable Upali on particulars of the monastic rule. This monk was well qualified for the task as the Buddha had taught him the whole of the Vinaya himself. The Elder Mahakassapa asked him specifically about the ruling on the first offence parajika, with regard to the subject, the occasion, the individual introduced, the proclamation, the repetition of the proclamation, the offence and the case of non-offence. Upali gave knowledgeable and adequate answers and his remarks met with the unanimous approval of the presiding Sangha. Thus, the Vinaya was formally approved.

The Elder Mahakassapa then turned his attention to Ananda in virtue of his reputable expertise in all matters connected with the Dhamma. Happily, the night before the Council was to meet, Ananda had attained Arahantship and joined the Council. The Elder Mahakassapa, therefore, was able to question him at length with complete confidence about the Dhamma with specific reference to the Buddha's sermons. This interrogation on the Dhamma sought to verify the place where all the discourses were first preached and the person to whom they had been addressed.

Ananda aided by his word-perfect memory was able to answer accurately and so the Discourses met with the unanimous approval of the Sangha. The First Council also gave its official seal of approval for the closure of the chapter on the minor and lesser rules, and approval for their observance. It took the monks seven months to recite the whole of the Vinaya and the Dhamma and those monks sufficiently endowed with good memories retained all that had been recited. This historic first council came to be known as the Pancasatika because five-hundred fully enlightened Arahants had taken part in it.

Some scholars deny that the First Council actually took place. According to the Macmillan *Encyclopedia of Buddhism* (2004), "... its historicity is questioned by virtually all Buddhist scholars. They argue that while it was not unlikely that a small group of Buddha's intimate disciples gathered after his death, a council held in the grand style described in the scriptures is almost certainly a fiction."

Mahakauyapa

Mahakauyapa (Mahakassapa) or Kauyapa was a brahman of Magadha, who became one of the principal disciples of Uakyamuni Buddha and who convened and directed the first council. Mahakauyapa is one of the most revered of the Buddha's early disciples. He is often depicted in statuary together with Ananda, each standing to one side of the Buddha.

Zen purports to lead its adherents to insights akin to that mentioned by Uakyamuni Buddha in his *Flower Sermon* in which he held up a white flower and just admired it in his hand. Mahakauyapa smiled faintly, and Uakyamuni Buddha picked that disciple as one who truly understood him and who was worthy to be his successor.

The words of the Uakyamuni Buddha addressed to Mahakauyapa are described below:

I possess the true Dharma eye, the marvellous mind of Nirvana, the true form of the formless, the subtle dharma gate that does not rest on words or letters but is a special transmission outside of the scriptures. This I entrust to Mahakauyapa.

Thus, a way within Buddhism developed which concentrated on direct experience rather than on rational creeds or revealed scriptures. Zen is a method of meditative religion which seeks to enlighten people in the manner that the Mahakauyapa experienced.

In the *Song of Enlightenment* of Onychia Xuanjue (665-713) — one of the chief disciples of Honing, the 6th patriarch of Chan Buddhism—it is written that Bodhidharma was the 28th patriarch in a line of descent from Mahakauyapa, a disciple of Uakyamuni Buddha, and the first patriarch of Chan Buddhism:

- Mahakauyapa was the first, leading the line of transmission;

- Twenty-eight Fathers followed him in the West;
- The Lamp was then brought over the sea to this country;
- And Bodhidharma became the First Father here:
- His mantle, as we all know, passed over six Fathers,
- And by them many minds came to see the Light.

According to Chinese legend, the monk Ji Gong is a reincarnation of Mahakauyapa (known as the Taming Dragon arhat). In Lotus Sutra Chapter 6 (Bestowal of Prophecy), the Buddha bestows prophecies of enlightenment on the disciples Mahakashyapa, Subhuti.

Maha Katyayana and Mahamaudgalyayana

Among those of the Buddha's disciples who were closest to him, there were two friends, Sariputta and Maha Moggallana, who were the chief disciples of the Buddha, the exemplary pair of disciples. There were also two brothers, Ananda and Anuruddha, who were likewise eminent "Fathers of the Order." In between these two pairs stands a great solitary figure, Pipphali Kassapa, who later was called Maha Kassapa, Kassapa the Great, to distinguish him from the others of the Kassapa clan, such as Kumara Kassapa and Uruvela Kassapa.

After Sariputta and Maha Moggallana had passed away, predeceasing the Buddha, it was Maha Kassapa who was held in greatest respect and reverence in the Order. But even after the Buddha's passing away, Maha Kassapa did not become the elected head of the Order of Monks, as it had been the Buddha's express wish that there should not be a supreme authoritative head of the Sangha. Shortly before his passing away, the Buddha had said: "That which I have proclaimed and made known, Ananda, as the Teaching and the Discipline (Dhamma-Vinaya), that shall be your Master when I am gone".

Yet the natural authority emanating from Maha Kassapa made him particularly honoured and venerated in the Sangha. There were many factors that contributed to his pre-eminent position after the death of the Master. He had been praised by the Buddha as being equal to him in many respects and he shared with the Master seven of the thirty-two "Marks of a Great Man." He had been the only monk with whom the Buddha had exchanged robes.

Maha Kassapa possessed to the highest degree the ten "qualities that inspire confidence." He was also a model of a disciplined and austere life devoted to meditation. So it is no wonder that he was elected to preside over the First Council of the Sangha which had been summoned on his urgent advice. It may have been on account of all these features of his personality and his life that, much later in China and Japan, Maha Kassapa came to be regarded as the first patriarch of Chan or Zen Buddhism.

Like the two chief disciples, Sariputta and Maha Moggallana, Maha Kassapa too descended from the brahman caste, and again like them, he was older than the Buddha. He was born in the Magadha country, in the village Mahatittha, as the son of the brahman Kapila and his wife Sumanadevi. He was called Pipphali. His father owned sixteen villages over which he ruled like a little king, so Pipphali grew up in the midst of wealth and luxury. Yet already in his young years there was in him the wish to leave the worldly life behind, and hence he did not want to marry.

When his parents repeatedly urged him to take a wife, he told them that he would look after them as long as they live, but that after their deaths he wanted to become an ascetic. Yet they insisted again and again that he take a wife, so to comfort his mother he finally agreed to marry — on the condition that a girl could be found who conformed to his idea of perfection. For that purpose he shaped a golden statue of a beautiful woman, had it bedecked with fine garments and ornaments, and showed it to his parents, saying:

"If you can find a woman like this for me, I shall remain in the home life." His parents approached eight brahmans, showered them with rich gifts, and asked them to take the image with them and travel around in search of a human likeness of it. The brahmans thought: "Let us first go to the Madda country, which is, as it were, a gold mine of beautiful women." There they found at Sagala a girl whose beauty equalled that of the image. She was Bhadda Kapilani, a wealthy brahman's daughter, aged sixteen, four years younger than Pipphali Kassapa. Her parents agreed to the marriage proposal, and the brahmans returned to tell of their success. Yet Bhadda Kapilani also did not wish to marry, as it was her wish, too, to live a religious life as a female ascetic. Such identity between her aspiration and Pipphali Kassapa's may well point to a kammic bond and affinity between them in the past, maturing in their present life and leading to a decisive meeting between them and a still more decisive separation later on.

When Pipphali heard that what he had thought most unlikely had actually occurred, he was — unhappy and sent the following letter to the girl: "Bhadda, please marry someone else of equal status and live a happy home life with him. As for myself, I shall become an ascetic. Please do not have regrets." Bhadda Kapilani, like-minded as she was, independently sent him a similar letter. But their parents, suspecting such an exchange would take place, had both letters intercepted on the way and replaced by letters of welcome.

So Bhadda was taken to Magadha and the young couple were married. However, in accordance with their ascetic yearning, both agreed to maintain a life of celibacy. To give expression to their resolve, they would lay a garland of flowers between them before they went to bed, determined not to yield to sensual desire.

This young wealthy couple lived thus happily and in comfort for many years. As long as Pipphali's parents lived, they did not even have to look after the estate's farms. But when his parents died, they took charge of the large property.

One day, however, when Pipphali Kassapa was inspecting the fields, it happened that he saw, as if with new eyes, what he had seen so often before. He observed that when his people slowed, many birds gathered and eagerly picked the worms from the furrows. This sight, so common to a farmer, now startled him. It now struck him forcefully that what brought him his wealth, the produce of his fields, was bound up with the suffering of other living beings. His livelihood was purchased with the death of so many worms and other little creatures living in the soil. Thinking about this, he asked one of his labourers: "Who will have to bear the consequences of such an action?" — "You yourself, sir," was the answer.

Shaken by that insight into kammic retribution, he went home and reflected: "If I have to carry along the burden of guilt for that killing, what use is all that wealth to me? It will be better if I give it all to Bhadda and go forth into the ascetic's life."

But at home, at about the same time, his wife had a similar experience. She too saw afresh with a deeper understanding what she had very often seen before. Sesamum seeds had been spread out in the open to dry, and crows and other birds ate the insects that had been attracted by the seeds. When Bhadda asked her servants who it was that had to account morally for the violent death of so many creatures, she was told that the kammic responsibility was hers. Then she thought: "If even by that much I commit a wrong, I won't be able to lift my head above the ocean of rebirths, even in a thousand lives. As soon as Pipphali returns, I shall hand over everything to him and leave to take up the ascetic life."

When both found themselves of one accord, they had pale-yellow cloth and clay bowls brought for them from the bazaar, and then shaved each other's head. They thus became like ascetic wanderers, and they made the aspiration: "Those who are Arahats in the world, to them we dedicate our going forth!" Slinging their almsbowls over their shoulders, they left the estate's manor, unnoticed by the house servants. But when they reached the next village, which belonged to the estate, the labourers and their families saw them. Crying and lamenting, they fell to the feet of the two ascetics and exclaimed: "Oh, dear and noble ones! Why do you want to make us helpless orphans?" — "It is because we have seen the three worlds to be like a house afire, therefore we go forth into the homeless life." To those who were serfs, Pipphali Kassapa granted their freedom, and he and Bhadda continued on their road leaving the villagers behind still weeping.

When walking on, Kassapa went ahead while Bhadda followed behind him. Considering this, Kassapa thought: "Now, this Bhadda Kapilani follows me close behind, and she is a woman of great beauty. Some people-could easily think, 'Though they are ascetics, they still cannot live without each other! It is unseemly what they are doing.' If they spoil their minds by such wrong thoughts or even spread false rumours, they will cause harm to themselves." So he thought it better that they separate. When they reached a crossroads Kassapa said: "Bhadda, you take one of these roads, and I shall go the other way." She said: "It is true, for ascetics a woman is an obstacle. People might think and speak badly about us. So please go your own way, and we shall now part." She then respectfully circumambulated him thrice, saluted him at his feet, and with folded hands she spoke: "Our close companionship and friendship that had lasted for an unfathomable past comes to an end today. Please take the path to the right and I shall take the other road." Thus they parted and went their individual ways, seeking the high goal of Arahatship, final deliverance from suffering. It is said that the earth, shaken by the power of their virtue, quaked and trembled.

Bhadda Kapilani

Let us first follow Bhadda Kapilani. Her road led her to Sravasti where she listened to the Buddha's discourses at the Jetavana monastery. As the Order of Nuns (Bhikkhuni Sangha) did not yet exist at that time, she took up residence at a nunnery of non-Buddhist female ascetics, not far from the Jetavana. There she lived for five years until she could obtain ordination as a bhikkhuni. It was not long afterward that she was able to attain to the goal of the holy life, Arahatship or Sainthood. One day she uttered the following verses in praise of Maha Kassapa and declaring her own attainment:

- Son of the Buddha and his heir is he,
- Great Kassapa — his mind serene, collected.
- Vision of previous lives is his,
- Heaven and hell he penetrates.
- The ceasing of rebirth he has obtained,
- And supernormal knowledge he has mastered.
- With these three knowledges possessed by him
- He is a brahman true, of threefold knowledge.
- So has she, too, Bhadda the Kapilani, gained for herself
- The threefold knowledge and has vanquished death.
- Having bravely vanquished Mara and his host,
- It is the last formation of a body that she bears.
- Seeing the world's deep misery, we both went forth
- And are now both free of cankers, with well-tamed minds.
- Cooled of passions, we have found deliverance;
- Cooled of passions, we have found our freedom.

As an arahant bhikkhuni, Bhadda devoted herself chiefly to the education of the younger nuns and their instruction in monastic discipline (Vinaya). In the Analysis of Nuns' Discipline (Bhikkhuni Vibhanga), instances are recorded involving her pupils which led to the prescribing of certain disciplinary rules for bhikkhunis. There were also two instances when Bhadda Kapilani had to bear the envy of another nun who was hostile towards Maha Kassapa, too. The nun Thullananda was learned in the Dhamma and a good preacher, but evidently she had more intelligence than gentleness of heart. She was self-willed and not prepared to change her conduct, as evidenced by several Vinaya texts.

When Bhadda, too, became a popular preacher of Dhamma, even preferred by some of Thullananda's own pupils, Thullananda became jealous. In order to annoy Bhadda, once she and her pupil nuns walked up and down in front of Bhadda's cell, reciting loudly. She was censured by the Buddha on that account. Another time, at Bhadda's request, she had arranged temporary living quarters for Bhadda when the latter visited Sravasti. But then, in another fit of jealousy, she threw her out of those quarters. Bhadda, however, being an arahant, was no longer affected by such happenings and looked at them with detachment and compassion.

The Buddha praised Bhadda as being the foremost among the nuns who could recollect past lives (Anguttara, Ones). The Pail commentaries and the Jataka stories leave us a record of some of her former lives in which she had been Kassapa's wife.

Past Lives of Kassapa and Bhadda Kapilani

At the time of the former Buddha Vipassi, they had been a poor brahman couple. They were so extremely poor that they had only one single upper garment, and hence only one of them at a time could go out of their hut. In the record of this story, the brahman was therefore called "he with one garment" *(ekasataka).* Though it may not be easy for us to understand such extreme poverty, it will be still more difficult to understand that there have been many people for whom that utter poverty did not mean subjective, personal suffering. This was so with those two beings who later were to be Kassapa and Bhadda. In their life as that poor brahman couple, they had lived in such perfect harmony that it was easier for them to bear their poverty. Both, one after the other, had listened to the sermons of the Buddha Vipassi. Through that Buddha's teaching, the value of giving and generosity became so deeply impressed on the mind of that brahman that he wanted to offer his only upper garment to the Order of Monks. But after he had so resolved, scruples came to his mind. As it was his and his wife's only upper garment, he thought that he should first consult his wife. How could they manage if they had no upper garment at all? But he resolutely pushed aside all such hesitation and offered the garment to the monks. Having done so, he clapped his hands and joyfully called out: "I have vanquished! I have vanquished!"When the king, who had listened to the Buddha Vipassi's sermon behind a curtain, heard that shout of victory and learned its reason, he sent sets of garments to the brahman and later made him his court chaplain. So the couple's plight had come to an end.

As a result of his selfless giving, the brahman was reborn in a celestial world. After parting from there he became a king on earth, a great benefactor of his people who generously supported ascetics and among them also the Paccekabuddhas living at that time. Bhadda was then his chief queen.

As to Bhadda, she was once the mother of a brahman youth who was a pupil of the Bodhisatta (the future Buddha) and wanted to become an ascetic. Kassapa was her husband, Ananda her son. Bhadda had wanted her son to know the worldly life before she would permit him to become an ascetic. But that knowledge and lesson came to the young brahman in a very thorough and drastic way. His teacher's mother fell passionately in love with him and was even ready to kill her son. This encounter with reckless passion caused in him a deep revulsion for worldly life, a thorough disgust with it. After that experience his parents gave him permission to go forth as an ascetic. Again, another time Kassapa and Bhadda had been the brahman parents of four sons who in the future were to be our Bodhisatta, Anuruddha, Sariputta and Maha Moggallana. All four wanted to become ascetics. At first the parents refused permission, but later they came to understand the fruits and benefits of the ascetic life, and they themselves became ascetics.

In still another life, two village headmen who were friends decided that if the children that they were expecting were to be of the opposite sex, they should marry. And so it happened. But in their previous life both children had been deities of the Brahma-world. Hence they had no desire for sensual pleasures and, with their parents' permission, chose the ascetic life.

Bhadda's only wrong act reported in the stories of her past lives was this: At a time between the appearance of Buddhas of the past, when only Paccekabuddhas lived, Bhadda was the wife of a landowner. One day, having quarrelled with her sister-in-law, she begrudged her the merit of offering almsfood to a Paccekabuddha who was on almsround. She took the Paccekabuddha's bowl and filled it with mud. But at once she felt remorse, took the bowl back, washed it, filled it with delicious and fragrant food and offered it to the Paccekabuddha.

In her next life she possessed wealth and great beauty, but her body exuded a loathsome odor. Her husband, who later was to be Kassapa, could not bear the noxious smell and left her. As she was beautiful, she had other suitors, but all her later marriages had the same end. She was full of despair and no longer saw any meaning in her life. Preparing to dispose of her property, she had her ornaments melted down and formed into a golden brick. Taking that golden brick with her, she went to the monastery where a stupa was being erected in honour of the Buddha Kassapa, who had just passed away. For the completion of the stupa she offered that golden brick with great devotion. After she had done that, her body became fragrant again, and her first husband, Kassapa, took her back.

Two lives before her present existence, Bhadda was queen of Benares and used to support several Paccekabuddhas. Deeply moved by their sudden death, she renounced her worldly life as a queen and lived a meditative life in the Himalayas. By the power of her renunciation and her meditative attainments, she was reborn in a Brahma-world, and so was Kassapa. After the end of the long life-span in the Brahma-world, both were reborn in the human world, in a brahman family, and were named Pipphali Kassapa and Bhadda Kapilani.

From these accounts we gather that in their former existences both had lived a life of purity in the Brahma-worlds and that both had repeatedly been ascetic renunciates. Hence, in their final existence, it was not difficult for them to keep to a life of celibacy, to give up all possessions, and to follow the Buddha's teaching up to its culmination in Arahatship.

How Kassapa Came to the Buddha

Continuing our story, we shall now return to Maha Kassapa. Where did he go after he had come to the crossroads? Tradition says that when the two separated, the earth shook by the force of the great virtue in their act of renunciation. The Buddha perceived this trembling of the earth, and he thus knew that an outstanding disciple was on the way to him. He then set out on the road himself, walking the distance of five miles to meet his future pupil— an act of compassion which later was often praised.

On the road between Rajagaha and Nalanda, the Master sat down under a fig tree, waiting for his future disciple. When Kassapa arrived at the spot and saw the radiance of the Buddha's countenance, sensing the enlightenment that shone through it, he thought, "This must be my Master for whose sake I have gone forth!" He approached the Buddha, and paying homage, fell at his feet and exclaimed: "The Exalted One, Lord, is my teacher, and I am his disciple!"

The Master said: "Sit down, Kassapa. I shall give you your heritage." He then gave the following three exhortations:

"You should train yourself thus, Kassapa: 'A keen sense of shame and fear of wrong-doing *(hiri-ottappa)* shall be present in me towards seniors, novices, and those of middle status in the Order.

"'Whatever teaching I hear that is conducive to something wholesome, I shall listen to with an attentive ear, examining it, reflecting on it, absorbing it with all my heart.

"'Mindfulness of the body linked with gladness shall not be neglected by me!' Thus should you train yourself."

Then both Master and disciple walked towards Rajagaha. On the way, the Buddha wanted to rest and went off the road to the root of a tree. Maha Kassapa then folded his double-robe fourfold and requested the Master to sit on it as this would bring him, Kassapa, much benefit for a long time. The Buddha sat down on Kassapa's robe and said: "Soft is your robe of patched cloth, Kassapa." Hearing this, Kassapa replied: "May the Blessed One, O Lord, accept this robe of patched cloth out of compassion for me!" — "But, Kassapa, can you wear these hempen, worn-out rag-robes of mine?" Full of joy, Kassapa said: "Certainly, Lord, I can wear the Blessed One's rough and worn-out rag-robes."

This exchange of robes can be regarded as a great distinction bestowed on Kassapa, an honour which was not shared by any other disciple. By that exchange of robes the Buddha may have intended to motivate Kassapa to observe some other "austere practices" *(dhutanga)* as for instance, wearing only the triple set of robes, going for alms and not omitting any houses on the almsround. This would be a mode of conduct in conformity with wearing the Buddha's patched rag-robes. Thus the commentator says. However, the Buddha's offer may have been a quite spontaneous act in response to his being offered Kassapa's robe.

Kassapa, indeed, actually took upon himself those thirteen austere practices allowed by the Buddha for the purpose of cultivating contentedness, renunciation, and energy. On a later occasion, Kassapa was said by the Buddha to be foremost among the bhikkhus who observed the austere practices (Anguttara, Ones). Kassapa's circle of personal disciples was also devoted to these practices.

It was only seven days after his ordination and the exchange of robes that Kassapa attained the goal he was striving for, Arahatship, the mind's final liberation from defilements. Recounting this episode to Ananda at a much later time, he declared: "For seven days, friend, I ate the almsfood of the country as one unliberated, then on the eighth day the final knowledge of Arahatship arose in me" (S. 16:11).

Kassapa's Relationship to the Buddha

The earlier account has already shown that there was a deep inner relationship between Kassapa and the Buddha. This relationship had its root in their past lives. According to the Jataka stories, Kassapa was connected with the Bodhisatta in nineteen existences, frequently through a close family bond. No less than six times Kassapa had been the Bodhisatta's father (J. 155, 432, 509, 513, 524, 540), twice he was his brother . 522), and often his friend or teacher. As it was thus not their first meeting, we can understand why such an immediate and strong devotion and wholehearted dedication towards the Buddha arose in Kassapa's heart at the first sight of the Master.

From Kassapa's final life, many conversations are reported between the Buddha and this great disciple. It happened on three occasions that the Master spoke to him: "Exhort the monks, Kassapa. Give them a discourse on the Dhamma, Kassapa. Either I, Kassapa, should exhort the monks, or you. Either I or you should give them a discourse on the Dhamma". These words imply a high recognition of Kassapa's ability, because not every arahant has the capacity to expound the Teaching well and effectively.

The commentary raises here the question why it was Kassapa who was placed by the Buddha on an equal footing in this respect, and not Sariputta and Maha Moggallana. The Buddha did so, says the commentary, because he knew that Sariputta and Maha Moggallana would not survive him, but Kassapa would. It could also be that both Sariputta and Maha Moggallana were no longer alive at that time.

Though the Buddha had highly praised Kassapa's ability as an exponent of the Dhamma, there were three occasions when Kassapa hesitated to instruct the monks after being asked by the Buddha to do so. He did not refuse because he wanted to avoid the effort and distraction of teaching, but because he found that those particular young monks were unresponsive to his admonitions.

In the first of the three instances, Kassapa said that it had now become difficult to speak to some of the monks; they were not amenable to advice, were intractable, and did not accept admonitions with respect. He had also heard that two monks boasted of their skill in preaching, saying: "Come, let us see who will preach more profusely, more beautifully, and at greater length!" When the Buddha was informed about this by Kassapa, he had these monks summoned and brought them back to reason, making them give up their immature conceit (S. 16:6). Hence we can see that Kassapa's negative report turned out to be of benefit to those monks. It was not done just for criticizing others.

On the second occasion, too, Kassapa did not wish to instruct monks who were not amenable to admonishment, who lacked faith in the good, who lacked shame and fear of wrong-doing, who lacked energy and understanding as to the good.

This was a statement in general about a certain section of the monks, without reference of individuals. Of these monks Kassapa said further that, in their state of decline, they are like the waning moon that daily loses in beauty (confidence), in roundness (shame), in splendour (fear of wrong-doing), in height (energy), and in width (wisdom).

Also on a third occasion the Buddha asked Kassapa to instruct the monks, and Kassapa expressed his reluctance for the same reason as before. It seems that this time, too, the Buddha did not urge Kassapa to change his mind and admonish the monks, but he himself spoke of the reasons for their conduct:

"Formerly, Kassapa, there were elders of the Order who were forest-dwellers,-living on almsfood, wearing rag-robes, using only the threefold set of robes, having few wants and being contented, living secluded and aloof from society, energetic, and they praised and encouraged such a way of life. When such elders or younger bhikkhus visited a monastery, they were gladly welcomed and honoured as being dedicated to the practice of the Dhamma. Then those who thus welcomed and honoured those noble monks would also strive to emulate them in their ways of life, and this would be of great benefit to them for a long time.

"But nowadays, Kassapa, those who are honoured when visiting a monastery are not monks of austere and earnest life, but those who are well known and popular and are amply provided with the requisites of a monk. These are made welcome and honoured, and their hosts try to emulate them, which will bring them harm for a long time. Hence one will be right in saying that such monks are harmed and overpowered by what does harm to a monk's life." — Paraphrased from S.16:8 On another occasion, Kassapa asked the Buddha: "What is the reason that formerly there were fewer rules, but more monks were established in the knowledge of Arahatship, while now there are more rules, but fewer monks are established in the knowledge of Arahatship?" The Buddha replied:

"So it happens, Kassapa, when beings deteriorate and the true Dhamma vanishes: then there are more rules and fewer Arahats. There will be, however, no vanishing of the true Dhamma until a sham Dhamma arises in the world. But when a sham Dhamma arises in the world, there will be more rules and fewer Arahats.

"But, Kassapa, it is not a cataclysm of the four elements — earth, water, fire and air — that makes the Dhamma disappear. Nor is the reason for its disappearance similar to the overloading of a ship that causes it to sink. It is rather the presence of five detrimental attitudes that causes the obscuration and disappearance of the Dhamma.

"These are the five: it is the lack of respect and regard for the Buddha, the Dhamma, the Sangha, the training, and for meditative concentration, on the part of monks and nuns, and male and female lay devotees. But so long as there is respect and regard for those five things, the Dhamma will remain free of obscuration and will not disappear."

It deserves to be noted that, according to this text, the male and female lay followers are also preservers of the Dhamma. We may conclude from this that even when the Dhamma has come to oblivion among the monks, it will still remain alive when honoured and practiced by the laity.

Other discourses in the Kassapa Samyutta deal chiefly with Maha Kassapa's austere way of life, which was highly praised and commanded by the Buddha. But on one occasion the Buddha reminded Kassapa that he had now grown old, and that he must find his coarse, worn-out rag-robes irksome to use. Therefore, the Buddha suggested, he should now wear robes offered by householders, accept also their invitations for alms offerings, and live near him. But Kassapa replied: "For along time I have been a forest-dweller, going the almsround, and wearing rag-robes; and such a life I have commanded to others. I have had few wants, lived contented, secluded, applying strenuous energy; and that too I have commanded to others."

The Buddha asked: "But for what reason do you live so?" Kassapa replied that he had two reasons: his own well being here and now, and his compassion for later generations which, when hearing about such a life, would emulate it. Then the Buddha said: "Well spoken, Kassapa, well spoken! You have lived for the happiness of many, out of compassion for the world, for the benefit and welfare of gods and men. You may then keep to your coarse rag-robes, go out for alms, and live in the forest ".

"This our Kassapa," said the Buddha, "is satisfied with whatever robes, almsfood, lodging, and medicine he obtains. For the sake of these he will not do anything that is unbefitting for a monk. If he does not obtain any of these requisites, he is not perturbed; and when he obtains them, he makes use of them without clinging or infatuation, not committing any fault, aware of (possible) dangers and knowing them as an escape (from bodily affliction). By the example of Kassapa, or by one who equals him, I will exhort you, monks. Thus admonished, you should practice in the same way".

The Buddha also mentioned that Kassapa was likewise exemplary in his relation to the laity. When going among the families on his almsround or on invitation, he did not think wishfully that people may give amply and give things of quality, that they may give quickly and respectfully. He had no such thoughts, but remained detached like the moon that sheds its mild light from a distance.

"When Kassapa goes among families, his mind is not attached, not caught up, not fettered. He rather thinks: 'Let those who want gain acquire gain! Let those who want merit do merit!' He is pleased and glad at the gains of others, just as he is pleased and glad at his own gains. Such a monk is fit to go among families.

"When he preaches the doctrine, he will not do so for the sake of personal recognition and praise, but for letting them know the Teaching of the Exalted One, so that those who hear it may accept it and practice accordingly. He will preach because of the excellence of the Teaching and out of compassion and sympathy." — Paraphrased from S.16:3,4.

But the strongest recognition of Maha Kassapa's achievement, the highest praise given him by the Buddha, may be found in a sutta where it is said that Maha Kassapa could attain at will, just like the Buddha himself, the four fine-material and the four immaterial meditative absorptions, the cessation of perception and feeling, and could also attain the six supernormal knowledges *(Albania),* which include the supernormal powers and culminate in the attainment of Nibbana (S.16:9). Here his powerful meditative achievements, equaling those of the Buddha, appear as a characteristic trait of Maha Kassapa's mind. It was because of that deep meditative calm that he could adapt himself, unperturbed, to all external situations and live as one of few wants, materially and socially.

In his verses preserved in the "Verses of the Elders" *(Theragatha)* Maha Kassapa praises again and again the peace of the Johne's (meditative absorptions). He was one who went from abundance to abundance. In his lay life he had lived in the abundance of wealth and harmony. As a monk he dwelt in the abundance of jhanic experience, furthered by his former life in the Brahma-world. While in some of the texts he appears to be very severe, this should not lead us to believe that he was harsh by nature.

When he occasionally rebuked others in stem words, he did so for pedagogical reasons in order to help them. This we shall see especially when we deal with his relationship to Ananda.

Encounters with Deities

Two meetings of Maha Kassapa with deities of lower or higher order have been recorded. They are related here because they illustrate his independence of spirit and his determination to keep to his austere way of living without accepting privileges from wherever they were offered.

There was a young female deity, called Laja, who remembered that she had obtained her present celestial happiness because in her previous human existence as a poor woman, she had offered parched rice to the Elder Maha Kassapa with a believing heart, uttering the aspiration: "May I be a partaker of the truth you have seen!" On her way home, while reflecting on her offering, she was bitten by a snake and died, and was immediately reborn in the Heaven of the Thirty-three gods, in the midst of great splendour.

This the deity, remembered, and in her gratitude she wanted now to serve the great Elder. Descending to earth, she swept the Elder's cell and filled the water vessels. After she had done that for three days, the Elder saw her radiant figure in his cell, and after questioning her, asked her to leave as he did not wish that monks of the future, knowing of it, should disapprove of him. His entreaties were of no avail; the deity rose into the air, filled with great sadness. The Buddha, aware of what had happened, appeared to the deity and consoled her by speaking of the worth of meritorious deeds and their great reward. But he also said that it had been Kassapa's duty to practice restraint.

In the other story it is told that Maha Kassapa, while living at the Pipphali Cave, had entered a period of seven days' uninterrupted meditation, spending the time in unbroken meditative posture. At the end of that period, after arising from that meditation, he went to Rajagaha on almsround. At that time there arose in five hundred female deities of Sakka's celestial realm the keen desire to offer almsfood to the venerable Maha Kassapa. With the food prepared, they approached the Elder, asking for his favour by accepting their offering. But he asked them to leave as he wanted to bestow his favour on the poor so that they could benefit from their meritorious deed.

As he did not yield to their repeated entreaties, they finally left. When Sakka, king of the gods, heard about their vain effort, a great desire arose in him as well to offer almsfood to that great Elder. To avoid being refused, he turned himself into an old weaver. When Maha Kassapa approached, he offered rice to him, and at the moment the rice was accepted it turned exceedingly fragrant. Then Maha Kassapa knew who this old weaver truly was, and he reproached Sakka: "You have done a grievous wrong, Kosiya. By doing so, you have deprived poor people of the chance to acquire merit. Do not do such a thing again!" – "We too need merit, revered Kassapa! We too are in need of it! But have I acquired merit or not by giving alms to you through deception?" – "You have gained merit, friend. Now Sakka, while departing, gave voice to the following "Solemn Utterance":

- Oh, almsgiving! Highest almsgiving!
- Well bestowed on Kassapa!.

Relations to Pupils and Fellow Monks

One so very dedicated to the meditative life as Maha Kassapa was cannot be expected to have been keen on accepting and training many pupils; and, in fact, the canonical texts mention only a few pupils of his.

One of Kassapa's few recorded discourses addressed to the monks deals with the subject of overestimating one's attainments:

"There may be a monk who declares he has attained to the highest knowledge, that of Arahatship. Then the Master, or a disciple capable of knowing the minds of others, examines and questions him. When they question him, that monk becomes embarrassed and confused. The questioner now understands that the monk has made this declaration through overrating himself out of conceit. Then, considering the reason for it, he sees that this monk has acquired much knowledge of the Teaching and proficiency in it, which made him declare his overestimation of himself to be the truth. Penetrating the mind of that monk, he sees that he is still obstructed by the five hindrances and has stopped half-way while there is still more to do."

Apart from the few instances where Maha Kassapa is speaking to unnamed monks or a group of monks, the texts record only his relationship to Sariputta and Ananda.

According to the Jatakas, in former lives Sariputta was twice the son of Kassapa and twice the brother of Kassapa ; he was once also Kassapa's grandson and his friend . In his verses, Kassapa tells that he once saw thousands of Brahma-gods descend from their heaven, pay homage to Sariputta, and praise him.

Two conversations between Maha Kassapa and Sariputta have been recorded in the Kassapa Samyutta. On both occasions it was at evening time, after meditation, that the venerable Sariputta went to see the venerable Maha Kassapa.

In the first text Sariputta asked: "It has been said, friend Kassapa, that without ardour and without fear of wrongdoing, one is incapable of gaining enlightenment, incapable of attaining Nibbana, incapable of attaining highest security, but that with ardour and with fear of wrong-doing, one is capable of such attainments. Now in how far is he incapable of such attainments and in how far is he capable of them?"

"When, friend Sariputta, a monk thinks: 'If bad and unwholesome states that have so far not arisen in me were to arise, this would bring me harm,' and if then he does not arouse ardour and fear of wrongdoing, then he is lacking ardour and fear of wrong doing. When he thinks: 'If bad and unwholesome states that have arisen now in me are not abandoned, this would bring me harm,' or: 'If unarisen wholesome states were not to arise, this would bring me harm,' or: 'If arisen wholesome states were to vanish, this would bring me harm,' if on these occasions, too, a monk does not arouse ardour and fear of wrong-doing, then he is lacking these qualities, and lacking them, he is incapable of attaining enlightenment, incapable of attaining Nibbana, incapable of attaining the highest security. But if a monk (on those four occasions for right effort) arouses ardour and fear of wrong-doing, he is capable of attaining enlightenment, capable of attaining Nibbana, capable of attaining the highest security".

On another occasion Sariputta asked Maha Kassapa some questions which one may not have expected: whether the Perfect One (Tathagata) exists after death, or does not exist, or (in some sense) both exists and does not exist, or neither exists nor does not exist.

In each case Maha Kassapa replies that this was not declared by the Exalted One. And when asked why not, he said: "Because it is of no benefit and does not belong to the fundamentals of the holy life, because it does not lead to turning away (from worldliness), nor to dispassion, cessation, (inner) peace, direct knowledge, enlightenment, and Nibbana."

"But what, friend, did the Exalted One declare?"

"This is suffering-_ so, friend, has the Exalted One declared. This is the origin of suffering — the cessation of suffering — the way to the cessation of suffering — so, friend, has the Exalted One declared. And why? Because it conduces to benefit and belongs to the fundamentals of the holy life, because it leads to turning away (from worldliness), to dispassion, cessation, (inner) peace, direct knowledge, enlightenment, and Nibbana" — S. 16:12

We have no tradition as to why Sariputta posed these questions, which for an arahant should have been fully clear. It is, however, not impossible that this conversation took place immediately after Kassapa's ordination and before his attainment of Arahatship, and that Sariputta wanted to test him in that way; or, perhaps, it was for the sake of other monks who may have been present.

The Majjhima Nikaya records a sutta (No. 32, Mahagosinga Sutta) in which Maha Kassapa participated in a group discussion with several other eminent disciples led by Sariputta. At the time these elders of the Order were residing in the Gosinga Forest along with the Buddha, and on a clear moonlit night they approached Sariputta for a discussion on the Dhamma. Sariputta declared: "Delightful is this Gosinga Forest, it is a clear moonlit night, the sala-trees are in full bloom, and it seems as if celestial scents are being wafted around."

Then he asked each distinguished elder in the group — Ananda, Revata, Anuruddha, Maha Kassapa, and Maha Moggallana — what kind of monk could illumine that Gosinga Forest. Maha Kassapa, like the others, replied according to his own temperament. He declared that a monk who could illumine the Gosinga Forest would be a forest-dweller, one who went on almsround, who wore rag-robes, who possessed only three robes, who had few wishes, was content, aloof, not gregarious, energetic, and who would speak in praise of each of these qualities. He would also possess virtue, concentration, wisdom deliverance and the knowledge and vision of deliverance, and would speak in praise of each of these attainments.

According to tradition, Maha Kassapa also had close connections in former lives with the venerable Ananda. Ananda had twice been his brother (J. 488,535), once his son (J. 450), once even the murderer of his son (J. 540), and in this life he was his pupil (Maha Vagga I, 74). The Kassapa Samyutta likewise has two conversations between them. They concern practical questions, while those with Sariputta referred to doctrine.

On the first occasion (related at S. 16:10) Ananda asked Kassapa whether he would go with him to the nunnery. Kassapa, however, refused and asked Ananda to go alone. But Ananda seemed to be keen that Kassapa should give a Dhamma talk to the nuns, and he repeated his request twice. Kassapa finally consented to go and gave a discourse to the nuns. But the result turned out to be quite different from what Ananda had expected. One of the nuns, Thullatissa by name, raised her voice to make a rather offensive remark: "How could the Revered Kassapa presume to speak Dhamma in the presence of the Revered Ananda, the learned sage? This is as if a needle peddler wanted to sell a needle to the needle maker."

Obviously this nun preferred the gentle preaching of Ananda to Kassapa's stern and sometimes critical approach, which may have touched on her own weaknesses.

When Kassapa heard the nun's remarks, he asked Ananda: "How is it, friend Ananda, am I the needle peddler and you the needle maker, or am I the needle maker and you the needle peddler?"

Ananda replied: "Be indulgent, venerable sir. She is foolish woman.

"Beware, friend Ananda, or else the Sangha may further examine you. How is it, friend Ananda, was it you to whom the Exalted One referred in the presence of the Sangha when saying: 'I, O monks, can attain at will the four fine-material and immaterial meditative absorptions, the cessation of perception and feeling, the six supernormal knowledges; and Ananda, too, can so attain'?"

"Not so, venerable sir."

"Or was it that he said: 'Kassapa, too, can so attain'?"

From the above account we see that the venerable Maha Kassapa did not think that Ananda's conciliatory reply was adequate, or did full justice to the situation. Thullatissa's remarks showed her personal attachment to Ananda, who has always been a favourite with women, and who had also given his strong support to the founding of the Order of Nuns (Bhikkhuni Sangha). This emotional relation of Thullatissa's to Ananda could not be put aside just by Ananda's general remark. Hence Kassapa responded in a way which, at first glance, appears rather harsh: "Beware, friend Ananda, or else the Sangha may further examine you!" This was to say that Ananda should not engage himself too much in ministering to the nuns, as on their part attachment such as that of Thullatissa's could grow from it, and cause others to entertain doubts about him. Kassapa's reply has therefore to be seen as the earnest advice of a taint-free arahant to one who had not yet reached that state. When, immediately after, Kassapa mentioned that the Buddha had declared his own meditative attainments equal with those of himself, and not Ananda's, this may be taken as pointing to the far different spiritual status of the two; and it may have served as a spur to Ananda to strive for those attainments. The nun Thullatissa, however, left the Order.

Another conversation between the venerable Maha Kassapa and Ananda arose on the following occasion. Once the venerable Ananda went on a walking tour in the Southern Hills, together with a large company of monks. This was at a time when thirty mostly young monks, pupils of the venerable Ananda, had given up the robe and had returned to the lay life. After the venerable Ananda had ended his tour, he came to Rajagaha and went to see the venerable Maha Kassapa. When he had saluted him and had sat down, Kassapa said this:

"What are the reasons, friend Ananda, for the sake of which the Blessed One had said that only three monks should take their alms meal among families?"

"There are three reasons, venerable sir: it is for restraining ill-behaved persons, for the well-being of good monks, and out of consideration for the lay families."

"Then, friend Ananda, why do you go on tour with those young new monks whose senses are unrestrained, who are not moderate in eating, not given to watchfulness? It seems you behave like one trampling the corn. It seems you destroy the faith of the families. Your following is breaking up, your new starters are falling away. This youngster truly does not know his own measure!" "Gray hairs are now on my head, venerable sir, and still we cannot escape being called 'youngster' by the venerable Maha Kassapa."

But the venerable Maha Kassapa repeated again the very same words he had spoken.

This could have ended this matter, as Ananda did not deny that the reproach was justified. He objected only to the hurtful way in which Maha Kassapa had expressed his censure. In response to the admonition, Ananda would have tried to keep his pupils under stricter discipline. But, again, this matter was complicated by a nun, Thullananda, who along with Thullatissa was one of the "black sheep" of the Bhikkhuni Order. She had heard that Ananda had been called a "youngster" by the venerable Maha Kassapa, and full of indignation, she voiced her protest saying that Kassapa had no right to criticize a wise monk like Ananda, as Kassapa had formerly been an ascetic of another school. In that way, Thullananda diverted the matter of monastic discipline into personal detraction. Besides, she was wrong, as our earlier account has shown. (Before meeting the Buddha, Kassapa had gone forth as an independent ascetic, not as a follower of another school.) Thullananda soon left the Order, just as the other wayward nun, Thullatissa, had done.

When the venerable Maha Kassapa heard Thullananda's utterance, he said to Ananda: "Rash and thoughtless are the words spoken by Thullananda the nun. Since I left the home life, I have had no other teacher than the Exalted One, the Holy One, the Perfectly Enlightened One" .

After the Buddha's Parinibbana

What remains to be said about Maha Kassapa's relation to Ananda is closely connected with his leading role in the Sangha after the passing away of the Buddha. At the demise of the Buddha, only two of the five most prominent disciples were present, the brothers Ananda and Anuruddha. Sariputta and Maha Moggallana had preceded the Master in death and Maha Kassapa, with a large company of monks, was just then wandering on the highroad from Pava to Kusinara. During that walk he happened to step aside from the road and sat down under a tree to rest. Just then a naked ascetic passed that way. The ascetic had with him a Mandarava (coral tree) flower, which is said to grow only in a celestial world. When Maha Kassapa saw this, he knew that something unusual must have happened for the flower to be found on earth. He asked the ascetic whether he had heard any news about his teacher, the Buddha, and the ascetic affirmed that he had, saying: "The recluse Gotama passed into Nibbana a week ago. This Mandarava flower I picked up from the place of cremation."

Among the monks who heard that message, only those who were Arahats like Maha Kassapa could remain composed and calm; but the others who were still unliberated from the passions lamented and wept: "Too soon has the Blessed One passed into Nibbana! Too soon has the Eye of the World vanished from our sight!"

But there was one monk, Subhadda by name, who had ordained in his old age. He addressed the other monks and said: "Enough, friends! Do not grieve, do not lament! We are well rid of that Great Ascetic. We have been troubled by his telling us: 'This is befitting, that is not befitting.' Now we can do what we like, and we won't have to do what we do not like."

It is not recorded that at that time the venerable Maha Kassapa gave a reply to those callous words. He may not have wished just then to strike a discordant note by censuring the monk or having him disrobed as he deserved. Hence he remained silent. But, as we shall see later, Maha Kassapa quoted that incident when he spoke of the need for summoning a council. Now, however, he admonished his group of monks not to lament, but to remember that impermanence is the nature of all conditioned things. He then continued his journey to Kusinara, together with his monks.

Until then it had not been possible to set the funeral pyre alight as the deities present wanted to wait until the venerable Maha Kassapa came and paid his last homage to the remains of the Master. When the venerable Maha Kassapa arrived at the place of cremation, he walked twice around the pyre, reverently, with clasped hands, and then, with bowed head paid his homage at the feet of the Tathagata. When his group of monks had done likewise, the pyre, it is said, burst into flames by itself.

Hardly had the bodily remains of the Tathagata been cremated when there arose a conflict about the distribution of the relics among the lay folk assembled and those who had sent messengers later. But the venerable Maha Kassapa remained aloof in that quarrel, as did the other monks like Anuruddha and Ananda. It was a respected brahman, Dona by name, who finally divided the relics into eight portions and distributed them among the eight claimants. He himself took the vessel in which the relics had been collected.

The venerable Maha Kassapa himself brought to King Ajatasattu of Magadha his share of the relics. Having done so, he turned his thoughts to the preservation of the Master's spiritual heritage, the Teaching (Dhamma) and the Discipline (Vinaya).

The necessity to do so was demonstrated to him by Subhadda's challenge of the monastic discipline, and his advocacy of moral laxity, which Maha Kassapa took as a warning. If that attitude were to spread, it would lead to the decline and ruin of both the Sangha and the Teaching. To prevent this at the very start, Maha Kassapa proposed holding a council by which the Dhamma and Vinaya could be reliably established and secured. With that suggestion, he turned to the monks gathered at Rajagaha. The monks agreed and at their request Maha Kassapa selected five hundred members, all but one of whom were Arahats. Ananda, however, at that time had not yet succeeded in reaching that final attainment, but as he excelled in remembering a large number of the Buddha's discourses, he too was admitted to complete the five hundred members of the First Council. All other monks were to leave Rajagaha for the duration of the council.

As the first item of the council's proceedings, the texts of the monastic discipline were recited by the venerable Upali, who was a Vinaya expert. The second item was the codification of the Teaching laid down in the discourses. Here it was Ananda who, on being questioned by the venerable Maha Kassapa, recited all those texts which were later compiled in the Five Collections *(Nikaya)* of the Sutta Pitaka. It was an outstanding feat of memory on his part.

Finally, some special matters concerning the Sangha were discussed. Among them, the venerable Ananda mentioned that the Buddha, shortly before his death, had permitted the abolishment of minor rules. When Ananda was asked whether he had inquired from the Buddha what these minor rules were, he had to admit that he had neglected to do so.

Now various opinions about this matter were expressed in the assembly. As there was no consensus, the venerable Maha Kassapa asked the assembly to consider that if they were to abolish rules arbitrarily, the lay followers and the public in general would reproach them for being in a hurry to relax discipline so soon after the Master's death. Hence Maha Kassapa suggested that the rules should be preserved intact without exception. And so it was decided (Culavagga, XI).

After the holding of the First Council, the high regard in which the venerable Maha Kassapa was held grew still greater, and he was seen as the de facto head of the Sangha. His seniority would have contributed to this, as he was then one of the oldest living disciples.

Later on, the venerable Maha Kassapa handed over the Buddha's almsbowl to Ananda, as a symbol of continuing the faithful preservation of the Dhamma. Thus Maha Kassapa, who had been generally recognized in the Order as the worthiest in succession, chose on his part Ananda as being the worthiest after him.

There is no report in the Pail literature about the time and circumstances of his death.

The Verses of Maha Kassapa

In the canonical "Verses of the Elders" *(Theragatha),* forty verses (1051-1091) are ascribed to the venerable Maha Kassapa. These stanzas mirror some of the great Elder's characteristic qualities and virtues: his austere habits and his contentedness; his strictness towards himself and brother monks; his independent spirit and his self-reliance; his love of solitude, shunning the crowds; his dedication to the practice of meditation and the peace of the Janus. These verses also show what does not appear in the prose texts: his sensitivity to the beauty of nature that surrounded him.

Here only a selection of the stanzas is given, which may be read in full in the translations by C.A.F. Rhys Davids and K.R. Norman.

An exhortation to the monks to practice contentment with regard to the four basic requisites of a monk's life.

Down from my mountain-lodge I came one day

And made my round for alms about the streets.

A leper there I saw eating his meal
And courteously I halted at his side. (1054)
He with his hand all leprous and diseased
Put in my bowl a morsel; as he threw,
A finger broke off and fell into my food. (1055)
At a wall nearby I ate my share,
Not at the time nor after felt disgust. (1056)
For only he who takes as they come
The scraps of food, cow's urine for medicine,
Lodging beneath a tree, the patchwork robe,
Truly is a man contented everywhere. (1057)

When Maha Kassapa was asked why, at his advanced age, he still climbed daily up and down the rock, he replied:

While some are very wearied as they climb the rocks,
An heir of the Buddha, mindful, self-possessed,
By force of the spirit fortified,
Does Kassapa ascend the mountain bow. (1058)
Returning from the daily round for alms,
He mounts again the rock and sits
In meditation rapt, not clinging anywhere,
For far from him has he put fear and dread. (1059)
Returning from his daily round for alms,
He mounts again the rock and sits
In meditation rapt, not clinging anywhere,
For he among those that burn is cool and still. (1060)
Returning from his daily round for alms,
He mounts again the rock and sits
In meditation rapt, not clinging anywhere,
His task is done, from cankers he is free. (1061)

People asked again why the venerable Maha Kassapa, at his age, wishes to live in forests and mountains. Does he not like monasteries such as the Veluvana Vihara and others?

These regions are delightful to my heart
When the Kareri creeper spreads its flower wreaths,
When sound the trumpet-calls of elephants.
These rocky heights delight my heart. (1062)
These rocks with hue of dark-blue clouds
Where streams are flowing, cool and crystal-clear,
With glow-worms covered (shining bright),
These rocky heights delight my heart. (1063)
Like towering peaks of dark-blue clouds,
Like splendid edifices are these rocks,
Where the birds' sweet voices fill the air,
These rocky heights delight my heart. (1064)
With glades refreshed by (cooling) rain,
Resounding with the calls of crested birds,
The cliffs resorted to by seers,
These rocky heights delight my heart. (1065)
Here is enough for me who, resolute,
Desires to meditate (in solitude).
Here is enough for me, a monk determined,
Who seeks to dwell in the highest goal's attainment. (1066)
Here is enough for me who, resolute,
Desires to live in happy ease (and free).
Here is enough for me who is on effort bent,
(Devoted to the practice) as a monk determined. (1064)
Like dark-blue blooms of flax they are,
Like autumn sky with dark-blue clouds,
With flocks of many kinds of birds,
These rocky heights delight my heart. (1068)
No crowds of lay folk have these rocks,
But visited by herds of deer.
With flocks of many kinds of birds,

These rocky heights delight my heart. (1069)
Wide gorges are there where clear water flows,
Haunted by monkeys and by deer,
With mossy carpets covered, moist,
These rocky heights delight my heart. (1700)
No music with five instruments
Can gladden me so much
As when, with mind collected well,
Right insight into Dhamma dawns. (1071)

In the following verses the venerable Maha Kassapa voices his own "Lion Roar."

In the whole field of the Buddha's following,
Except for the mighty Master himself,
I stand the foremost in ascetic ways;
No one practices them so far as I. (1087)
The Master has been served by me,
And all the Buddha's teaching has been done.
Low have I laid the heavy load I bore,
Cause for rebirth is found in me no more. (1088)
Gotama the immeasurable does not cling
To robe, to food or place of lodging.
Like spotless lotus blossom he is free from taints,
Bent on renunciation he transcends the three worlds. (1089)
The four foundations of mindfulness are his neck;
The great Seer has faith and confidence for hands;
Above, his brow is perfect wisdom; nobly wise,
He ever wanders with all desire quenched. (1090)

Second Buddhist Council

The Second Buddhist council took place in Vesali, about one hundred years after the Buddha's Parinibbana, in order to settle a serious dispute on Vinaya. The orthodox monks were able to convince the monks whose behaviour was under question.

Accounts of the dispute are preserved in the Vinaya texts of several of the early Buddhist schools. Virtually all scholars agree that this second council was a historical event.

Some time after the Second Council, schisms occurred within the monastic Sangha, which resulted in the formation of several subgroups such as Sthaviravada, Mahasanghika and Sarvastivada.

The dispute arose over the 'Ten Points.' This is a reference to claims of some monks breaking ten rules, some of which were considered major. The specific ten points were:

1. Storing salt in a horn.
2. Eating after midday.
3. Eating once and then going again to a village for alms.
4. Holding the Uposatha Ceremony with monks dwelling in the same locality.
5. Carrying out official acts when the assembly was incomplete.
6. Following a certain practice because it was done by one's tutor or teacher.
7. Eating sour milk after one had his midday meal.
8. Consuming strong drink before it had been fermented.
9. Using a rug which was not the proper size.
10. Using gold and silver.

The key issue was the use of 'gold and silver', which is an Indic idiom that includes any kind of money. The monks of Vesali had taken to wandering for alms with the specific goal of collecting money, to which the visiting monk Yasa objected. Some of the other points are also important, for example point 6, which would allow monks to not follow the Vinaya on any point which their teacher did not follow or practice. This behaviour was noted, became an issue and caused a major controversy. The monastic Sangha is structured so that all actions and decisions must be unanimously agreed upon through consensus. Since the monks accused of breaking these ten rules refused to be reprimanded or acknowledge fault, the Sangha was unable to resolve this dispute in any other way than by convening the *Second Buddhist Council.*

Some of the *Ten Points* were against minor rules. Before the Buddha's Parinibbana he told Ven. Ananda that the community may (unanimously) relinquish the minor rules of the Vinaya but at the First Buddhist Council there was uncertainty about which rules he was referring to and it was unanimously decided to keep the Vinaya as it was during the Buddha's lifetime. However, 100 years later some monks felt that certain rules could be relaxed.

The Second Buddhist Council made the unanimous decision not to relax any of the rules, and censured the behaviour of the monks who were accused of violating the *ten points*.

Third Buddhist Council

The Third Buddhist council was convened in about 250 BCE at Asokarama in Patiliputta, supposedly under the patronage of Emperor Asoka. The reason for convening the Third Buddhist Council is reported to have been to rid the Sangha of corruption and bogus monks who held heretical views. It was presided over by the Elder Moggaliputta Tissa and one thousand monks participated in the Council. However, the council is unrecognized and unknown to all Buddhist sources outside of the Theravada school, and its importance to these other schools is therefore debatable. Tradition has it that Asoka had won his throne through shedding the blood of all his father's son's except his own brother, Tissa Kumara, who eventually got ordained and achieved Arahantship.

Historical Background

The Theravadin account of the background to the Third Council is as follows: Emperor Asoka was crowned in the two hundred and eighteenth year after the Buddha's Mahaparinibbana. At first he paid only token homage to the Dhamma and the Sangha and also supported members of other religious sects as his father had done before him. However, all this changed when he met the pious novice-monk Nigrodha who preached him the Appamada-vagga. Thereafter he ceased supporting other religious groups and his interest in and devotion to the Dhamma deepened. He used his enormous wealth to build, it is said, eighty-four thousand pagodas and viharas and to lavishly support the bhikkhus with the four requisites. His son Mahinda and his daughter Sanghamitta were ordained and admitted to the Sangha.

Eventually, his generosity was to cause serious problems within the Sangha. In time the order was infiltrated by many unworthy men, holding heretical views and who were attracted to the order because of the Emperor's generous support and costly offerings of food, clothing, shelter and medicine. Large numbers of faithless, greedy men espousing wrong views tried to join the order but were deemed unfit for ordination.

Despite this they seized the chance to exploit the Emperor's generosity for their own ends and donned robes and joined the order without having been ordained properly. Consequently, respect for the Sangha diminished. When this came to light some of the genuine monks refused to hold the prescribed purification or Uposatha ceremony in the company of the corrupt, heretical monks.

When the Emperor heard about this he sought to rectify the situation and dispatched one of his ministers to the monks with the command that they perform the ceremony. However, the Emperor had given the minister no specific orders as to what means were to be used to carry out his command. The monks refused to obey and hold the ceremony in the company of their false and 'thieving' companions.

In desperation the angry minister advanced down the line of seated monks and drawing his sword, beheaded all of them one after the other until he came to the King's brother, Tissa who had been ordained. The horrified minister stopped the slaughter and fled the hall and reported back to the Emperor. Asoka was deeply grieved and upset by what had happened and blamed himself for the killings. He sought Thera Moggaliputta Tissa's counsel. He proposed that the heretical monks be expelled from the order and a third Council be convened immediately.

Council

So it was that in the seventeenth year of the Emperor's reign the Third Council was called. Thera Moggaliputta Tissa headed the proceedings and chose one thousand monks from the sixty thousand participants for the traditional recitation of the Dhamma and the Vinaya, which went on for nine months. The Emperor, himself questioned monks from a number of monasteries about the teachings of the Buddha. Those who held wrong views were exposed and expelled from the Sangha immediately. In this way the Bhikkhu Sangha was purged of heretics and bogus bhikkhus.

According to the Pail account, the Elder Moggaliputta Tissa, in order to refute a number of heresies and ensure the Dhamma was kept pure, compiled a book during the council called the Kathavatthu. This book consists of twenty-three chapters, and is a collection of discussions on the points of controversy. It gives refutations of the 'heretical' views held by various Buddhist sects on matters philosophical. The Kathavatthu is the fifth of the seven books of the Abhidhamma Pitaka. However, the historicity of this has been questioned, as the account preserved in the San Jian Lu Pi Po Sho, although otherwise almost identical, does not mention the Kathavatthu. Moggaliputtatissa told Ashoka that the doctrine taught by the Buddha was the Vibhajjavada, the Doctrine of Analysis. This term is used in various senses, and it is not clear exactly what it meant in this context. Traditionally, however, the Sri Lankan Theravadins and other mainland schools of Early Buddhism identified themselves as Vibhajjavada.

Results of Missions

The Dhamma missions to Sri Lanka and Kashmir and Gandhara were very successful, leading to a long-term presence and dominance of Buddhism in those areas.

It is not clear exacly how influential the interactions to Egypt and Greece may have been, but some authors have commented that some level of syncretism between Hellenist thought and Buddhism may have started in Hellenic lands at that time. They have pointed to the presence of Buddhist communities in the Hellenistic world around that period, in particular in Alexandria (mentioned by Clement of Alexandria), and to the pre-Christian monastic order of the Therapeutae (possibly a deformation of the Pail word "Theravada"), who may have "almost entirely drawn (its) inspiration from the teaching and practices of Buddhist asceticism" (Robert Linssen).

Possibly Buddhist gravestones from the Ptolemaic period have also been found in Alexandria, decorated with what may be depictions of the Dharma wheel (Tarn, "The Greeks in Bactria and India"). Commenting on the presence of Buddhists in Alexandria, some scholars have even pointed out that "It was later in this very place that some of the most active centres of Christianity were established" (Robert Linssen "Zen living"). In the 2nd century CE, the Christian theologian Clement of Alexandria recognized Bactrian

Buddhists (Sramanas) and Indian Gymnosophists for their influence on Greek thought:

"Thus philosophy, a thing of the highest utility, flourished in antiquity among the barbarians, shedding its light over the nations. And afterwards it came to Greece. First in its ranks were the prophets of the Egyptians; and the Chaldeans among the Assyrians; and the Druids among the Gauls; and the Sramanas among the Bactrians; and the philosophers of the Celts; and the Magi of the Persians, who foretold the Saviour's birth, and came into the land of Judaea guided by a star. The Indian gymnosophists are also in the number, and the other barbarian philosophers. And of these there are two classes, some of them called Sramanas, and others Brahmins." Clement of Alexandria

Moggaliputta-Tissa

Moggaliputta- Tissa (ca. 327 BC – 247 BC), (born in Pataliputra, Magadha (now Patna, India) was a Buddhist monk and scholar who lived in the 3rd century BC. David Kalupahana sees him as a predecessor of Nagarjuna in being a champion of the middle-way and a reviver of the original philosophical ideals of the Buddha.

He was the spiritual teacher of the Mauryan Emperor Ashoka, and his son Mahinda, who brought Buddhism to Sri Lanka. Moggaliputta-Tissa also presided over the Third Buddhist Council. According to the *Mahavamsa,* he had consented himself to be reincarnated as a human in order to chair the council, on the request of the *arahants* who has presided over the second.

He was the son of Mogalli of Pataliputra, as a Hindu in the brahmin caste as Tissa. According to the *Mahavamsa,* Tissa, who was thoroughly proficient in the Vedas, at a young age was sought after by the Buddhist monks Siggava and Candavajji for conversion, as they went on their daily alms round. At the age of seven, Tissa was angered when Siggava, a Buddhist monk, occupied his seat in his house and berated him. Siggava responded by asking Tissa a question about the *Cittayamaka* which Tissa was not able to answer, and he expressed a desire to learn the dharma, converting to Buddhism. After obtaining the consent of his parents, he joined the Sangha as Siggava's disciple, who taught him the *Vinaya* and Candavajji the *Abhidhamma Pitakas.* He later attained arahantship and became an acknowledged leader of the monks at Pataliputra. He became known as Moggaliputta-Tissa.

At a festival for the dedication of the Asokarama and the other *viharas* built by Ashoka, Moggaliputta-Tissa, in answer to a question, informed Ashoka that one becomes a kinsman of the Buddha's religion only by letting one's son or daughter enter the Sangha. Upon this suggestion, Ashoka had both his son Mahinda and daughter Sanghamitta ordained.

Moggaliputta acted as Mahinda's teacher until Mahinda was sent to propagate Buddhism in Sri Lanka. Later, due to the great gains which accrued to the *Sangha* through Ashoka's patronage of Buddhism, he perceived that the Order had become corrupt. He committed the monks to the leadership of Mahinda, and lived in self-imposed solitary retreat for seven years on the Ahoganga pabbata. Ashoka recalled him to Pataliputra after some monks had been murdered by royal officials. After some initial reluctance, he traveled by boat to Pataliputra, and was met at the landing place by Ashoka. Ashoka had a dream on the previous night which royal soothsayers interpreted to mean that an eminent ascetic would touch him on the right hand. As the Moggaliputta touched Ashoka's hand the royal guards were about to carry out an instantaneous death penalty. Ashoka restrained his guards and Moggaliputta took his hand as a sign that he accepted him as a disciple.

On the advice of Moggaliputta, Ashoka convened the Third Buddhist Council in Pataliputra, in the Asokarama, which was attended by some 1,000 monks in 253 BC. In his presence, Ashoka questioned the assembled monks on their views of various doctrines, and those who held views which were deemed to be contrary to Buddhism were disrobed. He compiled the *Kathavatthu,* in refutation of those views, and it was in this council that this text was approved and added to the *Abhidhamma.* Moggaliputta later made arrangements arising from the council to send monks outside of the Mauryan Empire to propagate Buddhism, and arranged for a Bodhi tree sapling to be sent to Sri Lanka.

He died at the age of eighty in the twenty-sixth year of Ashoka's reign and his relics were enshrined in a stupa in Sanchi along with nine other arahants.

Fourth Buddhist Council

Fourth Buddhist Council is the name of two separate Buddhist council meetings. The first one was held in the First Century BC, in Sri Lanka. In this fourth Buddhist council the Theravadin Pail Canon was for the first time committed to writing, on palm leaves. The second one was held by the Sarvastivada school, in Kashmir around the First Century AD.

Fourth Buddhist Council in Sri Lanka

The 1st Fourth Buddhist Council (Theravada tradition) was held in response to a year in which the harvests in Sri Lanka were particularly poor, and many monks subsequently died of starvation. Because the Pail Canon was in that time solely remembered by heart, the surviving monks recognized the danger of not writing the teachings of the Tipitaka down, so that even if some of the monks (whose duty it was to study and remember parts of the Tipitaka for later generations) died, the teachings would not be lost. This Fourth Buddhist Council took three years. The Fourth Buddhist Council was held in Tambapanni (Sri Lanka) under the patronage of King Vattagamani. The main reason for its convening was the realization that it was now not possible for the majority of monks to retain the entire Tipitaka in their memories as had been the case formerly for the Venerable Mahinda and those who followed him soon after. Therefore, as the art of writing had, by this time developed substantially it was thought expedient and necessary to have the entire body of the Buddha's teaching written down.

King Vattagamani supported the monk's idea and a council was held specifically to commit the entire Tipitaka to writing, so that the genuine Dhamma might be lastingly preserved. To this purpose, the Venerable Maharakkhita and five hundred monks recited the words of the Buddha and then wrote them down on palm leaves. This remarkable project took place in a cave called, the Aloka lena, situated in the cleft of an ancient landslip near what is now Matale. Thus the aim of the Council was achieved and the preservation in writing of the authentic Dhamma was ensured. In the Eighteenth Century, King Vijayarajasiha had images of the Buddha created in this cave.

After the Council, palm leaves books appeared, and were taken to other countries, such as Burma, Thailand, Cambodia and Laos. The Tipitaka and its commentaries were originally brought to Sri Lanka by the missionary monk Mahinda of the Third Buddhist Council.

Fourth Buddhist Council in Kashmir

The 2nd Fourth Buddhist Council (Sarvastivada tradition) is said to have been convened by the Kushan emperor Kanishka, perhaps around 100 CE at Jalandhar or in Kashmir. The Fourth Council of Kashmir is not recognized as authoritative in Theravada; reports of this council can be found scriptures which were kept in the Mahayana tradition. The Mahayana tradition based some of its scriptures on (refutations of) the Sarvastivadin Abhidharma texts, which were systematized at this council.

It is said that for the Fourth Council of Kashmir, Kanishka gathered 500 monks headed by Vasumitra, partly, it seems, to compile extensive commentaries on the (Sarvastivadin Abhidharma, although it is possible that some editorial work was carried out upon the existing canon itself. The main fruit of this Council was the vast commentary known as the Maha-Vibhasha ("Great Exegesis"), an extensive compendium and reference work on a portion of the Sarvastivadin Abhidharma.

Scholars believe that it was also around this time that a significant change was made in the language of the Sarvastivadin canon, by converting an earlier Prakrit version into Sanskrit. Although this change was probably effected without significant loss of integrity to the canon, this event was of particular significance since Sanskrit was the official holy language of Brahmanism in India, and was also being used by other thinkers (regardless of their specific religious or philosophical allegiance), thus enabling a far wider audience to gain access to Buddhist ideas and practices. For this reason, all major (Sarvastivad and Mahayana) Buddhist scholars in India thereafter wrote their commentaries and treatises in Sanskrit. Theravada however never switched to Sanskrit; the language of the Theravadin scriptures (Pail) came to be regarded as the natural language, the root language of all beings.

5

Schools of Buddhism

Schools of Buddhism are classified in various ways. Normal English-language usage (as given in dictionaries) divides Buddhism into Theravada (also known by the name Hinayana, which many consider pejorative) and Mahayana. The most common classification among scholars is threefold, with Mahayana split into East Asian (also known simply as Mahayana) and Vajrayana, or Tibetan Buddhism (although Vajrayana properly includes the Japanese Shingon school).

Classifications

The *Macmillan Encyclopedia of Religion* distinguishes three types of classification of Buddhism:

- Movements:
  * Hinayana
  * Mahayana
  * Vajrayana.
- Nikayas, or monastic fraternities, three of which survive at the present day:
  * Theravada, in Southeast Asia
  * Dharmaguptaka, in China, Korea and Vietnam
  * Mulasarvastivada, in the Tibetan tradition.
- Doctrinal schools.

Terminology

The terminology for the major divisions of Buddhism can be confusing, as Buddhism is variously divided by scholars and practitioners according to geographic, historical, and philosophical criteria, with different terms often being used in different contexts. The following terms may be encountered in descriptions of the major Buddhist divisions:

Conservative Buddhism

An alternative name for the early Buddhist schools.

Early Buddhist Schools

The schools into which Buddhism became divided in its first few centuries; only one of these survives as an independent school, Theravada

East Asian Buddhism

A term used by scholars to cover the Buddhist traditions of Japan, Korea, Singapore and most of China and Vietnam

Eastern Buddhism

An alternative name used by some scholars for East Asian Buddhism; also sometimes used to refer to all traditional forms of Buddhism, as distinct from Western(ized) forms.

Esoteric Buddhism

Usually considered synonymous with Vajrayana. Some scholars have applied the term to certain practices found within the Theravada, particularly in Cambodia.

Hinayana

Often interpreted as a pejorative term, used in Mahayana doctrine to denigrate its opponents. It is sometimes used to refer to the early Buddhist schools, including the contemporary Theravada, although the legitimacy of this is disputed. Its use in scholarly publications is controversial. By the Mahayana schools and groups in China, Korea, Tibet, and Japan the term is felt to be only slightly pejorative, or not pejorative at all. By some it is used with respect proper to teachings coming direct from the Buddha. The main use of the term in East Asian and Tibetan traditions is in reference to spiritual levels regardless of school. The literal meaning of Hinayana can also be interpreted as "the small vehicle," referring to a raft meant to carry one person, as an arhat, to nirvana through their own effort, in contrast to the "large vehicle" of Mahayana meant to carry many there at once, piloted by a bodhisattva.

Lamaism

An old term, still sometimes used, synonymous with Tibetan Buddhism; widely considered derogatory.

Mahayana

A movement that emerged out of early Buddhist schools, together with its later descendants, East Asian and Tibetan Buddhism. Vajrayana traditions are sometimes listed separately. The main use of the term in East Asian and Tibetan traditions is in reference to spiritual levels regardless of school.

Mainstream Buddhism

A term used by some scholars for the early Buddhist schools.

Mantrayana

Usually considered synonymous with Vajrayana. The Tendai school in Japan has been described as influenced by Mantrayana.

Newar Buddhism

A non-monastic, caste based Buddhism with patrilineal descent and Sanskrit texts.

Nikaya Buddhism or Schools

An alternative term for the early Buddhist schools.

Non-Mahayana

An alternative term for the early Buddhist schools.

Northern Buddhism

An alternative term used by some scholars for Tibetan Buddhism. Also, an older term still sometimes used to encompass both East Asian and Tibetan traditions. It has even been used to refer to East Asian Buddhism alone, without Tibetan Buddhism.

Secret Mantra

An alternative rendering of mantrayana, a more literal translation of the term used by schools in Tibetan Buddhism when referring to themselves.

Sectarian Buddhism

An alternative name for the early Buddhist schools.

Southeast Asian Buddhism

An alternative name used by some scholars for Theravada.

Southern Buddhism

An alternative name used by some scholars for Theravada.

Sravakayana

An alternative term sometimes used for the early Buddhist schools.

Tantrayana or Tantric Buddhism

Usually considered synonymous with Vajrayana. However, one scholar describes the tantra divisions of some editions of the Tibetan scriptures as including Sravakayana, Mahayana and Vajrayana texts. Some scholars, particularly Francois Bizot, have used the term "Tantric Theravada" to refer to certain practices found particularly in Cambodia.

Theravada

The traditional Buddhism of Sri Lanka, Burma, Thailand, Laos, Cambodia and parts of Vietnam, China, India, Bangladesh and Malaysia. It is the only surviving representative of the historical early Buddhist schools. The term 'Theravada' is also sometimes used to refer to all the early Buddhist schools.

Tibetan Buddhism

Usually understood as including the Buddhism of Tibet, Mongolia, Bhutan and parts of China, India and Russia, which follow the Tibetan tradition.

Vajrayana

A movement that developed out of Indian Mahayana, together with its later descendants. There is some disagreement on exactly which traditions fall into this category. Tibetan Buddhism is universally recognized as falling under this heading; many also include also the Japanese Shingon school.

Some scholars, also apply the term to the Korean milgyo

tradition, which is not a separate school. One scholar says, "Despite the efforts of generations of Buddhist thinkers, it remains exceedingly difficult to identify precisely what it is that sets the Vajrayana apart."

Early Schools

Numerous attempts have been made to tabulate these schools. Here is one.

- Sthaviravada.
  - Pudgalavada ('Personalist') (c. 280 BCE)
  - Sarvastivadin.
    - Vibhajjavada (prior to 240 BCE; during Aloka)
    - The ravada (c. 240 BCE)
    - Theravada subschools
    - Mahiuasaka (after 232 BCE)
    - Dharmaguptaka (after 232 BCE)
    - Kauyapa (after 232 BCE)
    - Vatsiputriya (under Aœoka) later name: SaCmitiya
    - Dharmottariya
    - Bhadrayaniya
    - Sannagarika
    - Mulasarvastivada (third and fourth centuries)
    - Sautrantika (between 50 BCE and c. 100 CE).
- Mahsa Cghika ('Majority', c. 380 BCE).
  - Ekavyaharikas (under Aœoka).
    - Lokottaravada.
  - Golulika (during Aœoka).
    - Bahurutiya (late third century BCE)
    - Prajnaptivada (late third century BCE)
    - Cetiyavada.
  - Caitika (mid-first century BCE)
    - Apara Aiel
    - Uttara Aiel

Sthaviravada

Sthaviravada literally means "Teaching Of The Elders," known today by its Pail name, The ravada. They were one of the two main movements in early Buddhism that arose from the Great Schism, the other being that of the Mahs Eghika. "The Elders" referred to those who had attained to one of the four levels of awakening (namely, Sotapanna, Sakadagami, Anagami and Arahant; the latter signaling final liberation)-and also generally to monks who had been ordained for over ten years-who were naturally the leaders of the community, and whose voice and views carried more weight than more junior monks; some scholars believe that this was the primary cause of the Schism.

The Sthaviravada were the proponents of an orthodox understanding of the Buddha's teachings which later became known in Pail as The ravada. They criticised the Mahs Eghika school for adding additional rules to the Patimokkha.

The Schism happened between the second (350 BC) and third (250 BC) Buddhist Council. According to the Mahavamsa, after the Second Council was closed, those taking the side of junior monks did not accept the verdict but held an assembly of their own attended by ten thousand calling it a Mahasangiti (Great convocation) from which the school derived its name Mahs Eghika.

Another belief on the cause of the Great Schism, were the disagreements in the five theories about an Arahant, put forward by Mahadeva, who later founded Mahs Eghika. The rest of the monks who rejected the five theories named themselves as "Sthaviravada" to differentiate from the Mahs Eghika.

The Sthaviravada doctrine survives today in The ravada (Thera and Sthavira being the Pail and Sanskrit forms of the same word meaning 'elder'). Little evidence exists suggesting doctrinal, practical, or genealogical distinction between The ravada and the Sthaviravada (after all, the only records of the "Sthaviravada" we have are, in fact, The ravada sources, and their counterparts in the Chinese Agamas). One source claims there is no historical evidence that The ravada school arose until around two centuries after the Great Schism which occurred at the Council of Pmaliputra." However, there are no records of an imagined Sthaviravada independent of, and other than, Theravada. The Theravada is often recognized as being a continuation of the Sthaviravada, after the Third Buddhist Council, and, in being such, is the school most representative of early Buddhist doctrine and practice.

Pudgalavada

The Pudgalavada or "Personalist" school of Buddhism broke off from the orthodox Sthaviravada (elders) school around 280 BCE. The Sthaviravadins interpreted the doctrine of anatta to mean that, since there is no true "self", all that we think of as a self (i.e., the subject of sentences, the being that transmigrates) is merely the aggregated skandhas. The Pudgalavadins asserted that, while there is no atman, there is a pudgala or "person", which is neither the same as nor different from the skandhas. The "person" was their method of accounting for karma, rebirth, and nirvana. Other schools held that the "person" exists only as a label, a nominal reality.

The Pudgalavadins were strongly criticized by the Theravadins (a record of a Theravadin attack on the pudgala is found in the Kathavatthu), Sarvastivadins, and Madhyamakas. Peter Harvey agrees with criticisms levelled against the Pudgalavadins by Moggaliputta-Tissa and Vasubandhu, and finds that there is no support in the suttas for their "person"-concept.

They were labelled heretical, and the sect eventually died out.

Sammitiya

The Sammitiya sect was an offshoot of the Vatsiputriya and one of twenty or so early schools of Buddhism in India. Like its predecessor, it claims the person (Sanskrit: *pudgala*) as a carrier of skandhas endures.

The distinguished Buddhologist Etienne Lamotte, using the writings of the Chinese traveller Xuanzang, asserted that the Sammitiya were in all likelihood the most populous non-Mahayanist sect in India, comprising double the number of the next largest sect, although scholar L. S. Cousins revised his estimate down to a quarter of all non-Mahayana monks, still the largest overall. The Sammitiya sect seems to have been particularly strong in the Sindh, where one scholar estimates 350 Buddhist monasteries were Sammitiya of a total of 450. This area was rapidly Islamized in the wake of the Arab conquest.

Xuanzang reported that the Sammitiya of Sind "have narrow

views and attack the Mahayana, while the Tibetan historian Taranatha reported that the Sammitiya were staunchly anti-Mahayanist and anti-Vajrayanist, with Sammitiya monks from the Sind burning tantric scriptures and destroying a silver image of Hevajra at Vajrasana monastery. The end of the Sammitya sect appears to coincide with the overall decline of Buddhism in India.

Vibhajjavada

Vibhajjavada is an umbrella classification for Buddhist denominations that promote *analysis* as a primary tool for developing 'insight'. This doctrine holds that the first step to insight is to be achieved by the aspirant's experience, critical investigation and reasoning; instead of by blind faith.

Nomenclature and Etymology

Vibhajjavada (Pail) or Vibhajyavada (Sanskrit). The word *Vibhajjavada* may be parsed into *Vibhajja*, loosely meaning "analysis" and *vada* holding the semantic field: "doctrine", "teachings". Hence, the term "Vibhajjavada" may be rendered into English as "the doctrine of analysis".

Vibhajjavadi as a Characteristic of Bodhi

The term *Vibhajjavadi* occurs in MN 99 and AN X.94, though not in the sense of a separate school, but as a characteristic of Bodhi and the Shakyamuni Buddha himself: "Now, by blaming what is blamable and praising what is praiseworthy, the Blessed One is a 'discriminating teacher' (*vibhajja-vada*) and is not one-sided in his teaching" (AN X.94).

Mahisasaka

Mahisasaka is one of the twenty schools of early Buddhism according to a Mahayana record. Its origins go back to the dispute in the Second Buddhist Council. Dharmaguptaka sect branch out from Mihisasaka sect toward the end of the 2nd or the beginning of the 1st century BC. Its vinaya was translated into Chinese in AD 434.

Kauyapa

Kauyapa (Sanskrit; Pail: Kassapiya or Kassapika) is an early Buddhist school. Their name is believed to be derived from

Kauyapa, one of the original missionaries sent by King Ashoka to the Himavant country. They are believed to have become an independent school ca. 190 BCE. According to the traditional chronicles of Sri Lanka, the Kauyapa were an offshoot of the Sarvastivadin (Sanskrit; Pail: Sabbatthavadi). According to the Kathavatthu commentary, the Kauyapa believed that past events exist in the present in some form.

Some tentatively attribute the Gander Dharmapada to the Kauyapa school.

Dharmaguptaka

The Dharmaguptaka are one of the eighteen or twenty schools of Early Buddhism, depending on one's source. It originated from another sect, Mahisasaka. It had a prominent role in early Central Asian and Chinese Buddhism, and its monastic rules are still in effect in some East Asian countries to this day.

Doctrinal Development

The Dharmaguptaka doctrine appears to have been characterized by an understanding of the Buddha as separate from Sangha so that his teaching is superior to the one given by Arahants. They also emphasise the merit of devotion to the religious monument (stupa), which often had pictorial representation of the stories Buddha's previous life as bodhisattva (Jatakas). Consequently, they regarded the path of bodhisasttva and the path of Buddhist discipline (sravaka-hearer) to be separate. Dharmaguptakas's tripitaka contain two new addition, Bodhisattvapitaka and Dharanipitaka.

School's Flourishing and Demise

The Gandharan Buddhist texts, the earliest Buddhist texts ever discovered, are apparently dedicated to the teachers of the Dharmaguptaka school. They tend to confirm a flourishing of the Dharmaguptaka school in northwestern India around the 1st century CE, with Gander as the canonical language, and this would explain the subsequent influence of the Dharmaguptakas in Central Asia and then northeastern Asia. According to Buddhist scholar A.K. Warder, the Dharmaguptaka originated in Aparanta.

Scholars over the years have asserted that the Dharmaguptaka were founded by a Greek monk:

One of the major missionaries was Yonaka Dhammarakkhita. He was, as his name indicates, a Greek monk, native of 'Alasanda' (Alexandria). He features in the Pail tradition as a master of psychic powers as well as an expert on Abhidhamma. He went to the Greek-occupied areas in the west of India. Long ago Przyluski, followed by Frauwallner, suggested that Dhammarakkhita be identified with the founder of the Dharmaguptaka school, since dhammarakkhita and dhammagutta have identical meaning. Since that time two pieces of evidence have come to light that make this suggestion highly plausible. One is the positive identification of very early manuscripts belonging to the Dharmaguptakas in the Gandhara region, exactly where we expect to find Yonaka Dhammarakkhita. The second is that the phonetic rendering of his name in the Sudassanavinayavibhasa evidently renders 'Dharmagutta' rather than 'Dhammarakkhita'.

The Dharmaguptaka vinaya was translated into Chinese by Buddhayasas in the early fifth-century, and thereafter became the predominant vinaya in Chinese Buddhist monasticism. When Hsuan-Tsang travelled in Asia during the 7th century however, he reported that the Dharmaguptakas had almost completely disappeared from India and Central Asia.

6

Theravada

Theravada literally, "the Teaching of the Elders" or "the Ancient Teaching", is the oldest surviving Buddhist school. It was founded in India. It is relatively conservative, and generally closest to early Buddhism, and for many centuries has been the predominant religion of Sri Lanka (about 70% of the population) and most of continental Southeast Asia (Cambodia, Laos, Burma, Thailand). Theravada is also practiced by minorities in parts of southwest China (by the Shan and Tai ethnic groups), Vietnam (by the Khmer Krom), Bangladesh (by the ethnic groups of Baruas, Chakma, and Magh), Malaysia and Indonesia, while recently gaining popularity in Singapore and the Western World. Today Theravada Buddhists number over 100 million worldwide, and in recent decades Theravada has begun to take root in the West and in the Buddhist revival in India.

History

Origin of the School

The Theravada school is ultimately derived from the Vibhajjavada (or 'doctrine of analysis') grouping which was a continuation of the older Sthavira (or 'teaching of the Elders') group at the time of the Third Buddhist Council around 250 BC, during the reign of Emperor Asoka in India. Vibhajjavadins saw themselves as the continuation of orthodox Sthaviras and after the Third Council continued to refer to their school as the Sthaviras/ There's ('The Elders'), their doctrines were probably similar to the older Sthaviras but were not completely identical. After the Third Council geographical distance led to the Vibhajjavadins gradually evolving into four groups: the Mahiuasaka, Kauyapa, Dharmaguptaka and the Tamraparniya. The Theravada is descended from the Tamraparniya, which means 'the Sri Lankan lineage'. Some sources claim that only the Theravada actually evolved directly from the Vibhajjavadins.

According to Buddhist scholar A.K. Warder, the Theravada "spread rapidly south from Avanti into Maharastra and Andhra and down to the Chola country (Kanchi), as well as Ceylon. For sometime they maintained themselves in Avanti as well as in their new territories, but gradually they tended to regroup themselves in the south, the Great Vihara (Mahavihara) in Anuradhapura, the capital of Ceylon, become the main centre of their tradition, Kanchi a secondary centre and the northern regions apparently relinquished to other schools." There is little information about the later history of Theravada Buddhism in India, and it is not known when it disappeared in its country of origin.

The name of Tamraparniya was given to the Sri Lankan lineage in India but there is no indication that this referred to any change in doctrine or scripture from the Vibhajjavadins, since the name points only to geographical location. The Theravadan accounts of its own origins mention that it received the teachings that were agreed upon during the Third Buddhist Council, and these teachings were known as the Vibhajjavada. In the 7th century, Chinese pilgrims Xuanzang and Yi Jing refer to the Buddhist school in Sri Lanka as 'Sthavira'. In ancient India, those schools that used Sanskrit as their religious language referred to this school as the 'Sthaviras', but those that use Pail as their religious language referred to this school as the 'Theres'. Both 'Sthaviras' (Sanskrit) and 'There's' (Pail) both literally mean 'The Elders'. The school has been using the name 'Theravada' for itself in a written form since at least the fourth century CE when the term appears in the *Dipavamsa*.

The Theravada school had also reached Burma around the time it arrived in Sri Lanka and something of a synergy gradually developed. Around the end of the tenth century C.E, for example, war in Sri Lanka had extinguished the Theravadan ordination lineage, and a contingent of Burmese monks had to be imported to rekindle it. Burmese and Sri Lankan Theravada reinforced each other sufficiently, so that by the time Buddhism died out in India in the eleventh century, it had established a stable home in these countries. Gradually the Theravada form of Buddhism spread to Thailand, Laos, and Cambodia.

Although the Theravada tradition was always reputed to be one of the more conservative schools, like the other Nikaya Buddhist schools in India at one point it included Mahayana practioners ("Mahayana-Theravada" or "Mahayana-Sthaviravada"), according to reports of Chinese pilgrims such as Xuanzang. Royal houses in Sri Lanka and Southeast Asia associated themselves closely with Buddhism. States in those areas strictly enforced orthodoxy, and ensured that Theravada remained traditionalist. This contrasts with the relationship of Buddhism to states throughout most of Buddhism's history in India.

History of the Tradition

According to Sinhalese tradition, Buddhism was first brought to Sri Lanka by Mahinda, who is believed to have been the son of the Mauryan emperor Asoka, in the third century BCE, as a part of the missionary activities of the Asokan era. In Sri Lanka, Mahinda established the Mahavihara Monastery of Anuradhapura. Later it became divided into three subgroups, known after their monastic centres as the Mahavihara, the Abhayagiri Vihara, and the Jetavanavihara. In 1164, with the guidance of two monks from a forest branch of the Mahavihara, the Sri Lankan King reunited all bhikkhus in Sri Lanka into the orthodox Mahavihara school.

A few years after the arrival of Sthavira Mahinda, Sanghamitta, who is also believed to be the daughter of Emperor Asoka, came to Sri Lanka. She started the first nun order in Sri Lanka, but the nun order died out in Sri Lanka in the 11th century and in Burma in the 13th. In 429 CE, by request of China's emperor, nuns from Anuradhapura were sent to China to establish the Nun Order. The order was then spread to Korea. In 1996, 11 selected Sri Lankan nuns were ordained fully as Bhikkhunis by a team of Theravada monks in concert with a team of Korean Nuns in India. There is disagreement among Theravada vinaya authorities as to whether such ordinations are valid. In the last few years the head of the Dambulla chapter of the Siyam Nikaya in Sri Lanka has carried out ordination ceremonies for hundreds of nuns. This has been criticized by some other leading figures in the Siyam Nikaya and Amarapura Nikaya, and the governing council of Burmese

Buddhism has declared that there can be no valid ordination of nuns in modern times, though some Burmese monks disagree with this.

According to Mahavamsa the Sri Lanka chronical, after the conclusion of the Third Buddhist Council, a missionary was also sent to Suvannabhumi where two monks Sona and Uttara, are said to have proceeded. Scholar opinions differ as to where exactly this land of Suvannabhumi is located, but Suvannabhumi is believed to be located somewhere in the area which now includes lower Burma, Thailand, Malay Peninsula and Sumatra Island.

The Mon and Pyu were among the earliest people to inhabit Burma. Recent archaeological research at a Pyu settlement in the Samon Valley (around 100 km south-east of Bagan) has shown that they had trade links with India from 500-400 BC and with China around 200 BC. Chinese sources which have been dated to around 240 A.D. mention a Buddhist kingdom by the name of Lin-Yang, which some scholars have identified as the ancient Pyu kingdom of Beikthano 300 km north of Yangon. The Burmese slowly became Theravadan when they came into contact with the Pyu and Mon civilization. The Thais also slowly became Theravadan as they came into contact with the Mon civilization.

Despite its success in Southeast Asia, Theravada Buddhism in China has generally been limited to areas bordering Theravada countries.

Modern Developments

The following modern trends or movements have been identified.

- modernism: attempts to adapt to the modern world and adopt some of its ideas; includes among other things.
    * green movement
    * syncretism with other Buddhist traditions
    * women's rights
    * gay rights.
- reformisms: attempts to restore a supposed earlier, ideal state of Buddhism; includes in particular the adoption of Western scholars' theories of original Buddhism (in recent times the "Western scholarly interpretation of Buddhism"

is the official Buddhism prevailing in Sri Lanka and Thailand.)

- ultimatism: tendency to concentrate on advanced teachings such as the Four Noble Truths at the expense of more elementary ones
- neo-traditionalism; includes among other things.
    - revival of ritualism
    - remythologization.
- insight meditation
- social action
- devotional religiosity
- reaction to Buddhist nationalism
- renewal of forest monks
- revival of samatha meditation.

Buddhist revivalism has also reacted against changes in Buddhism caused by colonialist regimes. Western colonialists and Christian missionaries deliberately imposed a particular type of Christian monasticism on Buddhist clergy in Sri Lanka and colonies in Southeast Asia, restricting monks' activities to individual purification and temple ministries.

Prior to British colonial control, monks in both Sri Lanka and Burma had been responsible for the education of the children of lay people, and had produced large bodies of literature. After the British takeover, Buddhist temples were strictly administered and were only permitted to use their funds on strictly religious activities. Christian ministers were given control of the education system and their pay became state funding for missions.

Foreign, especially British rule had an enervating effect on the sangha. According to Walpola Rahula, Christian missionaries displaced and appropriated the educational, social, and welfare activities of the monks, and inculcated a permanent shift in views regarding the proper position of monks in society through their institutional influence upon the elite.

Many monks in post-colonial times have been dedicated to undoing this paradigm shift. Movements intending to restore Buddhism's place in society have developed in both Sri Lanka and Burma.

Overview of Philosophy

Theravada promotes the concept of Vibhajjavada (Pail), literally "Teaching of Analysis." This doctrine says that insight must come from the aspirant's experience, critical investigation, and reasoning instead of by blind faith; however, the scriptures of the Theravadan tradition also emphasize heeding the advice of the wise, considering such advice and evaluation of one's own experiences to be the two tests by which practices should be judged.

In Theravada, the cause of human existence and suffering is identified as craving, which carries with it the defilements (*kilesas*). Those defilements that bind human to the cycle of rebirth are classified into a set of ten "Fetters", while those defilements that impede concentration are presented in a fivefold set called the "Five Hindrances". The level of defilement can be coarse, medium, and subtle. It is a phenomenon that frequently arises, remains temporarily and then vanishes. Theravadans believe defilements are not only harmful to oneself, but also harmful to others. They are the driving force behind all inhumanities a human being can commit.

Theravadian's believe these defilements are the habits born of ignorance (*avijja*) which afflict the minds of all unenlightened beings. It is believed that unenlightened beings are under the influence of the defilements, unenlightened beings cling to them through ignorance of the truth. But in reality, those mental defilements are nothing more than taints that have afflicted the mind and create suffering and stress. It is also believed that unenlightened beings cling to the body, assuming it as their own "*Self*", but in reality the body is an impermanent phenomenon formed from the four basic elements. Often characterized by earth, water, fire and air, in the early Buddhist texts these are defined to be abstractions representing the sensorial qualities solidity, fluidity, temperature, and mobility, respectively. The mental defilements' frequent instigation and manipulation of the mind is believed to have prevented the mind from seeing the true nature of reality. Unskillful behaviour in turn can strengthen the defilements, but following the Noble Eightfold Path can weaken or eradicate them.

It is also believed that unenlightened beings experience the world through their imperfect six sense doors (eye, ear, nose, tongue, tactile sense, and mind) and then use the mind clouded by defilements to form their own interpretation, perception and conclusion.

In such a condition the perception or conclusion made will be based on that being's own illusion of reality. In the state of *jhana* (deep concentration), the five physical sense doors will fade, the mental defilements will be suppressed, and wholesome mental traits will become strengthened. The mind can then be used to investigate and gain insight into the true nature of reality.

There are three stages of defilements. During the stage of passivity the defilements lies dormant at the base of the mental continuum as latent tendencies (*anusaya*), but through the impact of sensory stimulus it will manifest (*pariyutthana*) itself to the surface of consciousness in the form of unwholesome thoughts, emotions, and volitions. If they gather additional strength, the defilement will reach the dangerous stage of transgression (*vitikkama*), which will then involve physical or vocal actions.

It is believed that in order to be free from suffering and stress these defilements need to be permanently uprooted. Initially the defilements are restrained through mindfulness to prevent them from taking over the mind and bodily action. They are then uprooted through internal investigation, analysing, experiencing and understanding the true nature of those defilements by using *jhana*. This process needs to be repeated for each and every defilement. The practice will then lead the meditator to realize the Four Noble Truths, Enlightenment, and Nirvana. Nirvana is the ultimate goal of Theravadans. *Nirvana* is said to be the perfect bliss and the person is liberated from the repeated cycle of birth, illness, aging and death.

Theravadans believe that every individual is personally responsible for their own self-awakening and liberation, as they are the ones that were responsible for their own actions and consequences (Sanskrit: *karma*; Pail: *kamma*). Simply learning or believing in the true nature of reality as expounded by the Buddha is not enough, the awakening can only be achieved through direct experience and personal realization. An individual will have to follow and practice the Noble Eightfold Path as taught by the Buddha to discover the reality for themselves. In Theravada belief, Buddhas, gods or deities are incapable of giving a human being the awakening or lifting them from the state of repeated cycle of birth, illness, aging and death (*samsara*). For Theravadans, Buddha is only a Teacher of the Noble Eightfold Path, while gods or deities are still subject to anger, jealousy, hatred, vengeance, craving, greed, delusion, and death.

It is believed that some people who practice with earnestness and zeal can attain Nirvana within a single lifetime, as did many of the first few generations of Buddha's disciples. For others, the process may take multiple lifetimes, with the individual reaching higher and higher states of realization. One who has attained Nirvana is called an *Arahant*. It is believed that the Nirvana is most quickly attained as a disciple of Buddha, since Lord Buddha is believed to have possessed the ultimate knowledge on how to guide a person through the process of enlightenment.

According to the early scriptures, the Nirvana attained by *Arahants* is identical to that attained by the Buddha himself, as there is only one type of Nirvana. Buddha was superior to *Arahants* because the Buddha had discovered the path all by himself, and has taught it to others (i.e., metaphorically turning the wheel of Dhamma). *Arahants*, on the other hand, attained Nirvana due in part to the Buddha's teachings. Theravadans revere the Buddha as a single supremely gifted person but do recognize the existence of other such Buddhas in the distant past and future. Maitreya (Pail: Metteyya), for example, is mentioned very briefly in the Pail Canon as a Buddha who will come in the distant future.

Traditionally Theravadans can either have the conviction (or "faith") in the Buddha's teaching and practice the minor precepts in the hope of gaining some minor benefits or they can investigate and verify by direct experience the truth of the Buddha's teaching by practicing the *jhana* which is part of the Noble Eightfold Path for their own Enlightenment.

Fundamentals of Theravada

One thing that should be expressed first and foremost is that the Theravada philosophy is a continuous analytical process of life, not a mere set of ethics and rituals. The ultimate theory of Theravada uses the Four Noble Truths, also known as the Four Sublime Truths. In the simplest form these can be described as the problem, the cause, the solution and the pathway to solution (implementation).

The Four Noble Truths

The Four Noble Truths (or The Four Truths of the Noble Ones) is one of the most fundamental Buddhist teachings. This Dharma Enlightenment makes ordinary person become the Buddha (Khun Weera Boontanorm, 2000). In broad terms, these truths relate to suffering (or dukkha), its nature, its origin, its cessation and the path leading to its cessation. They are among the truths Siddhartha Gautama is said to have realized during his experience of enlightenment.

The Four Noble Truths appear many times, throughout the most ancient Buddhist texts, the Pail Canon. The early teaching and the traditional understanding in Theravada is that the Four Noble Truths are an advanced teaching for those who are ready for them. Mahayana Buddhism regards them as a preliminary teaching for people not ready for its own teachings.

Some may see "truths" as a mistranslation (one author cites "realities" as a possibly better choice: these are *things*, not statements, in the original grammar). However, the original Tibetan Lotsawas, who studied Sanskrit grammar thoroughly, did translate the term from Sanskrit into Tibetan as "bden pa" which has the full meaning of "truth".

Background

Why the Buddha is said to have taught in this way is illuminated by the social context of the time in which he lived. The Buddha was a Sramana – a wandering ascetic whose "aim was to discover the truth and attain happiness." He is said to have achieved this aim while under a bodhi tree near the River Neranjana; the Four Noble Truths are a formulation of his understanding of the nature of "suffering", the fundamental cause of all suffering, the escape from suffering, and what effort a person can go to so that they themselves can "attain happiness."

These truths are not expressed as a hypothesis or tentative idea; rather, the Buddha says:

These Four Noble Truths, monks, are actual, unerring, not otherwise. Therefore, they are called noble truths.

The Buddha says that he taught them......because it is beneficial, it belongs to the fundamentals of the holy life, it leads to disenchantment, to dispassion, to cessation of suffering, to peace, to direct knowledge, to enlightenment, to Nirvana. That is why I have declared it.

This teaching was the basis of the Buddha's first discourse after his enlightenment. In early Buddhism this is the most advanced teaching in the Buddha's Gradual Training.

A formal description of the Four Noble Truths follows:

1. Dukkha (suffering)- This can be somewhat broadly classified into three categories. Inherent suffering, or the suffering one undergoes in all the worldly activities, what one suffers in day-to-day life: birth, aging, diseases, death, sadness, etc. In short, all that one feels from separating from 'loving' attachments and/or associating with 'hating' attachments is encompassed into the term. The second class of suffering, called Suffering due to Change, implies that things suffer due to attaching themselves to a momentary state which is held to be 'good'; when that state is changed, things are subjected to suffering. The third, termed 'Sankhara Dukkha', is the most subtle. Beings suffer simply by not realizing that they are mere aggregates with no definite, unchanging identity.
2. Dukkha Samudaya (cause of suffering)-Craving, which leads to Attachment and Bondage, is the cause of suffering. Formally, this is termed 'Tanha'. It can be classified into three instinctive drives. 'Kama Tanha' is the Craving for any pleasurable sense object (which involves sight, sound, touch, taste, smell and mental perceptives). 'Bhava Tanha' is the Craving for attachment to an ongoing process, which appears in various forms, including the longing for existence. 'Vibhava Tanha' is the Craving for detachment from a process, which includes non-existence and causes the longing for self-annihilation.
3. Dukkha Nirodha (cessation of suffering)-One cannot possibly adjust the whole world to one's taste in order to eliminate suffering and hope that it will remain so forever. This would violate the chief principle of Change. Instead, one adjusts one's own mind through detachment so that the Change, of whatever nature, has no effect on one's peace of mind. Briefly stated, the third Noble Truth implies that elimination of the cause (craving) eliminates the result

(suffering). This is inferred in the scriptural quote by The Buddha, 'Whatever may result from a cause, shall be eliminated by the elimination of the cause'.

4. Dukkha Nirodha Gamini Patipada (pathway to freedom from suffering)-This is the Noble Eightfold Pathway towards freedom or Nirvana. The path can roughly be rendered into English as right view, right intention, right speech, right actions, right livelihood, right effort, right mindfulness and right concentration.

Noble Eightfold Path

"Eightfold Path" redirects here. For the physics concept, see Eightfold way (physics). For the form of policy analysis, see Eightfold Path (policy analysis).

The Dharma wheel, often used to Represent the Noble Eightfold Path

The Noble Eightfold Path is one of the principal teachings of the Buddha, who described it as the way leading to the cessation of suffering (*dukkha*) and the achievement of self-awakening. It is used to develop insight into the true nature of phenomena (or reality) and to eradicate greed, hatred, and delusion. The Noble Eightfold Path is the fourth of the Buddha's Four Noble Truths; the first element of the Noble Eightfold Path is, in turn, an understanding of the Four Noble Truths. It is also known as the *Middle Path* or *Middle Way*.

All eight elements of the Path begin with the word "right", which translates the word *samyanc* (in Sanskrit) or *Samoa* (in Pail). These denote completion, togetherness, and coherence, and can also suggest the senses of "perfect" or "ideal" and practised by all the previous Buddhas. The Noble Eightfold Path is a practice said to lead its practitioner toward self-awakening and liberation. The path was taught by the Buddha to his disciples so that they, too, could follow it.

In the same way I saw an ancient path, an ancient road, traveled by the Rightly Self-mindfulness, right concentration...I followed that path. Following it, I came to direct knowledge of aging & death, direct knowledge of the origination of aging & death, direct knowledge of the cessation of aging & death, direct knowledge of the path leading to the cessation of aging &

death...Knowing that directly, I have revealed it to monks, nuns, male lay followers & female lay followers... —Nagara Sutta

The practice of the Noble Eightfold Path varies from one Buddhist school to another. Depending on the school, it may be practiced as a whole, only in part, or it may have been modified. Each Buddhist lineage claims the ability to implement the path in the manner most conducive to the development of its students.

The Practice

According to the *bhikkhu* (monk) and scholar Walpola Rahula, the divisions of the noble eightfold path "are to be developed more or less simultaneously, as far as possible according to the capacity of each individual. They are all linked together and each helps the cultivation of the others." Bhikkhu Bodhi explains that "with a certain degree of progress all eight factors can be present simultaneously, each supporting the others. However, until that point is reached, some sequence in the unfolding of the path is inevitable".

According to the discourses in the Pail and Chinese canons, right view, right resolve, right speech, right action, right livelihood, right effort, and right mindfulness are used as the support and requisite conditions for the practice of right concentration. Understanding of the right view is the preliminary role, and is also the forerunner of the entire Noble Eightfold Path. The practitioner should first try to understand the concepts of right view. Once right view has been understood, it will inspire and encourage the arising of right intention within the practitioner. Right intention will lead to the arising of right speech. Right speech will lead to the arising of right action. Right action will lead to the arising of right livelihood. Right livelihood will lead to the arising of right effort. Right effort will lead to the arising of right mindfulness. The practitioner must make the right effort to abandon the wrong view and to enter into the right view. Right mindfulness is used to constantly remain in the right view. This will help the practitioner restrain greed, hatred and delusion.

Once these support and requisite conditions have been established, a practitioner can then practice right concentration more easily. During the practice of right concentration, one will need to use right effort and right mindfulness to aid concentration practice. In the state of concentration, one will need to investigate and verify his or her understanding of right view. This will then result in the arising of right knowledge, which will eliminate greed, hatred and delusion. The last and final factor to arise is right liberation.

Wisdom (Prajna Panna)

"Wisdom", sometimes translated as "discernment" at its preparatory role, provides the sense of direction with its conceptual understanding of reality. It is designed to awaken the faculty of penetrative understanding to see things as they really are. At a later stage, when the mind has been refined by training in moral discipline and concentration, and with the gradual arising of right knowledge, it will arrive at a superior right view and right intention.

Right view

Right view can also be translated as "right perspective", "right vision" or "right understanding". It is the right way of looking at life, nature, and the world as they really are. It is to understand how reality works. It acts as the reasoning for someone to start practicing the path. It explains the reasons for human existence, suffering, sickness, aging, death, the existence of greed, hatred, and delusion. It gives direction and efficacy to the other seven path factors. Right view begins with concepts and propositional knowledge, but through the practice of right concentration, it gradually becomes transmuted into wisdom, which can eradicate the fetters of the mind. Understanding of right view will inspire the person to lead a virtuous life in line with right view. In the Pail and Chinese canons, it is explained thus:

And what is right view? Knowledge with reference to stress (dukkha can also be translated as suffering), knowledge with reference to the origination of stress (or suffering), knowledge with reference to the cessation of stress (or suffering), knowledge with reference to the way of practice leading to the cessation of stress (or suffering): This is called right view.

There are two types of right view:

1. View with taints: this view is mundane. Having this type of view will bring merit and will support the favourable existence of the sentient being in the realm of samsara.
2. View without taints: this view is supramundane. It is a factor of the path and will lead the holder of this view

toward self-awakening and liberation from the realm of samsara.

Right view has many facets; its elementary form is suitable for lay followers, while the other form, which requires deeper understanding, is suitable for monastics. Usually, it involves understanding the following reality:

1. Moral law of karma: Every action (by way of body, speech, and mind) will have karmic results (a.k.a. reaction). Wholesome and unwholesome actions will produce results and effects that correspond with the nature of that action. It is the right view about the moral process of the world.
2. The three characteristics: everything that arises will cease (impermanence). Mental and body phenomena are impermanent, source of suffering and not-self.
3. Suffering: Birth, aging, sickness, death, sorrow, lamentation, pain, grief, distress, and despair are suffering. Not being able to obtain what one wants is also suffering. The arising of craving is the proximate cause of the arising of suffering and the cessation of craving is the proximate cause of the cessation of the suffering. The quality of ignorance is the root cause of the arising of suffering, and the elimination of this quality is the root cause of the cessation of suffering. The way leading to the cessation of suffering is the noble eightfold path. This type of right view is explained in terms of Four Noble Truths.

Right view for monastics is explained in detail in the *Sammdimmhi Sutta* ("Right View Discourse"), in which Ven. Sariputta instructs that right view can alternately be attained by the thorough understanding of the unwholesome and the wholesome, the four nutriments, the twelve *nidanas* or the three taints. "Wrong view" arising from ignorance (*avijja*), is the precondition for wrong intention, wrong speech, wrong action, wrong livelihood, wrong effort, wrong mindfulness and wrong concentration. The practitioner should use right effort to abandon the wrong view and to enter into right view. Right mindfulness is used to constantly remain in right view.

The purpose of right view is to clear one's path of the majority of confusion, misunderstanding, and deluded thinking. It is a means to gain right understanding of reality. Right view should be held with a flexible, open mind, without clinging to that view as a dogmatic position. In this way, right view becomes a route to liberation rather than an obstacle.

Right Intention

Right intention can also be known as "right thought", "right resolve", "right conception", "right aspiration" or "the exertion of our own will to change". In this factor, the practitioner should constantly aspire to rid themselves of whatever qualities they know to be wrong and immoral. Correct understanding of right view will help the practitioner to discern the differences between right intention and wrong intention. In the Chinese and Pail Canon, it is explained thus:

And what is right resolve? Being resolved on renunciation, on freedom from ill will, on harmlessness: This is called right resolve.

It means the renunciation of the worldly things and an accordant greater commitment to the spiritual path; good will; and a commitment to non-violence, or harmlessness, towards other living beings.

Ethical Conduct (Uila Sila)

For the mind to be unified in concentration, it is necessary to restrain from unwholesome deeds of body and speech to prevent the faculties of bodily action and speech from becoming tools of the defilements. Ethical conduct is used primarily as aids for mental purification.

Right Speech

Right speech, deals with the way in which a Buddhist practitioner would best make use of their words. In the Pail Canon, it is explained thus:

And what is right speech? Abstaining from lying, from divisive speech, from abusive speech, and from idle chatter: This is called right speech.

The *Samannaphala Sutta, Kevatta Sutta* and *Cunda Kammaraputta Sutta* elaborate :

Abandoning false speech...He speaks the truth, holds to the truth, is firm, reliable, no deceiver of the world...

Abandoning divisive speech...What he has heard here he does

not tell there to break those people apart from these people here...Thus reconciling those who have broken apart or cementing those who are united, he loves concord, delights in concord, enjoys concord, speaks things that create concord...

Abandoning abusive speech...He speaks words that are soothing to the ear, that are affectionate, that go to the heart, that are polite, appealing and pleasing to people at large...

Abandoning idle chatter...He speaks in season, speaks what is factual, what is in accordance with the goal, the Dhamma, and the Vinaya. He speaks words worth treasuring, seasonable, reasonable, circumscribed, connected with the goal...

The *Abhaya Sutta* elaborates:

In the case of words that the Tathagata knows to be unfactual, untrue, unbeneficial (or: not connected with the goal), unendearing and disagreeable to others, he does not say them.

In the case of words that the Tathagata knows to be factual, true, unbeneficial, unendearing and disagreeable to others, he does not say them.

In the case of words that the Tathagata knows to be factual, true, beneficial, but unendearing and disagreeable to others, he has a sense of the proper time for saying them.

In the case of words that the Tathagata knows to be unfactual, untrue, unbeneficial, but endearing and agreeable to others, he does not say them.

In the case of words that the Tathagata knows to be factual, true, unbeneficial, but endearing and agreeable to others, he does not say them.

In the case of words that the Tathagata knows to be factual, true, beneficial, and endearing and agreeable to others, he has a sense of the proper time for saying them. Why is that? Because the Tathagata has sympathy for living beings.

Right Action

Right action can also be translated as "right conduct". As such, the practitioner should train oneself to be morally upright in one's activities, not acting in ways that would be corrupt or bring harm to oneself or to others. In the Chinese and Pail Canon, it is explained as:

And what is right action? Abstaining from taking life, from stealing, and from illicit sex [or sexual misconduct]. This is called right action. —Saccavibhanga Sutta

And what, monks, is right action? Abstaining from taking life, abstaining from stealing, abstaining from unchastity: This, monks, is called right action. —Magga-vibhanga Sutta

For the lay follower, the *Cunda Kammaraputta Sutta* elaborates:

And how is one made pure in three ways by bodily action? There is the case where a certain person, abandoning the taking of life, abstains from the taking of life. He dwells with his...knife laid down, scrupulous, merciful, compassionate for the welfare of all living beings. Abandoning the taking of what is not given, he abstains from taking what is not given. He does not take, in the manner of a thief, things in a village or a wilderness that belong to others and have not been given by them. Abandoning sensual misconduct, he abstains from sensual misconduct. He does not get sexually involved with those who are protected by their mothers, their fathers, their brothers, their sisters, their relatives, or their Dhamma; those with husbands, those who entail punishments, or even those crowned with flowers by another man. This is how one is made pure in three ways by bodily action.

For the monastic, the *Samannaphala Sutta* adds:

Abandoning uncelibacy, he lives a celibate life, aloof, refraining from the sexual act that is the villager's way.

Right Livelihood

Right livelihood. This means that practitioners ought not to engage in trades or occupations which, either directly or indirectly, result in harm for other living beings. In the Chinese and Pail Canon, it is explained thus:

And what is right livelihood? There is the case where a disciple of the noble ones, having abandoned dishonest livelihood, keeps his life going with right livelihood: This is called right livelihood.

The five types of businesses that are harmful to undertake are:

1. Business in weapons: trading in all kinds of weapons and instruments for killing.
2. Business in human beings: slave trading, prostitution, or the buying and selling of children or adults.

3. Business in meat: "meat" refers to the bodies of beings after they are killed. This includes breeding animals for slaughter.
4. Business in intoxicants: manufacturing or selling intoxicating drinks or addictive drugs.
5. Business in poison: producing or trading in any kind of toxic product designed to kill.

Samadhi: Mental Discipline, Concentration, Meditation

Samadhi is literally translated as "concentration", it is achieved through training in the higher consciousness, which brings the calm and collectedness needed to develop true wisdom by direct experience.

Right Effort

Right effort can also be translated as "right endeavor". In this factor, the practitioners should make a persisting effort to abandon all the wrong and harmful thoughts, words, and deeds. The practitioner should instead be persisting in giving rise to what would be good and useful to themselves and others in their thoughts, words, and deeds, without a thought for the difficulty or weariness involved. In the Chinese and Pail Canon, it is explained thus:

And what, monks, is right effort?

(i) There is the case where a monk generates desire, endeavors, activates persistence, upholds and exerts his intent for the sake of the non-arising of evil, unskillful qualities that have not yet arisen.

(ii) He generates desire, endeavors, activates persistence, upholds and exerts his intent for the sake of the abandonment of evil, unskillful qualities that have arisen.

(iii) He generates desire, endeavors, activates persistence, upholds and exerts his intent for the sake of the arising of skillful qualities that have not yet arisen.

(iv) He generates desire, endeavors, activates persistence, upholds and exerts his intent for the maintenance, non-confusion, increase, plenitude, development, and culmination of skillful qualities that have arisen:

This, monks, is called right effort.

Although the above instruction is given to the male monastic order, it is also meant for the female monastic order and can be practiced by lay followers from both genders.

The above four phases of right effort mean to:

1. Prevent the unwholesome that has not yet arisen in oneself.
2. Let go of the unwholesome that has arisen in oneself.
3. Bring up the wholesome that has not yet arisen in oneself.
4. Maintain the wholesome that has arisen in oneself.

Right Mindfulness

Right mindfulness, also translated as "right memory", "right awareness" or "right attention". Here, practitioners should constantly keep their minds alert to phenomena that affect the body and mind. They should be mindful and deliberate, making sure not to act or speak due to inattention or forgetfulness. In the Pail Canon, it is explained thus:

And what, monks, is right mindfulness?

(i) There is the case where a monk remains focused on the body in and of itself—ardent, aware, and mindful—putting away greed and distress with reference to the world.

(ii) He remains focused on feelings in and of themselves—ardent, aware, and mindful—putting away greed and distress with reference to the world.

(iii) He remains focused on the mind in and of itself—ardent, aware, and mindful—putting away greed and distress with reference to the world.

(iv) He remains focused on mental qualities in and of themselves—ardent, aware, and mindful—putting away greed and distress with reference to the world.

This, monks, is called right mindfulness.

Although the above instruction is given to the male monastic order, it is also meant for the female monastic order and can be practiced by lay followers from both genders..

Bhikkhu Bodhi, a monk of the Theravada tradition, further explains the concept of mindfulness as follows:

The mind is deliberately kept at the level of *bare attention,* a detached observation of what is happening within us and around us in the present moment. In the practice of right mindfulness the mind is trained to remain in the present, open, quiet, and alert, contemplating the present event. All judgments and interpretations have to be suspended, or if they occur, just registered and dropped.

The Maha Satipatthana Sutta also teaches that by mindfully observing these phenomena, we begin to discern its arising and subsiding and the Three Characteristics of Dharma in direct experience, which leads to the arising of insight and the qualities of dispassion, non-clinging, and release

Right Concentration

Right concentration, as its Pail and Sanskrit names indicate, is the practice of concentration (*samadhi*). As such, the practitioner concentrates on an object of attention until reaching full concentration and a state of meditative absorption (*jhana*). Traditionally, the practice of samadhi can be developed through mindfulness of breathing (*anapanasati*), through visual objects (*kasina*), and through repetition of phrases. Samadhi is used to suppress the five hindrances in order to enter into jhana. Jhana is an instrument used for developing wisdom by cultivating insight and using it to examine true nature of phenomena with direct cognition. This leads to cutting off the defilements, realizing the dhamma and, finally, self-awakening. During the practice of right concentration, the practitioner will need to investigate and verify their right view. In the process right knowledge will arise, followed by right liberation. In the Pail Canon, it is explained thus:

And what is right concentration?

(i) Herein a monk aloof from sense desires, aloof from unwholesome thoughts, attains to and abides in the first meditative absorption [jhana], which is detachment-born and accompanied by applied thought, sustained thought, joy, and bliss.

(ii) By allaying applied and sustained thought he attains to, and abides in the second jhana, which is inner tranquillity, which is unification (of the mind), devoid of applied and sustained thought, and which has joy and bliss.

(iii) By detachment from joy he dwells in equanimity, mindful, and with clear comprehension and enjoys bliss in body, and attains to and abides in the third jhana, which the noble ones [ariyas] call "dwelling in equanimity, mindfulness, and bliss".

(iv) By giving up of bliss and suffering, by the disappearance already of joy and sorrow, he attains to, and abides in the fourth jhana, which is neither suffering nor bliss, and which is the purity of equanimity – mindfulness.

This is called right concentration.

Although this instruction is given to the male monastic order, it is also meant for the female monastic order and can be practiced by lay followers from both genders.

According to the Pail and Chinese canon, right concentration is dependent on the development of preceding path factors:

The Blessed One said: "Now what, monks, is noble right concentration with its supports and requisite conditions? Any singleness of mind equipped with these seven factors – right view, right resolve, right speech, right action, right livelihood, right effort, and right mindfulness – is called noble right concentration with its supports and requisite conditions. —Maha-cattarisaka Sutta

The Acquired Factors

In the *Mahacattarisaka Sutta* which appears in the Chinese and Pail canons, the Buddha explains that cultivation of the noble eightfold path leads to the development of two further factors, which are right knowledge/insight (*Samoa-naga*) and right liberation/release (*Samoa-vimutti*). These two factors fall under the category of wisdom (*Panna*).

Right Knowledge and Right Liberation

Right knowledge is seeing things as they really are by direct experience, not as they appear to be, nor as the practitioner wants them to be, but as they truly are. A result of Right Knowledge is the tenth factor-Right liberation

These two factors are the end result of correctly practicing the noble eightfold path, which arise during the practice of right concentration. The first to arise is right knowledge: this is where deep insight into the ultimate reality arises. The last to arise is right liberation: this is where self-awakening occurs and the practitioner has reached the pinnacle of their practice.

The Noble Eightfold Path and Cognitive Psychology

In the essay "Buddhism Meets Western Science", Gay Watson explains: Buddhism has always been concerned with feelings, emotions, sensations, and cognition. The Buddha points both to cognitive and emotional causes of suffering. The emotional cause is desire and its negative opposite, aversion. The cognitive cause is ignorance of the way things truly occur, or of three marks of existence: that all things are unsatisfactory, impermanent, and without essential self.

The noble eightfold path is, from this psychological viewpoint, an attempt to change patterns of thought and behaviour. It is for this reason that the first element of the path is right understanding (*samm-dimmhi*), which is how one's mind views the world. Under the wisdom (*Pañna*) subdivision of the noble eightfold path, this worldview is intimately connected with the second element, right thought, which concerns the patterns of thought and intention that controls one's actions. These elements can be seen at work, for example, in the opening verses of the *Dhammapada*:

- All experience is preceded by mind,
- led by mind,
- made by mind.
- Speak or act with a corrupted mind,
- And suffering follows
- As the wagon wheel follows the hoof of the ox.
- All experience is preceded by mind,
- Led by mind,
- Made by mind.
- Speak or act with a peaceful mind,
- And happiness follows
- Like a never-departing shadow. Audio/Audio Source.

Thus, by altering one's distorted worldview, bringing out "tranquil perception" in the place of "perception polluted", one is able to ease suffering. Watson points this out from a psychological standpoint:

Research has shown that repeated action, learning, and memory can actually change the nervous system physically, altering both synaptic strength and connections. Such changes may be brought about by cultivated change in emotion and action; they will, in turn, change subsequent experience.

The Three Characteristics

These are the three characteristics of all conditioned phenomena in Theravada thought.

1. Anicca (impermanence): Change is. All conditioned phenomena are subject to Change, including physical characteristics, qualities, assumptions, theories, knowledge, etc. Nothing is permanent, because, for something to be permanent, there has to be an unchanging cause behind it. Since all causes are recursively bound together, there can be no ultimate unchanging cause.
2. Dukkha (suffering)- Craving causes suffering, since what is craved is transitory, changing, and perishing. The craving for impermanent things causes disappointment and sorrow. There is a tendency to label practically everything in the world, as either 'good', 'comfortable' or 'satisfying', as opposed to 'bad', 'uncomfortable', and 'unsatisfying'. Since we label things in terms of 'like' or 'dislike', we create suffering for ourselves. If one succeeds in giving up the tendency to label things and free himself from the instincts that drive him towards attaining what he himself labels collectively as 'liking', he attains the ultimate freedom. The problem, the cause, the solution and the implementation, all of these are within oneself, not outside.
3. Anatta (not-self)- The concept 'Anatta' can be rendered as *lack of fixed, unchanging identity*; there is no permanent, essential Self. A living being is a composite of the five aggregates (*khandhas*), which is the physical forms (*rupa*), feelings or sensations (*vedana*), perception (*sanna*), mental formations (*sankhara*), and consciousness (*vinnana*), none of which can be identified as one's *Self*. From the moment of conception, all entities (including all living beings) are subject to a process of continuous change. A practitioner should, on the other hand, develop and refine his or her mind to a state so as to see through this phenomenon.

Direct realization of these three characteristics leads to freedom from worldly bonds and attachments, thus leading to the state where one is completely, ultimately free, the state which is termed Nirvana, which literally means 'Freedom'.

The Three Noble Disciplines

The pathway towards Nirvana, or the Noble Eightfold Pathway is sometimes stated in a more concise manner, known as the Three Noble Disciplines. These are known as discipline (*sila*), training of mind (*samadhi*) and wisdom (*Panna*).

Meditation

Meditation (Pail: *Bhavana*) means the positive reinforcement of one's mind. Broadly categorized into Samatha and Vipassana, Meditation is the key tool implemented in attaining jhana. Samatha literally means "to make skillful", and has other renderings also, among which are "tranquilizing, calming", "visualizing", and "achieving". Vipassana means "insight", or "abstract understanding". In this context, Samatha Meditation makes a person skillful in concentration of mind. Once the mind is sufficiently concentrated, Vipassana allows one to see through the veil of ignorance.

In the Pail Canon discourses, the Buddha frequently instructs his disciples to practice samadhi (concentration) in order to establish and develop jhana (full concentration). Jhana is the instrument used by the Buddha himself to penetrate the true nature of phenomena (through investigation and direct experience) and to reach Enlightenment. Right Concentration (*Samoa-samadhi*) is one of the elements in the Noble Eightfold Path. Samadhi can be developed from mindfulness with breathing (*anapanasati*), from visual objects (*kasina*), and repetition of phrases. The traditional list contains 40 objects of meditation (*kammammhâna*) to be used for Samatha Meditation. Every object has a specific goal; for example, meditation on the parts of the body (*kayanupassana* or *kayagathasathi*) will result in a lessening of attachment to our own bodies and those of others, resulting in a reduction of sensual desires. Metta (loving kindness) generates the feelings of goodwill and happiness toward ourselves and other beings; metta practice serves as an antidote to ill-will, wrath and fear.

Levels of Attainment

Through practice, (Theravadan) practitioners can achieve four stages of enlightenment:

1. Stream-Enterers-Those who have destroyed the first three fetters (false view of *Self*, doubt, and clinging to rites and rituals) will be safe from falling into the states of misery (they will not be born as an animal, peta (ghost), or hell being). At most they will have to be reborn only seven more times before attaining Nirvana.
2. Once-Returners-Those who have destroyed the first three fetters and have lessened the fetters of lust and hatred will attain Nirvana after being born once more in the world.
3. Non-Returners-Those who have destroyed the five lower fetters, which bind beings to the world of the senses. Non-returners will never again return to the human world and after they die, they will be born in the high heavenly worlds, there to attain Nirvana. Attaining the state of non-returner is portrayed in the early texts as the ideal goal for laity.
4. Arahants-Those who have reached Enlightenment, realized Nirvana, and have reached the quality of deathlessness are free from all the fermentations of defilement. Their ignorance, craving and attachments have ended. Attaining the state of arahant is portrayed in the early texts as the ideal goal for monastics.

Scriptures

The Theravada school upholds the Pail Canon or Tipitaka as the most authoritative collection of texts on the teachings of Gautama Buddha. The Sutta and Vinaya portion of the Tipitaka shows considerable overlap in content to the Agamas, the parallel collections used by non-Theravada schools in India which are preserved in Chinese and partially in Sanskrit, Prakrit, and Tibetan, and the various non-Theravada Vinayas. On this basis, both these sets of texts are generally believed to be the oldest and most authoritative texts on Buddhism by scholars. It is also believed that much of the Pail Canon, which is still used by Theravada communities, was transmitted to Sri Lanka during the reign of Asoka. After being orally transmitted (as was the custom in those days for religious texts) for some centuries, were finally committed to writing in the last century BCE, at what the Theravada usually reckons as the fourth council, in Sri Lanka. Theravada is one of the first Buddhist schools to commit the whole complete set of its

Buddhist canon into writing. Much of the material in the Canon is not specifically "Theravadan", but is instead the collection of teachings that this school preserved from the early, non-sectarian body of teachings. According to Peter Harvey:

The Theravadans, then, may have *added* texts to the Canon for some time, but they do not appear to have tampered with what they already had from an earlier period.

The Pail Tipitaka consists of three parts: the Vinaya Pitaka, Sutta Pitaka and Abhidhamma Pitaka. Of these, the Abhidhamma Pitaka is believed to be a later addition to the first two pitakas, which, in the opinion of many scholars, were the only two pitakas at the time of the First Buddhist Council. The Pail Abhidhamma was not recognized outside the Theravada school.

In the 4th or 5th century CE Buddhaghosa Thera wrote the first Pail commentaries to much of the Tipitaka (which were based on much older manuscripts, mostly in old Sinhalese), and after him many other monks wrote various commentaries, which have become part of the Theravada heritage. These texts, however, do not enjoy the same authority as the Tipitaka does. The Tipitaka is composed of 45 volumes in the Thai edition, 40 in the Burmese and 58 in the Sinhalese, and a full set of the Tipitaka is usually kept in its own (medium-sized) cupboard.

The commentaries, together with the Abhidhamma, define the specific Theravada heritage. Related versions of the Sutta Pitaka and Vinaya Pitaka were common to all the early Buddhist schools, and therefore do not define only Theravada, but also the other early Buddhist schools, and perhaps the teaching of Gautama Buddha himself.

Theravada Buddhists consider much of what is found in the Chinese and Tibetan scriptural collections to be apocryphal, meaning that they are not authentic words of the Buddha.

Tripimaka

The Tripimaka is the Sanskrit term used by Westerners for a Buddhist canon of scriptures. Asian Buddhists of the Theravada Buddhist school use the term Tipitaka to refer to the Pail Canon. Other Buddhist schools use other terms for their own collection of scriptures, such as Kangyur. Each of the Early Buddhist Schools had their own recension of the Tripitaka, which mainly differed on the subject of Abhidhamma. In terms of Vinaya and Sutras, the contents were remarkably similar.

Early Buddhism

The Tripitaka writings of some or all the Early Buddhist Schools, which were originally memorized and recited orally by disciples, fall into three general categories and are traditionally classified in three baskets (*tri-pimaka*). The following is the most common order.

The first category, the *Vinaya Pimaka,* was the code of ethics to be obeyed by the early *saegha,* monks and nuns. According to the scriptural account, these were invented on a day-to-day basis as the Buddha encountered various behaviour problems with the monks.

The second category, the *Sktra Pimaka* (literally "basket of threads", Pail: *Sutta Pimaka*), consists primarily of accounts of the Buddha's teachings. The Sktra Pimaka has numerous subdivisions: it contains more than 10,000 Sutras.

The third category is the Abhidharma Pimaka. This is applied to very different collections in different versions of the Tripimaka. In the Pail Canon of the Theravada there is an *Abhidhamma Pimaka* consisting of seven books. An *Abhidharma Pimaka* of the Sarvastivadin school survives, also in seven books, six in Chinese and one in Tibetan. These are different books from the Pail ones though there are some common material and ideas. Another work surviving in Chinese, the *Uariputrabhidharmauastra,* may be all or part of another Abhidharma Pimaka. At least some other early schools of Buddhism had Abhidharma Pimakas, which are now lost.

According to some sources, some early schools of Buddhism had five or seven pitakas. According to some scholars, some early schools of Buddhism had no Abhidharma.

Mahayana Buddhism

In the Mahayana a mixed attitude to the term Tripimaka developed. On the one hand, a major Mahayana scripture, the Lotus Sutra, uses the term to refer to the above literature of the early schools, as distinct from the Mahayana's own scriptures, and this usage became quite common in the tradition. On the other hand, the term Tripimaka had tended to become synonymous with Buddhist scriptures, and thus continued to be used for the Chinese and Tibetan collections, even though their contents do not really fit the pattern of three pimakas. In the Chinese tradition, the texts are classified in a variety of ways, most of which have in fact four or even more pimakas or other divisions. In the few that attempt to follow a genuine threefold division the term Abhidharma Pitaka is used to refer vaguely to non-canonical literature, whether Indian or Chinese, with only the other two pimakas being regarded as strictly canonical. In the Tibetan tradition, on the other hand, when attempts are made to explain the application of the term Tripimaka to the Kanjur, the Tibetan canon of scripture, the Abhidharma Pimaka is considered as consisting of the Prajnaparamita.

The Chinese form of Tripimaka, "Sanzang", was sometimes used as an honorary title for a Buddhist monk who has mastered all the Tripimaka canons, most notably in the case of the Tang Dynasty monk Xuanzang, whose pilgrimage to India to study and bring Buddhist text back to China was portrayed in the novel *Journey to the West* as "Tang Sanzang". Due to the popularity of the novel, the term in "Sanzang" is often erroneously understood as a name of the monk Xuanzang. One such screen version of this is the popular 1979 Monkey (TV series).

7

Vinaya Pitaka

The Vinaya Pimaka is a Buddhist scripture, one of the three parts that make up the Tripitaka. Its primary subject matter is the monastic rules for monks and nuns. The name Vinaya Pimaka (*vinayapimaka*) is the same in Pail, Sanskrit and other dialects used by early Buddhists in India, and means basket of discipline.

Surviving Versions

Six versions survive complete, of which three are still in use.

- The Pail version of the Theravada, included in the Pail Canon, translated by I. B. Horner as *The Book of the Discipline*, 1938-66, 6 volumes, Pail Text Society, Bristol.
  * Suttavibhanga (-vibhaEga): commentary on the Patimokkha, with much of its text embedded.
    - Mahavibhanga (Maha-) dealing with monks
    - Bhikkhunivibhanga (bhikkhuni-) dealing with nuns.
  * Khandhaka: 22 chapters on various topics
  * Parivara: analyses the rules from various points of view.
- 'Dul-ba, Tibetan translation of the Mulasarvastivada version; this is the version used in the Tibetan tradition.
  * Vinayavastu: 16 skandhakas (khandhakas) and the start of the 17th
  * Pratimokshasutra of monks
  * Vinayavibhanga of monks
  * Pratimokshasutra of nuns

  * Vinayavibhanga of nuns
  * Vinayakshudrakavastu: rest of the 17th skandhaka and others
  * Vinayottaragrantha: appendices, including Upalipariprccha, which corresponds to a chapter of the Parivara.
- Ssm-fen Lu UVR (Taisho catalogue number 1428), Chinese translation of the Dharmaguptaka version; this is the version used in the Chinese tradition and its derivatives in Korea, Vietnam and the Ritsu school in Japan (most Buddhist clergy in Japan do not follow the Vinaya, but rather follow the Mahayana [Bodhisattva] Precepts, a result of the successful Tendai school campaign).
  * Bhikshuvibhanga dealing with monks
  * Bhikshunivibhanga dealing with nuns; translated by Ann Heirman as *Rules for Nuns According to the Dharmaguptakavinaya*, Part II, Motilal Banarsidass, Delhi, 2002
  * Skandhaka
  * Samyuktavarga
  * Vinayaikottara, corresponding to a chapter of the Parivara.
- Shih-sung Lu (T1435), translation of Sarvastivadin version.
  * Bhikshuvibhanga
  * Skandhaka
  * Bhikshunivibhanga
  * Ekottaradharma, similar to Vinayaikottara
  * Upalipariprccha
  * Ubhayatovinaya
  * Samyukta
  * Parajikadharma
  * Sanghavasesha
  * Kusaladhyaya.
- Wu-fen Lu (T1421), translation of Mahisasaka version.
  * Bhikshuvibhanga

  * Bhikshunivibhanga
  * Skandhaka.
- Mo-ho-seng-ch'i Lu (T1425), translation of Mahasanghika version (the nuns' rules have been translated by the late Professor Hirakawa as *Monastic Discipline for the Buddhist Nuns*, Patna, 1982).
  * Bhikshuvibhanga
  * Bhikshunivibhanga
  * Skandhaka.

In addition, portions of various versions survive in various languages.

Origins

Each school traditionally claimed that its own version was compiled at the First Council shortly after the Buddha's death, and recited by Upali, with little later addition. As the versions are different, scholars do not take this literally. However, as the different versions are fairly similar, most scholars consider most of the Vinaya to be fairly early, that is, dating from before the separation of schools. However, Dr. Gregory Schopen, Professor of Sanskrit, Tibetan, and Buddhist Studies in the University of Texas at Austin, argues against this assumption on various grounds. He suggests that similarities may be due to later standardization. He also points out that many inscriptions from early times on show that monks owned property, contrary to the Vinaya. He argues that there is no evidence that this represents a decline from an early period of observance, and suggests that the Vinaya may be an attempt by a self-appointed elite to impose their standards on everyone else.

Contents

The Pail version of the Patimokkha, the code of conduct that applies to Buddhist monastics, contains 227 major rules for bhikkhus and 311 major rules for bhikkhunis. The Vibhanga section(s) of Vinaya Pitaka constitute(s) a commentary on these rules, giving detailed explanations of them along with the origin stories for each rule. The Khandhaka/Skandhaka sections give numerous supplementary rules grouped by subject, again with origin stories. The Buddha called his teaching the "Dhamma-

Vinaya", emphasizing both the philosophical teachings of Buddhism as well as the training in virtue that embodies that philosophy.

In the collected Chinese editions of the Scriptures the Vinaya pitaka has a broader sense, including all four Chinese vinayas listed above, parts of others, non-canonical vinaya literature, lay vinaya and bodhisattva vinaya.

Place in the Tradition

According to the scriptures, in the first years of the Buddha's teaching the sangha lived together in harmony with no vinaya, as there was no need, because all of the Buddha's early disciples were highly realized if not fully enlightened. As the sangha expanded situations arose which the Buddha and the lay community felt were inappropriate for Samoans. According to tradition, the first rule to be established was the prohibition against sexual acts. The origin story tells of an earnest monk whose family was distraught that there was no male heir and so persuaded the monk to impregnate his wife. According to tradition, all three, the monk, his wife and son who both later ordained, eventually became fully enlightened arahants.

The vinaya is very important to Buddhists-

"Whatever Dhamma and Vinaya I have pointed out and formulated for you, that will be your Teacher when I am gone." (Mahaaparinibbaana Sutta, [D.16]).

Abhidhamma Pitaka

The Abhidhamma Pitaka (abhidhammapimaka) is the last of the three pitakas, that is, baskets, constituting the Pail Canon, the scriptures of Theravada Buddhism.

The Abhidhamma pitaka is a detailed scholastic reworking of doctrinal material appearing in the Suttas, according to schematic classifications. It does not contain systematic philosophical treatises, but summaries or enumerated lists..

Translations

The first five books and part of the seventh of the Abhidhamma Pitaka have been translated by the Pail Text Society and offers an option to order them through their website.

Nature of Abhidhamma

Abhidhamma has been variously described as philosophy, psychology, metaphysics etc. L. S. Cousins says that the abhidhamma methodology looks at things in terms of occasions or events instead of sequences or processes.

Origins

Tradition holds that the Buddha thought the Abhidhamma out immediately after his enlightenment then taught it to the gods some years later. Later the Buddha repeated it to Sariputta who then handed it on to his disciples. This tradition is also evident in the Parivara, a very late addition to the Vinaya Pitaka, which mentions in a concluding verse of praise to the Buddha that *this best of creatures, the lion, taught the three pitakas..*

Scholars, however, generally date the Abhidhamma works to originating some time around the third century BCE, 100 to 200 years after the death of the Buddha. Therefore the seven Abhidhamma works are generally claimed by scholars not to represent the words of the Buddha himself, but those of disciples and great scholars. Dr. Rupert Gethin however said that important elements of abhidhamma methodology probably go back to the Buddha's lifetime. A. K. Warder and Dr. Peter Harvey both suggested early dates for the matikas on which most of the Abidhamma books are based. Abhidhamma started out as elaboration of the suttas, but later developed independent doctrines.

As the last major division of the canon, the Abhidhamma Pitaka has had a checkered history. It was not accepted as canonical by the Mahasanghika school and several other schools. Another school included most of the Khuddaka Nikaya within the Abhidhamma Pitaka. Also, the Pail version of the Abhidhamma is a strictly Theravada collection, and has little in common with the Abhidhamma works recognized by other Buddhist schools. The various Abhidhamma philosophies of the various early schools have no agreement on doctrine and belong to the period of 'Divided Buddhism' (as opposed to Undivided Buddhism). The earliest texts of the Pail Canon have no mention of (the texts of) the Abhidhamma Pitaka. The Abhidhamma is also not mentioned in some reports of the First Buddhist Council, which do mention the existence of the texts of the Vinaya and either the five Nikayas or the four Agamas. Other accounts do include the Abhidhamma.

In the Theravadin Abhidhamma Pitaka, unlike the Abhidharma Pitaka of the Sarvastivadin school, ontological theorizing is absent, and the question of ontological status of dharmas remains a moot point. The notion of *sabhava* (Sanskrit: *svabhava*) is only utilized in late Theravadin texts. The doctrine of momentariness is also a late addition to Theravada thought. It only appears at the time of Buddhaghosa.

Dhammasangani

The Dhammasangani begins with a matika (translated as matrix) which lists classifications of dhammas (translated as phenomenas, ideas, states, etc). The matika starts with 22 threefold classifications, such as good/bad/unclassified, and then follows with 100 twofold classifications according to the Abhidhamma method. Many of these classifications are not exhaustive, and some are not even exclusive. The matika ends with 42 twofold classifications according to the sutta method; these 42 are only used in the Dhammasangani, whereas the other 122 are used in some of the other books as well.

The main body of the Dhammasangani is in four parts. The first part goes through numerous states of mind, listing and defining by lists of synonyms, factors present in the states. The second deals with material form, beginning with its own matika, classifying by ones, twos and so on, and explaining afterwards. The third explains the book's matika in terms of the first two parts, as does the fourth, by a different method (and omitting the sutta method).

Vibhanga

The Vibhanga consists of 18 chapters, each dealing with a different topic. For example the first chapter deals with the five aggregates. A typical chapter consists of three parts. The first of these parts explains the topic according to the sutta method, often word-for-word as in actual suttas. The second is Abhidhamma explanation, mainly by lists of synonyms as in the Dhammasangani. The third employs questions and answers, based on the matika, such as "How many aggregates are good?"

Dhatukatha

This book covers both the matika and various topics, mostly from the Vibhanga, relating them to the 5 aggregates, 12 bases and 18 elements. The first chapter is fairly simple: "In how many aggregates etc. are good dhammas etc. included?" The book progressively works up to more complicated questions: "From how many aggregates etc. are the dhammas dissociated from attention etc. dissociated?"

Puggalapannatti

This book starts with its own matika, which begins with some standard lists but then continues with lists of persons grouped numerically from ones to tens. This latter portion of the matika is then explained in the main body of the work. Most of the lists of persons and many of the explanations are also found in the Anguttara Nikaya.

Kathavatthu

This book consists of more than two hundred debates on questions of doctrine. It does not identify the participants. The commentary says the debates are between the Theravada and other schools, which it identifies in each case. These identifications are mostly consistent with what is known from other sources about the doctrines of different schools.

Yamaka

This book consists of ten chapters, each dealing with a different topic; for example, the first deals with roots. A typical chapter (there are a number of divergences from this pattern) is in three parts. The first part deals with questions of identity: "Is good root root?" "But is root good root?" The entire Yamaka consists of such pairs of converse questions, with their answers. Hence its name, which means pairs. The second part deals with arising: "For someone for whom the form aggregate arises, does the feeling aggregate arise?" The third part deals with understanding: "Does someone who understands the eye base understand the ear base?"

Patthana

This book deals with 24 conditions in relation to the matika: "Good dhamma is related to good dhamma by root condition", with details and numbers of answers.

Place in the Tradition

The importance of the Abhidhamma Pitaka in classical Sinhalese Buddhism is suggested by the fact that it came to be furnished, not only, like much of the canon, with a commentary and a sub-commentary on that commentary, but even with a subsubcommentary on that sub-commentary. On the other hand, this relentless sub-commenting might be illustrative of what has been called "Shastra-vasna" or The Lust for Scriptures rather than a true effort at Nirvana, as envisioned by the Buddha. In more recent centuries, Burma has become the main centre of abhidhamma studies.

Sutta Pitaka

The Sutta Pitaka is the second of the three divisions of the Tipitaka or Pail Canon, the great Pail collection of Buddhist writings, the scriptures of Theravada Buddhism. The Sutta Pitaka contains more than 10,000 suttas (teachings) attributed to the Buddha or his close companions.

Origins

The scriptures tell how the First Council held shortly after the Buddha's death collected together the discipline (vinaya), and the dhamma in five collections. Tradition holds that little was added to the Canon after this. Scholars are more skeptical, but differ in their degrees of scepticism. Dr. Richard Gombrich, Academic Director of the Oxford Centre for Buddhist Studies, former Boden Professor of Sanskrit at Oxford University and former President of the Pail Text Society, thinks most of the first four nikayas go back to the Buddha, in content but not in form. The late Professor Hirakawa Akira says that the First Council collected only short prose passages or verses expressing important doctrines, and that these were expanded into full length suttas over the next century.

Digha Nikaya

The Digha Nikaya (dighanikaya; "Collection of Long Discourses") is a Buddhist scripture, the first of the five nikayas, or collections, in the Sutta Pitaka, which is one of the "three baskets" that compose the Pail Tipitaka of Theravada Buddhism. Some of the most commonly referenced suttas from the Digha Nikaya include the Maha-parinibbana Sutta (DN 16), which described the final days and death of the Buddha, the Sigalovada Sutta (DN 31) in which the Buddha discusses ethics and practices for lay followers, and the Samannaphala (DN 2), Brahmajala Sutta (DN 1) which describes and compares the point-of-view of Buddha and other ascetics in India about the universe and time (past, present, and future); and Potthapada (DN 9) Suttas, which describe the benefits and practice of samatha meditation.

Correspondence with the Dirgha Agama

The Digha Nikaya corresponds to the *Dirgha Agama* found in the Sutra Pitikas of various Sanskritic early Buddhists schools, fragments of which survive in Sanskrit. It contains 30 Sutras in contrast to the 34 suttas of the Theravadin Digha Nikaya. In addition, portions of the Sarvastivadin school's Dirgha Agama survive in Sanskrit and in Tibetan translation.

Divisions

The Digha Nikaya consists of 34 discourses, broken into three groups:

- Silakkhandha-vagga – The Division Concerning Morality (suttas 1-13); named after a tract on monks' morality that occurs in each of its suttas (in theory; in practice it is not written out in full in all of them); in most of them it leads on to the Janus (the main attainments of samatha meditation), the cultivation of psychic powers and becoming an arahant
- Maha-vagga – The Great Division (suttas 14-23)
- Patika-vagga – The Patika Division (suttas 24-34)

The individual discourses are:

1. Brahmajala Sutta : mainly concerned with 62 types of wrong view
2. Samannaphala Sutta: King Ajatasattu of Magadha asks the Buddha about the benefits in this life of being a samana (most often translated as "recluse"); the Buddha's main reply is in terms of becoming an arahant by the path outlined above
3. Ambattha Sutta: Ambattha the brahmin is sent by his teacher to find whether the Buddha possesses the 32 bodily marks, but on arrival he is rude to the Buddha on grounds of descent; the Buddha responds that he is actually higher born than Ambattha and that society treats aristocrats like himself as higher ranking than brahmins, but that he considers those fulfilled in conduct and wisdom as higher,

and he explains conduct and wisdom as above

4. Sonadanta Sutta
   a) the Buddha asks Sonadanda the brahmin what are the qualities that make a brahmin; Sonadanda gives five, but the Buddha asks if any can be omitted and beats him down to two, morality and wisdom, which he explains as above
5. Kutadanta Sutta: Kutadanta the brahmin asks the Buddha how to perform a sacrifice (Rhys Davids considers this an example of a peculiar straight-faced sort of humour to be found in texts such as this); the Buddha replies by telling of one of his past lives, as chaplain to a king, where they performed a sacrifice which consisted of making offerings, with no animals killed; Kutadanta asks whether there are any better sacrifices, and the Buddha recommends in succession going to the Three Refuges, taking the Five Precepts and the path as above
6. Mahali Sutta (Mahali-): in reply to a question as to why a certain monk sees divine sights but does not hear divine sounds, the Buddha explains that it is because of the way he has directed his meditation; he then reports the following sutta
7. Jaliya Sutta: asked by two brahmins whether the soul and the body are the same or different, the Buddha describes the path as above, and asks whether one who has fulfilled it would bother with such questions
8. Kassapa Sihanada Sutta: Maha Sihanada Sutta (Maha-) or Sihanada Sutta; the word sihanada literally means lion's roar: this discourse is concerned with asceticism
9. Potthapada Sutta : asked about the cause of the arising of sanna, usually translated as perception, the Buddha says it is through training; he explains the path as above up to the Johne's and the arising of their perceptions, and then continues with the first three formless attainments; the sutta then moves on to other topics, the self and the unanswered questions
10. Subha Sutta: Ananda explains the path as above
11. Kevaddha Sutta or Kevatta Sutta: Kevaddha asks the

Buddha why he does not gain disciples by working miracles; the Buddha explains that people would simply dismiss this as magic and that the real miracle is the training of his followers

12. Lohicca Sutta: on good and bad teachers
13. Tevijja Sutta: asked about the path to union with Brahma, the Buddha explains it in terms of the path as above, but ending with the four brahmaviharas; the abbreviated way the text is written out makes it unclear how much of the path comes before this; Professor Gombrich has argued that the Buddha was meaning union with Brahma as synonymous with nirvana
14. Mahapadana Sutta: mainly telling the story of a past Buddha up to somewhat after his enlightenment; the story is similar to that of "our" Buddha
15. Maha Nidana Sutta: on dependent origination
16. Maha Parinibbana Sutta: story of the last few months of the Buddha's life, his death and funeral and the distribution of his relics
17. Mahasudassana Sutta: story of one of the Buddha's past lives, as a king; the description of his palace has close vebal similarities to that of the Pure Land, and Dr. Rupert Gethin has suggested this as a precursor
18. Janavasabha Sutta: King Bimbisara of Magadha, reborn as the god Janavasabha, tells the Buddha that his teaching has resulted in increased numbers of people being reborn as gods (according to the Buddhist scriptures, Bimbisara was a Buddhist, but the Jain scriptures say he was a Jain)
19. Maha-Govinda Sutta: story of a past life of the Buddha
20. Mahasamaya Sutta: long versified list of gods coming to honour the Buddha
21. Sakkapanha Sutta: the Buddha answers questions from Sakka, ruler of the gods (a Buddhist version of Indra)
22. Maha Satipatthana Sutta: the basis for one of the present-day Burmese vipassana meditation traditions; many people have it read or recited to them on their deathbeds
23. Payasi Sutta or Payasi Rajanna Sutta: dialogue between the sceptical prince of the title and a monk

24. Patika Sutta or Pathika Sutta : a monk has left the order because he says the Buddha does not work miracles; most of the sutta is taken up with accounts of miracles the Buddha has worked
25. Udumbarika Sihanada Sutta or Udumbarika Sutta: another discourse on asceticism
26. Cakkavatti Sihanada Sutta or Cakkavatti Sutta: story of humanity's decline from a golden age in the past, with prophecy of eventual return
27. Agganna Sutta: another decline story
28. Sampasadaniya Sutta: Sariputta praises the Buddha
29. Pasadika Sutta: the Buddha's response to the news of the death of his rival, the founder of Jainism, covering various topics
30. Lakkhana Sutta: explains the actions of the Budha in his previous lives leading to his 32 bodily marks; thus it describes practices of a bodhisattva (perhaps the earliest such description)
31. Singalovada Sutta, Singala Sutta, Singalaka Sutta or Sigala Sutta: traditionally regarded as the lay vinaya
32. Atanatiya Sutta: gods give the Buddha a poem for his followers, male and female, monastic and lay, to recite for protection from evil spirits; it sets up a mandala or circle of protection and a version of this sutta is classified as a tantra in Tibet and Japan
33. Sangiti Sutta; L. S. Cousins has tentatively suggested that this was the first sutta created as a literary text, at the Second Council, his theory being that sutta was originally a pattern of teaching rather than a body of literature; it is taught by Sariputta at the Buddha's request, and gives lists arranged numerically from ones to tens (cf. Anguttara Nikaya); a version of this belonging to another school was used as the basis for one of the books of their Abhidharma Pitaka
34. Dasuttara Sutta: similar to the preceding sutta but with a fixed format; there are ten categories, and each number has one list in each; this material is also used in the Patisambhidamagga

Majjhima Nikaya

The Majjhima Nikaya is a Buddhist scripture, the second of the five nikayas, or collections, in the Sutta Pitaka, which is one of the "three baskets" that compose the Pail Tipitaka of Theravada Buddhism. This Nikaya consists of 152 discourses attributed to the Buddha and his chief disciples. The Majjhima Nikaya corresponds to the *Madhyama Agama* found in the Sutra Pitikas of various Sanskritic early Buddhists schools, fragments of which survive in Sanskrit and in Tibetan translation. A complete Chinese translation from the Sarvastivadin recension appears in the Chinese Buddhist canon, where it is known as the *Zhong Ahanjing*. The Madhyama Agama of the Sarvastivadin school contains 222 Sutras, in contrast to the 152 suttas in the Pail Majjhima Nikaya.

Samyutta Nikaya

The Samyutta Nikaya (SaCyutta Nikya SN, "Connected Discourses" or "Kindred Sayings") is a Buddhist scripture, the third of the five nikayas, or collections, in the Sutta Pitaka, which is one of the "three baskets" that compose the Pail Tipitaka of Theravada Buddhism. Because of the abbreviated way parts of the text are written, the total number of suttas is unclear. The editior of the Pail Text Society edition of the text made it 2889, Bodhi in his translation has 2904, while the commentaries give 7762. A study by Dr. Rupert Gethin gives the totals for the Burmese and Sinhalese editions as 2854 and 7656, respectively, and his own calculation as 6696; he also says the total in the Thai edition is unclear. The suttas are grouped into five vaggas, or sections. Each vagga is further divided into samyuttas, or chapters, each of which in turn contains a group of suttas on a related topic.

Correspondence with the SaCyukta Agama

The Samyutta Nikaya corresponds to the *SaCyukta Agama* found in the Sutra Pitikas of various Sanskritic early Buddhists schools, fragments of which survive in Sanskrit and in Tibetan translation. A complete Chinese translation from the Sarvastivadin recension appears in the Chinese Buddhist canon, where it is known as the *Za Ahanjing*; meaning "the mixed Agama". A comparison of the Sarvastivadin, Kauyapa, and Theravadin texts reveals a considerable consistency of content, although each recension contains sutras/suttas not found in the others.

Selections

- anthology published by Buddhist Publication Society, Kandy, Sri Lanka
- *Nidana Samyutta,* published in Burma; reprinted Sri Satguru, Delhi.

Divisions

The vaggas contained in this Nikaya are (the numbering of chapters [*samyuttas*] here refers to the PTS and Burmese editions; the Sinhalese and Thai editions divide the text up somewhat differently):

Part I. Sagatha-vagga (SN chapters 1-11) a collection of suttas containing verses (Pail, *sagatha*), many shared by other parts of the Pail canon such as the Theragatha, Therigatha, Suttanipata, Dhammapada and the Jatakas.

Part II. Nidana-vagga (SN chapters 12-21) a collection of suttas primarily pertaining to causation (Pail, *nidana*).

Part III. Khandha-vagga (SN chapters 22-34) a collection of suttas primarily pertaining to the five aggregates (Pail, *khanda*).

Part IV. Salayatana-vagga (SN chapters 35-44) a collection of suttas primarily pertaining to the six sense bases (Pail, *salayatana*), including the "Fire Sermon" (*Adittapariyaya Sutta*).

Part V. Maha-vagga (SN chapters 45-56) the largest – that is, great (Pail, *maha*) – collection consists of the following chapters:

Ch 45. the Noble Eightfold Path

Ch 46. the Seven Factors of Enlightenment

Ch 47. the Four Establishment of Mindfulness

Ch 48. the Faculties

Ch 49. the Four Right Striving

Ch 50. the Five Powers

Ch 51. the Four Bases for Spiritual Power

Ch 52. Anuruddha discourses

Ch 53. the Johne's

Ch 54. Mindfulness of Breathing

Ch 55. Factors of Stream-entry

Ch 56. the Truths.

Anguttara Nikaya

The Anguttara Nikaya is a Buddhist scripture, the fourth of the five nikayas, or collections, in the Sutta Pitaka, which is one of the "three baskets" that comprise the Pail Tipitaka of Theravada Buddhism. This Nikaya consists of several thousand discourses ascribed to the Buddha and his chief disciples arranged in eleven nipatas, or books, according to the number of dhaṁma items referenced in them.

The Anguttara Nikaya corresponds to the *Ekottara Agama* ("Increased by One Discourses") found in the Sutra Pitikas of various Sanskritic early Buddhists schools, fragments of which survive in Sanskrit. A complete version survives in Chinese translation by the name *Zcngyi Ahanjing*; it is thought to be from either the MahasaCghika or Sarvastivadin recensions. According to Keown, "there is considerable disparity between the Pail and the Sarvastivadin versions, with more than two-thirds of the Sutras found in one but not the other compilation, which suggests that much of this portion of the Sutra Pimaka was not formed until a fairly late date."

Divisions

The nipatas in this Nikaya are:

- The Book of Ones
- The Book of Twos
- The Book of Threes
- The Book of Fours
- The Book of Fives
- The Book of Sixes
- The Book of Sevens
- The Book of Eights
- The Book of Nines
- The Book of Tens
- The Book of Elevens.

Appreciation

Translator Bhikkhu Bodhi wrote: "In Anguttara Nikaya, persons are as a rule not reduced to mere collections of aggregates, elements and sense-bases, but are treated as real centres of living experience engaged in a heartfelt quest for happiness and freedom from suffering." (from Intro to Samyutta Nikaya)

Khuddaka Nikaya

The Khuddaka Nikaya (-Nikaya; "Minor Collection") is the last of the five nikayas, or collections, in the Sutta Pitaka, which is one of the "three baskets" that compose the Pail Tipitaka, the scriptures of Theravada Buddhism. This Nikaya consists of fifteen (Thailand), seventeen (Sri Lanka), or eighteen books (Burma) in different editions on various topics attributed to the Buddha and his chief disciples.

Professor Hirakawa Akira has stated that the Khuddaka Nikaya represent a stage in the development of the Pail Canon/Agamas in which new material was not added any more to the rest of the Sutta Pitaka, but was added to a Khuddaka Pitaka instead. This Khuddaka Pitaka was the repository for materials that were left out of the four Agamas/Nikayas (the Digha Nikaya, Majjhima Nikaya, Samyutta Nikaya and Anguttara Nikaya) and thus included both early and late texts. Some of the schools that included a Khuddaka Pitaka in their canons were the Mahisasaka, Dharmaguptaka and Mahasanghika. The Khuddaka Nikaya of the Theravada school is the only extant example of such a Khuddaka Pitaka.

Divisions

This Nikaya contains some or all of the following texts:

1. Khuddakapatha
2. Dhammapada
3. Udana
4. Itivuttaka
5. Suttanipata
6. Vimanavatthu
7. Petavatthu
8. Theragatha
9. Therigatha
10. Jataka
11. Niddesa

12. Patisambhidamagga
13. Apadana
14. Buddhavamsa
15. Cariyapitaka
16. Nettipakarana or Netti (included in Burmese and Sinhalese editions, but not in Thai edition)
17. Petakopadesa (included in Burmese and Sinhalese editions, but not in Thai edition)
18. Milindapanha (included in Burmese edition, but not in Sinhalese and Thai editions).

The introduction to the Sumangalavilasini, the commentary on the Digha Nikaya compiled in the fourth or fifth century by Buddhaghosa on the basis of earlier commentaries that no longer survive, says that the reciters of the Digha listed 2-12 in this Nikaya, while the reciters of the Majjhima Nikaya listed 2-15. Later, it gives a listing of the contents of the Canon also found in the introductions to the commentaries on the Vinaya and Abhidhamma Pitakas, which gives 1-15 for this Nikaya, though it also includes an alternative classification in which the Vinaya and Abhidhamma are also included in this Nikaya, so that the five nikayas are a classification of the whole Canon, not just the Sutta Pitaka. Scholars conclude on the basis of these lists that 13-15 were added later, and 1 later still.

Both surviving sub-commentaries on the passage about reciters explain the apparent difference between the reciters as being, not a substantive disagreement on the contents of the Canon, but merely a nominal one on its classification. Thus they say for example that the Digha reciters did regard 15 as canonical but counted it as part of 10 instead of a separate book. Similarly, the more recent sub-commentary, compiled by the head of the Burmese sangha about two centuries ago, says that 16 and 17 were counted as part of 11 and/or 12. The full list of 18 books are included in the inscriptions approved by the Burmese Fifth Council and in the printed edition of the text recited at the Sixth Council.

Dating the Books of the Khuddaka Nikaya

Oliver Abeynayake has the following to say on the dating of the various books in the Khuddaka Nikaya:

'The Khuddaka Nikaya can easily be divided into two strata, one being early and the other late. The texts Sutta Nipata, Itivuttaka, Dhammapada, Therigatha (Theragatha), Udana and Jataka belong to the early stratum. The texts Khuddakapatha, Vimanavatthu, Petavatthu, Niddesa, Patisambhida, Apadana, Buddhavamsa and Cariyapitaka can be categorized in the later stratum.'

Lay and Monastic Life

Traditionally, Theravada Buddhism has observed a distinction between the practices suitable for a lay person and the practices undertaken by ordained monks (and, in ancient times, nuns). While the possibility of significant attainment by laymen is not entirely disregarded by the Theravada, it occupies a position of significantly less prominence than in the Mahayana and Vajrayana traditions. This distinction-as well as the distinction between those practices advocated by the Pail Canon, and the folk religious elements embraced by many monks-have motivated some scholars to consider Theravada Buddhism to be composed of multiple separate traditions, overlapping though still distinct. Most prominently, the anthropologist Melford Spiro in his work *Buddhism and Society* separated Burmese Theravada into three groups: *Apotropaic Buddhism* (concerned with providing protection from evil spirits), *Kammatic Buddhism* (concerned with making merit for a future birth), and *Nibbanic Buddhism* (concerned with attaining the liberation of Nirvana, as described in the Tipitaka). He stresses that all three are firmly rooted in the Pail Canon. These categories are not accepted by all scholars, and are usually considered non-exclusive by those who employ them.

The role of lay people has traditionally been primarily occupied with activities that are commonly termed 'merit making' (falling under Spiro's category of kammatic Buddhism). Merit making activities include offering food and other basic necessities to monks, making donations to temples and monasteries, burning incense or lighting candles before images of the Buddha, and chanting protective or merit-making verses from the Pail Canon. Some lay practitioners have always chosen to take a more active role in religious affairs, while still maintaining their lay status. Dedicated lay men and women sometimes act as trustees or custodians for their temples, taking part in the financial planning and management of the temple. Others may volunteer significant time in tending to the mundane needs of local monks (by cooking, cleaning, maintaining temple facilities, etc.). Lay activities have traditionally not extended to study of the Pail scriptures, nor the practice of meditation, though in the 20th Century these areas have become more accessible to the lay community, especially in Thailand.

A number of senior monastics in the Thai Forest Tradition, including Ajahn Buddhadasa, Luang Ta Maha Bua, Ajahn Plien Pányapatipo, Ajahn Pasanno, and Ajahn Jayasaro, have begun teaching meditation retreats outside of the monastery for lay disciples.

In the UK, Ajahn Chah a disciple of Ajahn Mun, set up a monastic lineage at Chithurst in West Sussex, "Cittaviveka", with his disciple Ajahn Sumedho, then "Amaravati" in Hertfordshire was founded which has a retreat centre for lay retreats. Ajahn Sumedho extended this to Harnham in Northumberland as Aruna Ratanagiri under the present guidance of Ajahn Munindo, another disciple of Ajahn Chah.

Nirvana, the highest goal of Theravada Buddhism, is attained through study and the practice of morality, meditation and wisdom (sila, samadhi, Panna). The goal of Nirvana (and its associated techniques) have traditionally been seen as the domain of the fully ordained monastic, whereas many of the same techniques can be used by laypeople to generate happiness in their lives, without focusing on Nirvana. Monastic roles in the Theravada can be broadly described as being split between the role of the (often urban) scholar monk and the (often rural or forest) meditation monk. Both types of monks serve their communities as spiritual teachers and officiants by presiding over spiritual ceremonies and providing instruction in basic Buddhist morality and teachings.

Scholar monks undertake the path of studying and preserving the Pail literature of the Theravada. They may devote little time to the practice of meditation, but may attain great respect and renown by becoming masters of a particular section of the Pail Canon or its commentaries. Masters of the Abhidhamma, called Abhidhammika, are particularly respected in the scholastic tradition.

Meditation monks, often called forest monks because of their association with certain wilderness-dwelling traditions, are considered to be specialists in meditation. While some forest monks may undertake significant study of the Pail Canon, in general meditation monks are expected to learn primarily from their meditation experiences and personal teachers, and may not know more of the Tipitaka than is necessary to participate in liturgical life and to provide a foundation for fundamental Buddhist teachings.

More so than the scholastic tradition, the meditation tradition is associated with the attainment of certain supernatural powers described in both Pail sources and folk tradition. These powers include the attainment of Nirvana, mind-reading, supernatural power over material objects and their own material bodies, seeing and conversing with gods and beings living in hell, and remembering their past lives. These powers are called Albania. Sometimes the remain of the cremated bone fragment of an accomplished forest monk is believed able to transfom itself into crystal-like relics (sarira-dhatu).

Ordination

The minimum age for ordaining as a Buddhist monk is 20 years, reckoned from conception. However, boys under that age are allowed to ordain as novices (samanera), performing a ceremony such as *Shinbyu* in Burma. Novices shave their heads, wear the yellow robes, and observe ten basic precepts. Although no specific minimum age for novices is mentioned in the scriptures, traditionally boys as young as seven are accepted. This tradition follows the story of the Lord Buddha's son, Rahula, who was allowed to become a novice at the age of seven. Monks follow 227 rules of discipline, while nuns follow 311 rules.

In most Theravada countries, it is a common practice for young men to ordain as monks for a fixed period of time. In Thailand and Burma, young men typically ordain for the 3 month Rain Retreat (vassa), though shorter or longer periods of ordination are not rare. Traditionally, temporary ordination was even more flexible among Laotians. Once they had undergone their initial ordination as young men, Laotian men were permitted to temporarily ordain again at any time, though married men were expected to seek their wife's permission. Throughout Southeast Asia, there is little stigma attached to leaving the monastic life. Monks regularly leave the robes after acquiring an education, or when compelled by family obligations or ill-health.

Ordaining as a monk, even for a short period, is seen as having many virtues. In many Southeast Asian cultures, it is seen as a means for a young man to 'repay' his parents for their work and effort in raising him, because the merit from his ordination accrues to them as well. Thai men who have ordained as a monk may be seen as more fit husbands by Thai women, who refer to men who have served as monks with a colloquial term meaning 'cooked' to indicate that they are more mature and ready for marriage. Particularly in rural areas, temporary ordination of boys and young men traditionally gave peasant boys an opportunity to gain an education in temple schools without committing to a permanent monastic life.

In Sri Lanka, temporary ordination is not practiced, and a monk leaving the order is frowned upon. The continuing influence of the caste system in Sri Lanka may play a role in the taboo against temporary ordination and leaving the monkhood. Though Sri Lankan monastic nikayas are often organized along caste lines, men who ordain as monks temporarily pass outside of the conventional caste system, and as such during their time as monks may act (or be treated) in a way that would not be in line with the expected duties and privileges of their caste.

Monastic Practices

The practices usually vary in different sub-schools and monasteries within Theravada. But in the most orthodox forest monastery, the monk usually models his practice and lifestyle on that of the Buddha and his first generation of disciples by living close to nature in forest, mountains and caves. Forest monasteries still keep alive the ancient traditions through following the Buddhist monastic code of discipline in all its detail and developing meditation in secluded forests.

In a typical daily routine at the monastery during the 3 month vassa period, the monk will wake up before dawn and will begin the day with group chanting and meditation. At dawn the monks will go out to surrounding villages bare-footed on alms-round and will have the only meal of the day before noon by eating from the bowl by hand. Most of the time is spent on Dhamma study and meditation. Sometimes the abbot or a senior monk will give a Dhamma talk to the visitors. Laity who stay at the monastery will have to abide by the traditional eight Buddhist precepts.

After the end of the Vassa period, many of the monks will go out far away from the monastery to find a remote place (usually in the forest) where they can hang their umbrella tents and where it is suitable for the work of self-development. When they go wandering, they walk barefoot, and go wherever they feel inclined. Only those requisites which are necessary will be carried along. These generally consist of the bowl, the three robes, a bathing cloth, an umbrella tent, a mosquito net, a kettle of water, a water filter, razor, sandals, some small candles, and a candle lantern.

The monks do not fix their times for walking and sitting meditation, for as soon as they are free they just start doing it; nor do they determine for how long they will go on to meditate. Some of them sometimes walk from dusk to dawn whereas at other times they may walk from between two to seven hours. Some may decide to fast for days or stay at dangerous places where ferocious animals live in order to aid their meditation.

Those monks who have been able to achieve a high level of attainment will be able to guide the junior monks and lay Buddhists toward the four degrees of spiritual attainment.

Lay Devotee

In Pail the word for a male lay devotee is Upasaka. Upasaka is its female equivalent. One of the duties of the lay followers, as taught by the Buddha, is to look after the needs of the monk/nuns. They are to see that the monk/nuns do not suffer from lack of the four requisites: food, clothing, shelter and medicine. As neither monks nor nuns are allowed to have an occupation, they depend entirely on the laity for their sustenance. In return for this charity, they are expected to lead exemplary lives.

In Burma and Thailand, the monastery was and is still regarded as a seat of learning. In fact today about half of the primary schools in Thailand are located in monasteries. Religious rituals and ceremonies held in a monastery are always accompanied by social activities. In times of crisis, it is to the monks that people bring their problems for counsel.

Traditionally, a ranking monk will deliver a sermon four times a month: when the moon waxes and wanes and the day before the new and full moons. The laity also have a chance to learn meditation from the monks during these times.

It is also possible for a lay disciple to become enlightened. As Bhikkhu Bodhi notes, "The Suttas and commentaries do record a few cases of lay disciples attaining the final goal of Nirvana. However, such disciples either attain Arahantship on the brink of death or enter the monastic order soon after their attainment. They do not continue to dwell at home as Arahant householders, for dwelling at home is incompatible with the state of one who has severed all craving."

Influences

According to the linguist Zacharias P. Thundy the word "Theravada" may have been Hellenized into "Therapeutae", to name a coenobitic order near Alexandria described around the 1st century CE. The similarities between the Therapeutae and Buddhist monasticism, combined with Indian evidence of Buddhist missionary activity to the Mediterranean around 250 BC (the Edicts of Asoka), have been pointed out. The Therapeutae would have been the descendants of Asoka's emissaries to the West, and would have influenced the early formation of Christianity. However, the Macmillan *Encyclopedia of Buddhism* states that theories of influences of Buddhism on early Christianity are without historical foundation.

Monastic Orders within Theravada

Theravada monks typically belong to a particular *Nikaya,* variously referred to as monastic orders or fraternities. These different orders do not typically develop separate doctrines, but may differ in the manner in which they observe monastic rules. These monastic orders represent lineages of ordination, typically tracing their origin to a particular group of monks that established a new ordination tradition within a particular country or geographic area. In Sri Lanka caste plays a major role in the division into nikayas. Some Theravada Buddhist countries appoint or elect a sangharaja, or Supreme Patriarch of the Sangha, as the highest ranking or seniormost monk in a particular area, or from a particular Nikaya. The demise of monarchies has resulted in the suspension of these posts in some countries, but patriarchs have continued to be appointed in Thailand. Burma and Cambodia ended the practice of appointing a sangharaja for some time, but the position was later restored, though in Cambodia it lapsed again.

- *Bangladesh*:
  - Sangharaj Nikaya
  - Mahasthabir Nikaya.
- *Burma* (Myanmar):
  - Thudhamma Nikaya
  - Shwekyin Nikaya
  - Dvara Nikaya.
- *Sri Lanka*:
  - Siam Nikaya.
    - Malwaththa
    - Asgiriya.
    - Waturawila (or Mahavihara Vamshika Shyamopali Vanavasa Nikaya).
  - Amarapura NikayaMany Sub orders including.
    - Dharmarakshitha
    - Kanduboda (or Swejin Nikaya)
    - Tapovana (or Kalyanavamsa).
  - Romania Nikaya.
    - Galduwa (or Kalyana Yogashramaya Samsthava)
    - Delduwa.
- *Thailand and Cambodia.*
  - Maha Nikaya
  - Dhammayuttika Nikaya.

Festivals and Customs

Theravada Spiritual festivals:

1. Magha Puja
2. Vesakha Puja
3. Asalha Puja
4. Uposatha
5. Vassa (Rain Retreat).

Sarvastivada

Sarvastivada is an early school of Buddhism that held to 'the existence of all dharmas in the past, present and future, the 'three times'. The Abhidharma Kosabhacya, a later text, states:

"25c-d. He who affirms the existence of the dharmas of the three time periods [past, present and future] is held to be a Sarvastivadin. "

Origination and History

According to scholar Charles Prebish, There is a great deal of mystery surrounding the rise and early development of the Sarvastivadin school. On the one had, we have the tradition of Asokakakapoka's council, stating that the schismatic group in the Sangha was expelled from Magadha, migrating to northwestern India and evolving into the Sarvastivadin school. On the other hand, we have the attempts of several scholars to ascribe the rise of the school to one of Asoka's missions—that sending Majjhantika to Gandhara, an early seat of the school. This episode corresponds well with one Sarvastivadidn tradition stating that Madhyantika (the Sanskrit counterpart of the Pail Majjhantika) converted the city of Kasmir, which seems to have close ties with Gandhara. Still another tradition established a community of Sarvastivadin monks at Mathura, founded by the patriarch Upagupta. Be that as it may, unit the rain of King Kanishka, around the turn of the Christian era, the history of the school is at best sketchy.

The enjoyed the patronage of Kanishka, during which time they were greatly strengthened, and became one of the dominant shravaka sects for the next thousand years.

Relation to the Mulasarvastivada

A number of theories have been posited by academics as to how the two are related, which Bhikkhu Sujato summaries as follows:

The uncertainty around this school has led to a number of hypotheses. Frauwallner's theory holds that the Mulasarvastivada Vinaya is the disciplinary code of an early Buddhist community based in Mathura, which was quite independent in its establishment as a monastic community from the Sarvastivadins of Kaumir (although of course this does not mean that they were different in terms of doctrine). Lamotte, opposing Frauwallner, asserts that the Mulasarvastivada Vinaya was a late Kaumir compilationmade to complete the Sarvastivadin Vinaya. Warder suggests that the

Mulasarvastivadins were a later development of the Sarvastivada, whose main innovations were literary, the compilation of the large Vinaya and the Saddharmasm [tyupasthana Sutra, which kept the early doctrines but brought the style up to date with contemporary literary developments.

Enomoto pulls the rug out from all these theories by asserting that Sarvastivadin and Mulasarvastivadin are really the same. Meanwhile, Willemen, Dessein, and Cox have developed the theory that the Sautrantikas, a branch or tendency within the Sarvastivadin group of schools, emerged in Gandhara and Bactria around 200 CE. Although they were the earlier group, they temporarily lost ground to the Kaumir Vaibhauika school due to the political influence of KaGicka. In later years the Sautrantikas became known as Mulasarvastivadins and regained the ascendancy. I have elsewhere givenmy reasons for disagreeing with the theories of Enomoto and Willemen et al. Neither Warder nor Lamotte give sufficient evidence to back up their theories. We are leftwith Frauwallner's theory, which in this respect has stood the test of time.

Name

Sarvastivada is a Sanskrit term, which can be glossed as: "the theory of all exists". The Pail equivalent is Sabbatthivada.

Although there is some dispute over how the word "Sarvastivada" is to be analysed, the general consensus is that it is to be parsed into three parts: *sarva* "all" or "every" + *asti* "exist" + *vada* "speak", "say" or "theory". This equates perfectly with the Chinese term, which is literally "the sect that speaks of the existence of everything", as used by Hsuan Tsang and other translators.

Philosophy

Though the Sarvastivadins would themselves claim that their teaching of 'all exists' (sarvasti) is a direct teaching of the Buddha himself, as shown by their attributing the earliest Abhidharma texts to direct disciples of the Buddha, notably to Sariputra and constant reference to the sutras throughout, the school in its entirety is more rightly to be considered as part of the age of scholastic Buddhism. It was the most influential school in the northwestern part of India. In a Chinese context, the word *Abhidharma* refers to the Sarvastivada Abhidharma, although at a minimum the

Dharmaguptaka, Pudgalavada and Theravada also had abhidharmas. During the first century BC, in the Gandharan cultural area (consisting of Oddiyana, Gandhara and Bactria, Tokharistan, across the Khyber Pass), the sthaviriyas used Gander to write their literature in the Kharocmhi script. During this time, the Sarvastivada Abhidharma primarily consisted of the *Abhidharmahrdaya* authored by Dharmashresthin, a native from Tokharistan, and the *Ashtagrantha* authored/compiled by Katyayaniputra.

Both texts were translated by Samghadeva in 391 A.D. and in 183 A.D. respectively, but they were not completed until 390 in Southern China. Although the sarvastitva was the central thesis, there were different theories on how 'sarvam' and even 'asti' were actually to be explained and understood among the Gandharan diverse Sarvastivadins. Vasubandhu's *Koshabhasya*, an elaborate yoga manual based on the Hrdaya, describes four main theses on sarvasti: 'There are four types of Sarvastivadins accordingly as they teach a difference in existence (*bhavanyathatva*), a difference in characteristic (*laksananyathatva*), a difference in condition (*avasthanyathatva*), and mutual difference (*anyonyathatva*).

Later Sarvastivada takes a combination of the first and third theses as its model. It was on this basis that the school's doctrines were defended in the face of growing external, and sometimes even internal, criticism.

The doctrines of Sarvastivada were not confined to 'all exists', but also include the theory of momentariness (*ksanika*), conjoining (*samprayukta*) and simultaneity (*sahabhu*), conditionality (*hetu* and *pratyaya*), the culmination of the spiritual path (*marga*), and others. These doctrines are all inter-connected and it is the principle of 'all exists' that is the axial doctrine holding the larger movement together when the precise details of other doctrines are at stake. The Sarvastivada was also known by other names, particularly *hetuvada* and *yuktivada*. Hetuvada comes from hetu – 'cause', which indicates their emphasis on causation and conditionality.

Yuktivada comes from yukti – 'reason' or even 'logic', which shows their use of rational argument and syllogism. When the Sarvastivada school held a synod in Kashmira during the reign of Kanishka II (ca. 158-176), the Gandharan most important text, the Astagrantha of Katyayaniputra was rewritten in Sanskrit making necessary revisions. This revised text was now known as

Jbanaprasthana, Course of Knowledge. Though the Gandharan Astagrantha had many vibhasas, the new Kashmira Astagrantha i.e. the Jnanaprasthana had a Sanskrit Mahavibhasa, compiled by the Kashmira Sarvastivada synod.

The Jnanaprasthana and its Mahavibhasa, which took more than a generation to complete, were then declared the Vaibhasika orthodoxy, said to be 'Buddha's word', Buddhabhasita. This new Vaibhasika orthodoxy, however, was not readily accepted by the Gandharan Sarvastivadins, though gradually they adapted their views to the new Kawmira orthodoxy. The Gandharan Sarvastivadins used the same Vinaya from Mathura. As a matter of fact, their Abhidharma was meant for meditational practices. They made use of the Hrdaya which is a manual for attaining arhat. However, the long Gandharan Vinaya was abridged to a Sanskrit Dashabhanavara in the Kashmira synod by removing the avadanas and jatakas, stories and illustrations.

After the declaration of the Vaibhasika orthodoxy, the Gandharan non-vaibhasika Sarvastivadins, the majority, were called 'sautrantikas' (those who uphold the sutras). Interestingly, the Kawmira orthodoxy, the Vaibhasikas disappeared in the later part of the 7th century. Subsequently, the old Gandharan Sarvastivadins, the non-vaibhasika sautrantikas, were named 'Mulasarvastivadins', who then at a later went to Tibet. It has been suggested that the minority Vaibhasikas were absorbed into the majority Sautrantika Sarvastivadins as a possible result of the latter's adaptations. Moreover, Mishrakabhidharmahrdaya, a title which means that 'Sautrantika views were mixed with vaibhasika views' was composed by Dharmatrata in the 4th century in Gandharan area.

Vasubandhu (ca.350-430), a native from Purusapura in Gandhara, composed his Kowa based on this text and the Astagrantha. While in Kawmira, he wrote his karikas which were well received there but he faced intense opposition, notably from Samghabhadra, a leading Sarvastivada pundit, when he composed his bhasya. By his bhasya, Vasubandhu made it clear to the Vaibhasikas that he was a Sautrantika, which is why he was fiercely opposed by the Sarvastivada vaibhasikas in Kawmira. In reply to Vasubhandhu's bhasya, Samghabhadra wrote a text, the Nyananusara 'according to reason'. This work is presently only extant in Chinese (from Xuanzang's translation and little is known of it in English).

For a critical examination of the Sarvastivadin interpretation of the Samyuktagama, see David Kalupahana, *Causality: The Central Philosophy of Buddhism.* For a Sautrantika refutation of the Sarvastivadin use of the Samyuktagama, see Theodore Stcherbatsky, *The Central Conception of Buddhism and the Meaning of the Word Dharma.*

Texts

Sutra Pitika

Scholars at present have "a nearly complete collection of sutras from the Sarvastivada school" thanks to a recent discovery in Afghanistan of roughly two-thirds of Dirgha-Agama in Sanskrit. The Madhyama and Saayukta Agamas have long been available in Chinese translation. The Sarvastivada is therefore the only early school besides the Theravada for which we have a roughly complete sutra collection, although unlike the Theravada it has not all been preserved in the original language.

Abhidharma

The Sarvastivada Abhidharma consists of seven texts. The texts of the Sarvastivadin Abhidharma are:

- Sangitiparyaya ('Discourses on Gathering Together').

Sangitiparyaya or Samgiti-paryaya-sastra ("recitation together") is one of the seven Sarvastivada Abhidharma Buddhist scriptures. It was composed by Mahakausthila (according to the Sanskrit and Tibetan sources) or Sariputra (according to the Chinese sources).

Structurally, the Samgitiparyaya is similar to the Dharmaskandha, though earlier, as the latter is mentioned in the former. It is basically a matrka on the early teachings, arranged in groups of dharmas by number, similar to the Ekottarikagama.

This text, as the name implies, is essentially a commentary on the Samgitisutra (T 9, Dighanikaya no. 33). This also indicates that the contents are more a gathering together and assemblage of the Buddha's Dharma, than any new theory or discussion. The background to the first recital of the Samgitisutra, as the Jains fell into disarray after the death of the Mahavir, and the Buddhist Samgha gathered together to recite the core teachings of the Dharma to prevent such a split in their own religion, perhaps indicates the fear of present or impending schism arising in the Samgha on the part of those who compiled this Abhidharma work, some time later. The Samgitisutra is also the basis of a commentarial work, in the later Yogacara-bhumi-sastra, some several hundred years later.

Yin Shun notes it being mentioned in the Mulasarvastivada Vinayavyakaraga, indicating its early inclusion in the Sarvastivada canon. As this text has some 14 references to the Dhatuskandha, "as the Dhatuskandha states", it is also clear that this is post Dhatuskandha in composition. The Chinese Taisho reverses the order of the two. Obviously they are very closely related

Dharmaskandha ('Aggregation of Dharmas')

Dharmaskandha or Dharma-skandha-sastra is one of the seven Sarvastivada Abhidharma Buddhist scriptures. Dharmaskandha means "collection of dharmas". It was composed by Sariputra (according to the Sanskrit and Tibetan sources) or Maudgalyayana (according to Chinese sources). The Chinese edition was translated by Xuanzang, and appears as:

It begins with a matrka as a summary of the topics, showing its antiquity, as these were supposedly only assigned by the Buddha himself. It presents 21 subjects, the first 15 of which concern the practice of the spiritual path, and the realization of its fruits. The 16th deals with "various issues". Subjects 17 to 20 deal with the enumeration of the ayatanas, dhatus and skandhas as encompassing "all dharmas". The 21st is regards dependent origination.

Frauwallner concludes that the Dhatuskandha is from a period before then split between the Sanskrit and Pail Abhidharma traditions, based on its correlation with the Pail Vibhanga. He thus dates it to pre-Ashoka Buddhism. Yin Shun notes it being mentioned in the Mulasarvastivada Vinayavyakaraga, indicating its early inclusion in the Sarvastivada canon. These two combined, would suggest the Mulasarvastivada having its own canon at quite an early date.

Yin Shun also cites three points for considering this text to be sourced in a pre-sectarian Abhidharma. It similar analysis of rupa to the Sariputta Abhidhamma and the Dhammapariyaya (considered to be the oldest Abhidharma texts of any tradition). No mention of avijnapti-rupa, as per the Sariputta Abhidhamma;

and Yin Shun. The emphasis on the five indriya and five bala, as paramount in the spiritual path

Prajnaptisastra ('Treatise on Designations')

Prajnaptisastra or Prajnapti-sastra is one of the seven Sarvastivada Abhidharma Buddhist scriptures. The word *Prajnaptisastra* means "designation" (of dharmas). It was composed by Maudgalyayana (according to the Sanskrit, Tibetan and MPPU) or Mahakatyayana (according to Puguang).

The importance of this text is shown in its being quoted 135 times by the MVS, though these references are not exclusively Sarvastivada in nature. The format is of matrka, followed by question and answer explanations, with references to the sutras for orthodoxy.

Willemen, Dessein & Cox assign this text to the next period, based on its "abstract principles of organization" and "complexity of doctrinal analysis". However, though the content is different from the Samgiti and Dharmaskandha, one could scarcely consider it more abstract in nature. It simply reflects the nature of the Sutras upon which it is based. In fact, it has relatively more direct references to the Sutras for its overall size than many of the developed texts, and a similar use of questions and answers as the Samgita.

Dhatukaya ('Body of Elements')

Dhatukaya or Dhatukaya-sastra is one of the seven Sarvastivada Abhidharma Buddhist scriptures.

Dhatukaya means "group of elements". It was written by Purna (according to Sanskrit and Tibetan sources), or Vasumitra (according to Chinese sources).

This comparatively short text bears similarities with the Pail Sthaviravada text, the Dhatukatha, in style and format, though it uses a different matrka. It also bears a close connection with the Prakaranapada, through several items common to both. In its sevenfold division of dharmas in particular, it does provide, a closer look at the various divisions of dharmas, in particular citta and caitasika, with its conjoined and non-conjoined aspects. As it is not mentioned in the Mahavibhasa, this also suggests it is either a later text, or originally a fragment removed from an earlier text.

Vijnanakaya ('Body of Consciousness')

Vijnanakaya or Vijnanakaya-sastra is one of the seven Sarvastivada Abhidharma Buddhist scriptures. "Vijnanakaya" means "group of consciousness".

Vijnanakaya is the first Abhidharma text that is not attritubted to a direct disciple of the Buddha, but written some 100 years after the Buddha's parinirvana, according to Xuanzang's disciple Puguang. Yin Shun however, concludes it was composed around the first century CE, and was influenced by the Jnanaprasthana, though differs in several aspects. In this regard, he likens it to the Prakaranapada, which is also a different position on the Sarvastivada as a whole.

This is an esteemed Sarvastivada text wherein the Sarvastivada is upheld against Vibhajyavada objections, in the first of its six sections. It is here that the theory of Sarvastivada, the existence of all dharmas through past, present and future, is first presented. Interestingly, the issue is only brought up when Moggaliputta-tissa makes the standard claim of the Vibhajyavada, "past and future (dharmas) do not exist, (only) present and unconditioned (dharmas) do exist". The Vaginae-kaya has four main theses to refute this:

1. The impossibility of two simultaneous cittas
2. The impossibility of karma and vipaka being simultaneous
3. That vaginae only arises with an object
4. Attainments are not necessarily present.

In addition to refuting the Vibhajyavada view, the second section is a refutation of the Vatsiputriya Pudgalavada claim of: "the paramartha of the arya [truths] can be attained, can be realized by the 'pudgala', present and complete, therefore it is certainly [the case] that the 'pudgala' exists". The Sarvastivada take the title 'Sunyavada' in order to refute this claim, though this is obviously meaning "empty of pudgala", rather than the later Sunyavada of the Mahayana, i.e. the *Madhyamaka*. The first refutation centres around the two extremes of "absolute identity" and "absolute difference". The second hinges on the continuity of the existence of the skandhas in the past, present and future – Sarvastivada – proper. The third and fourth sections concern the causal condition, and the conditioning object of vaginae respectively. The fifth includes the two other conditions, the immediate condition and predominant condition. These conditions are discussed in terms of their realm, nature, temporal location, etc. in a format that came to be standard for the Sarvastivada Abhidharma. Such a system also appears in Abhidharma type analysis of dharmas in the Mahaprajnaparamita Sutra and its Upadesa. The remaining five sections are doctrinal elaborations of the Sarvastivada school, including issues regarding perception, dependent origination and conditionality

Prakaranapada ('Exposition')

Prakaranapada or Prakaranapada-sastra, composed by Vasumitra, is one of the seven Sarvastivada Abhidharma Buddhist scriptures.

Prakaranapada is the major text of the central Abhidharma period. It influenced other non-Sarvastivada schools, though not in the polarizing manner that the later Jnanaprasthana and Vibhasha texts did. Its format for dharma analysis is used, for example, by the Maha-Prajna-paramitopadesa, which also states that the first four chapters where composed by Vasumitra, with the other four chapters by Kasmira arhats. Yin Shun considers this Vasumitra to be the same Vasumitra who appears in the Mahavibhasa later.

This seems to indicate that before the later formalization of Sarvastivada doctrines, the Vaginae-kaya and Prakaranapada were perhaps representative of several differing lines of thought, though were only later over-shadowed by the Vibhasha and its orthodoxy. It would be interesting to perhaps trace some of these differences through the likes of Buddhadeva and Dharmatrata, as they are presented in the Vibhasha.

Prakaranapada contains two systems of dharma classification, one fivefold, the other sevenfold. It was the former fivefold system that later became the standard format, and was important for the establishment of the respective characteristics, nature and functions of the various dharmas, especially the caitasika and citta-viprayukta-dharmas. The sevenfold system bears some similarities to Pail Abhidhamma, and seems to made of categories of dharmas that are all sutra based.

It also expands on the traditional fourfold theory of conditionality, by introducing some 20 types of condition, in paired dharmas. Although these are not the later sixfold classification, this may have opened the door for later innovation.

Jnanaprasthana ('Foundation of Knowledge')

Jnanaprasthana or Jnanaprasthana-sastra, composed by Katyayaniputra is one of the seven Sarvastivada Abhidharma Buddhist scriptures. Jnanaprasthana means "establishment of knowledge".

The tradition of the Mahavibhasa states that it was taught by the Buddha himself, but differs as to the circumstances. It was later Katyayaniputra who was responsible for the compilation thereof. The Maha-Prajna-paramitopadesa (which actually refers to the Astaskandha) states that 100 years after the Buddha's demise, there arose doctrinal disputes among the great masters, giving rise to distinctly named schools.

Xuanzang maintained that it was written some three centuries after the Buddha, which would be c. 150 BCE. The orthodox Vibhca takes this as the 'root' Abhidharma, though references are sometimes made to the Prakara Gapda in the same terms. It became known as the 'body' of the Abhidharma, with the six remaining texts of the early period known as the 'legs' or 'supports'. This is based on textual authority, and not a temporal definition, given the respective historical order of these seven treatises. That is, the Jnanaprasthana is not sourced from the six legs, but neither is it directly sourced from the Sutras. This is also a reminder that these texts were all probably in a state of constant revision and update, for possibly several hundred years. There are thus mutual reference and borrowing of format and content, that cannot be summarily described by a simply sequential order.

The outline of the text more closely approximates that earliest of models, the Sariputra Abhidharma, than those specifically Sarvastivada treatises. This is evidenced in its use of the samyojanas, Prajna, karma, indriya, mahabhuta, dhyana and drsti as main divisions. A similar system is later continued through into the Kosa, and Hrdaya texts. Prior to this is a division of "assorted issues". The analysis is of three main types, according to Yinshun:

1. Analysis of the sutras themselves – in order to find the actual underlying principle, rather than acceptance of the content at face value, which could lead to apparent

contradiction. This indicates the Abhidharmika standpoint of taking the Abhidharma as pramana in understanding the doctrine.

2. Analysis of the nature, or characteristics, of individual dharmas. Rather than the use of Sutra categories pertaining to spiritual praxis, the tendency here is to group by type. Thus, dharmas are assigned as either rupa, citta, caitasika or citta-viprayukta – the conditioned dharmas, and also the unconditioned dharmas. Specifics as to each type are given, as well as detailed discussions of related dharmas. These are then again categorized according to their being with or without outflows; visible or non-visible; past, present or future; as to realm; and so forth.
3. Analysis of the relationship between various dharmas. As the preceding analysis lends itself to plurality, and the possibility of falling into independent Sackhya-type realities, this analysis completes the Buddhist teaching of dependent origination, preventing such an error. Using kcanika theory, it establishes the six-fold conditionality theory, that would later be a special feature of the Sarvastivada. This is the earliest text in which the theory appears. It also includes some detail on citta-viprayukta-dharmas.

The influence of the Vijnanaprasthana is seen strongly in the Vibhasha, and this influenced the subsequent Hrdaya texts, and also the Kosa and commentaries.

Following these, are the texts that became the authority of the Vaibhashikas, the Kasmiri Sarvastivada Orthodoxy:

Mahavibhasa ("Great Commentary", on the Jnanaprasthana)

The Abhidharma Mahvibhca Uastra is an ancient Buddhist text.

The Vibhasa Compendia

Vibhasa is a term meaning 'compendium', 'treatise' or simply 'explanation', derived from vibhas, 'to speak' or 'to explain'. Evidence strongly indicates that there were originally many different Vibhas texts, mainly commenting on the Jnanaprasthana, but also commenting on other Abhidharma texts too. The relationship between all these texts is very complex, as there is mutual influence, and the texts underwent some development from initial inception to completion. The Taisho has three, however, which are compendiums on the Jnanaprasthana, and its six legs: the Abhidharma Mahavibhasa Sastra (T1545), the Abhidharma Vibhasa Sastra (T1546) and the Vibhasa Sastra (T1547).

Abhidharma Mahavibhasa Sastra, by Katyayaniputra

Of these three, the Abhidharma Mahvibhca Sastra is considered prominent. Its authorship is traditionally attributed to five hundred arhats, some 600 years after the Parinirvana of the Buddha. Its compilation, however, is attributed to a certain Katyayaniputra.

Contents

As such an immense text, it contains a huge array of material. This includes the discussion of basically every doctrinal issue of the day, as presented by not only non-Sarvastivada views, such as the Vibhajyavada, Pudgalavada, Mahasa Cghika, and others; but also non-Buddhist systems, such as the Sackhya, the Vaiecika, and others; and finally of the Sarvastivada itself, as represented by its various learned and venerable leaders.

With regards the former two, their 'unorthodox' and 'incorrect' doctrines are taken to task from the perspective of the Buddhist Sarvastivada. With regards the latter, several views are often expressed as more detailed descriptions of Sarvastivada doctrines. These are often open ended, with no particular explanation favoured over another, though sometimes a particular explanation is extolled as being particularly clear and in harmony with the teachings.

Due to both of the above reasons, the Vibhas literature is particularly useful in not only understanding this school, but in also getting a good perspective on the general state of the Buddha Dharma, and other other non-Buddhist religions at the time.

Mulasarvastivada

The Mulasarvastivada was an early school of Buddhism, developed in India during the 2nd century A.D. and prevalent in Tibet for centuries thereafter. Its vinaya is extant in Tibetan (9th century translation) and Chinese (5th century translation), and to some extent in the original Sanskrit. Its relationship to the

Sarvastivada school is a matter of dispute; modern scholars lean towards classifying them as independent.

Tibetan Emperor Ralpacan restricted Buddhist ordination to the Mulasarvastivadin line.

Sautrantika

The Sautrantika were an early school of Buddhist philosophy, generally believed to be descended from the Sthaviravada by way of their immediate parent school, the Sarvastivadins. Their name means literally "those who rely upon the sutras", and indicated their rejection of the Abhidharma texts of other early Buddhist schools. The Sarvastivadins sometimes referred to them as the Drcmntika school, meaning "those who utilize the method of examples". This latter name may have been a pejorative label. It is also possible that the name 'Darcmantika' identifies a predecessor tradition, or another related, but distinct, doctrinal position; the exact relationship between the two terms is unclear. Charles Willemen identifies the Sautrantika as a Western branch of the Sarvastivadins, active in the Gandhara area, who split from the Sarvastivadins sometime before 200 CE, when the Sautrantika name emerged. Other scholars are less confidant of a specific identification for the Sautrantika; Nobuyoshi Yamabe calls specifying the precise identity of the Sautrantika "one of the biggest problems in current Buddhist scholarship."

The Sautrantika differed from their parent school, the Sarvastivadins, on matters of ontology. While the Sarvastivadins Abhidharma described a complex system in which past, present, and future phenomena are all held to have some form of their own existence, the Sautrantika subscribed to a doctrine of "extreme momentariness" that held that only the present moment existed. They seem to have regarded the Sarvastivadin position as a violation of the basic Buddhist principle of impermanence (anicca). The Sarvastivadin Abhidharma also broke down human experience in terms of a variety of underlying phenomena (a view similar to that held by the modern Theravada abhidhamma); the Sautrantika believed that experience could not be differentiated in this manner.

They used the concept of an auraya (substrate, refuge) to explain the continuity of consciousness through rebirth, whereas the Pudgalavadins and the Vatsiputriya school posited a *pudgala* (a 'personal entity' distinct from the five skandha), and where non-Buddhist Indian philosophy typically referred to an atman. Vasubandhu, one of the Indian monastic scholars primarily responsible for articulating the doctrines of the Yogacara school, was sympathetic to the Sautrantika on many doctrinal issues, and wrote critiques of the Vaibhashika tradition from a Sautrantika perspective.

No separate monastics code specific to the Sautrantika has been found, nor is the existence of any such separate disciplinary code evidenced in other texts; this indicates that they were likely only a doctrinal division within the Sarvastivadin school.

MahasaCghika

The Mahasa Cghika also transliterated "Mahasanghika," and "Mahasamghika") (lit. "Great[er]-Community" or majority) was one of the early Buddhist schools in ancient India which is now extinct (i.e. its ordination lineage does not continue). The origins of the Mahasa Cghika sect of Buddhism are still extremely uncertain, and the subject of intense debate among scholars. The reason for the intensity of interest in the origins of the Mahasa Cghika school is that their Vinaya recension appears in several ways to represent an older redaction overall, and so has important implications for the history of the Vinaya recensions of all sects.

Location

The Mahs Cghikas were primarily situated in Northwestern India but also with an important presence in southeast India around Amaravati and Nagarjunakonda.

Origins

As one would expect with the history of the sectarian period, the different sects each have their own accounts. The account by the Theravada sect, found in the Dipavamsa, seems to be merely a mythic account designed to glorify the Theravada sect itself, written at a time when the historical situation had been forgotten.

According to one account, the Mahasacghika sect was formed in the first Buddhist schism around 320 BCE. It split from the Sthaviravada (Elders) school over disputes about the authenticity of certain texts which the Mahscghikas claimed had been invented by the Elders and were not genuine Word of the Buddha

(Buddhavacana). In this account, they did not join the third buddhist council.

There are several other accounts: from the Sammitiya sect, the Sarvastivadin sect and others.

The Mahscghikas' own account of their origins states that they divided from the Sthaviravadins on friendly terms at a meeting convened by the King following King Pushyamitra who persecuted Buddhism, probably meaning Agnimitra; therefore after the Third Council. It is not clear from this account that this division would have counted as a formal 'schism' in the technical sense. The issue was, according to them, that the Elders had composed a new redaction of the Vinaya. According to them, the King (and implicitly the writers too) acknowledged both redactions as valid, but it was considered that the monks must choose to follow one or the other; they could not vacilate between both. So those who followed the old Vinaya edition were called the Mahscghikas, and those who followed the new edition were called the Sthaviras. The Mahscghikas' account gives each of the major sects listed, with the colour of the robe that they wear.

Vinaya Recension

The Mahasacghika Vinaya recension is essentially very similar to the other recensions, as they all are to each other. However, relatively, the Mahasacghika recension differs most from the other recensions in structure, nevertheless the rules are generally identical in meaning, if the Vibhangas (explanations) are compared. The features of the Mahasacghika Vinaya recension which suggest that it might be an older redaction are, in brief, these:

The *Bhiksu-prakirnaka* and *Bhiksuni-prakirnaka* and the *Bhiksu-abhisamacarika-dharma* sections of the Mahasacghika Vinaya are generally equivalent to the *Khandhakas/Skhandhakas* of the Sthavira derived schools. However, their structure is simpler, and according to recent research by Clarke, the structure follows a *matika* (Matrix) which is also found embedded in the Vinayas of several of the Sthavira schools, suggesting that it is presectarian. The sub-sections of the *Prakirnaka* sections are also titled *pratisamyukta* rather than Skandhaka/Khandhaka. *Pratisamyukta/Patisamyutta* means a section or chapter in a collection organised by subject; the '*Samyukta*-principle', like the *Samyutta-Nikaya/Samyukta-Agama*. Scholars such as Master Yin Shun, Choong Moon Keat, and Bhikkhu Sujato have argued that the *Samyutta/Samyukta* represents the earliest collection among the Nikayas/Agamas, and this may well imply that it is also the oldest *organising principle* too. (N.B. this does not necessarily say anything about the age of the contents).

There are also fewer stories in general in the Vinaya of the subsidiary school, the Mahasacghika-Lokottaravada (Lokuttaravada), and many of them give the appearance of badly connected obvious interpolations, whereas in the structure of the Sthavira recensions the stories are integrated into the whole scheme which must originally have been a brilliantly artistic literary composition. In the formulations of some of the pratimoksha rules also, the phrasing (though generally identical in meaning to the other recensions) often appears to represent a clearer but less streamlined version, which suggests it might be older. This is particularly noticeable in the *Bhiksuni-Vinaya,* which has not been as well preserved as the *Bhiksu-Vinaya* in general in all the recensions. Yet the formulation of certain rules which seem very confused in the other recensions (e.g. *Bhikkhuni Sanghadisesa* three = six in the Ma-L) seems to better represent what would be expected of a root formulation which could lead to the variety of confused formulations we see (presumably later) in the other recensions. The formulation of this rule (as an example) also reflects a semi-parallel formulation to a closely related rule for Bhiksus which is found in a more similar form in all the Vinayas.

Abhidhamma

The Abhidhamma was not accepted as canonical by the Mahasanghika school.

Prominent Persons

Atisha was ordained in the MahasaCghika lineage. However, because the Tibetan Emperor Ralpacan had decreed that only the Mulasarvastivadan order would be permitted in Tibet, he did not ordain anyone.

Ekavyaharaka

The Ekavyaharaka school of Buddhism split from the MahsaCghikas during the reign of Acœoka. The Ekavyaharikas emphasized the transcendence of the Buddha, asserting that he was eternally enlightened and essentially non-physical.

The Lokottaravada may be an offshoot of the Ekavyaharikas.

Etymology

The Sanskrit *Ekavyaharaka* is composed of three elements: *Ekavyaharaka Eka* means "one" "oneness", "solitary", "a certain one," etc. *Vihara* means "doing", "performing", "action", "practice", "conduct", "behaviour", etc. The suffix *ka* means "school." Taken together the term *Ekavyaharaka* can be translated as "The School of One Practice," "The School of the Practice of Oneness," "The School of Unified Activity," etc.

Lokuttaravada

Lokottaravada was one of the twenty schools of early Buddhism, according to Mahayana doxological sources compiled by Bhavyaviveka, Vinitadeva and others, and was a sub-group which emerged from the Mahasanghika sect. The Mahavastu, the only complete surviving Mahasanghika text in Sanskrit, is attributed to the Lokottaravadins. The Lokottaravadins asserted that there are no real things in the world except two kinds of emptiness (sunyata), that is, sunyata of persons and sunyata of things. The Buddha is transcendent (lokottara) and his life(s) and physical manifestation are mere appearance.

Prajnaptivada

The Prajnaptivada (Conceptualist) school of Buddhism split from Golulikas in late third century BCE. The Prajnaptivadins were early articulators of the two truths doctrine that is so important to Mahayana Buddhism, where it is usually found in the tension between upaya and Prajna. The Prajnaptivadins distinguished between sacvrti (conventional) and paramartha (ultimate) truth, and between tattva dharmas (real phenomena) and pranapti ones (mere concepts). They grouped the senses and their objects, along with basic elements, as mere concepts, while identifying the skandhas and suffering as real.

There is evidence that the Prajnaptivadins were an influence on Nagarjuna, who is also among the storied promulgators of the two truths doctrine (using some of the same technical terms), and who in his Mulamadhyamakakarika only cites one text by name, that being the Kaccayanagotta Sutta, of which the Prajnaptivadins were known to be fond.

Caitika

The Caitika school of Buddhism split from MahasaCghaka in the middle of the first century BCE. It later gave rise to the Apara Aiel and Uttara Aiel schools. All three emphasized the supernatural character of the Buddha. The school also included an early version of the Bodhisattva ideal (as opposed to the earlier arhat ideal); this would later become vitally important to Mahayana Buddhism.

Twenty Sects

The following lists the twenty sects described as Hinayana in some Mahayana texts:

Sthaviravada split into the 11 sects:

- Sarvastivadin
- Haimavata
- Vatsiputriya
- Dharmottara
- Bhadrayaniya
- Sammitiya
- Channagirika
- Mahisasaka
- Dharmaguptaka
- Kasyapiya
- Sautrantika.

Sthaviravada Haimavata:

- Sarvastivadin
- Vatsiputriya
- Dharmottara
- Bhadrayaniya
- Sammitiya
- Channagirika
- Mahisasaka
- Dharmaguptaka
- Kasyapiya
- Sautrantika.

Mahasanghika split into 9 sects:

- Ekavyaharaka
- Lokottaravadin
- Kaukkutika
- Bahussrutiya
- Prajnaptivada
- Caitika
- Aparasaila
- Uttarasaila.

Mahasanghika:

- Ekavyaharaka Caitika
- Lokottaravadin Aparasaila
- Kaukkutika – Uttarasaila
- Bahussrutiya
- Prajnaptivada

Influences on East Asian Schools

The following later schools used the Vinaya of the Dharmaguptaka:

- Chinese Buddhism, especially the Vinaya School
- Korean buddhism, especially Gyeyul
- Vietnamese Buddhism
- Japanese Ritsu

The following involve philosophical influence:

- The Japanese Jojitsu is considered by some an offshoot of Sautrantika; others consider it to be derived from Bahusrutiya
- The Chinese/Japanese Kusha school is considered an offshoot of Sarvastivada, influenced by Vasubandhu.

Theravada subschools

The different schools in Theravada often emphasize different aspects (or parts) of the Pail Canon and the later commentaries, or differ in the focus on (and recommended way of) practice. There are also significant differences in strictness or interpretation of the Vinaya.

- *Bangladesh*:
  - Sangharaj Nikaya
  - Mahasthabir Nikaya.
- *Burma*:
  - Thudhamma Nikaya.
    - Vipassana tradition of Mahasi Sayadaw and disciples.
  - Shwekyin Nikaya
  - Dvaya Nikaya or Dvara Nikaya.
- *Sri Lanka*:
  - Siam Nikaya
    - Waturawila (or Mahavihara Vamshika Shyamopali Vanavasa Nikaya).
  - Amarapura Nikaya.
    - Kanduboda (or Swejin Nikaya)
    - Tapovana (or Kalyanavamsa).
  - Romania Nikaya.
    - Galduwa (or Kalyana Yogashramaya Samsthava)
    - Delduwa.
  - forest Nikaya.
- *Thailand*.
  - Maha Nikaya.
    - Dhammakaya Movement.
  - Thammayut Nikaya.
    - Thai Forest Tradition
    - Tradition of Ajahn Chah.

Mahayana Schools

- Madhyamaka.
  - Prasangika
  - Svatantrika
  - Sanlun (Three Treatise school).
    - Sanron.
  - Maha-Madhyamaka (Jonangpa).

- Yogacara
  * Cittamatra in Tibet
  * Wei-Shi (Consciousness-only school) or Faxiang (Dharma-character school).
    - Beopsang
    - Hosso.
- Tathagatagarbha.
  * Daúabhumika (absorbed into Huayan)
  * Huayan (Avatacasta).
    - Hwaeom
    - Kegon.
- Chan/Zen/Seon/Thien.
  * Caodong.
    - Soto
    - Keizan line
    - Jakuen line
    - Giin line.
  * Linji.
    - Rinzai
    - Obaku
    - Fuke
    - Won Buddhism: Korean Reformed Buddhism.
- Pure Land (Amidism).
  * Judo Shu
  * Judo Shinshu.
- Tiantai (Lotus Sutra School).
  * Cheontae
  * Tendai (also contains Vajrayana elements).
- Nichiren.
  * Nichiren Shu
  * Nichiren Shush
  * Nipponzan Myohoji
  * Soka Gakkai.

Tantric Schools

- Tibetan Buddhism.
  - Nyingma
  - New Bon (synthesis of Yungdrung Bon and Nyingmapa)
  - Kadam
  - Sakya.
    - Ngor-pa
    - Tsar-pa.
  - Jonang
  - Gelug
  - Kagyu:
    - Shangpa Kagyu
    - Marpa Kagyu:
    - Rechung Kagyu
    - Dagpo Kagyu:
    - Karma Kagyu (or Kamtshang Kagyu)
    - Tsalpa Kagyu
    - Baram Kagyu
    - Pagtru Kagyu (or Phagmo Drugpa Kagyu):
    - Taglung Kagyu
    - Trophu Kagyu
    - Drukpa Kagyu
    - Martsang Kagyu
    - Yerpa Kagyu
    - Yazang Kagyu
    - Shugseb Kagyu
    - Drikung Kagyu.
  - Rime movement (ecumenical movement).
- Japanese Mikkyo.
  - Shingon
  - Tendai (derived from Tiantai but added tantric practices)
  - Shinnyo-en.

8

Hinayana

Hinayana is a Sanskrit and Pail term literally meaning: "the low vehicle", "the inferior vehicle", or "the deficient vehicle".

The term appeared around the 1st or 2nd century CE. Its use in scholarly publications is controversial. There are differing views on the use and meaning of the term, both among scholars and within Buddhism.

The legitimacy of using the term Hinayana to refer to the early Buddhist schools is disputed while use of Hinayana to refer to the contemporary Theravada is seen as pejorative.. In the Chinese, Korean, Vietnamese and Japanese languages, the term means small vehicle, and in the Tibetan language the word means "small" or "lesser" vehicle..

Etymology

The word Hinayana is formed of China : "low", "inferior", "deficient", "defective", and yana: "vehicle", where "vehicle" means "a way of going to enlightenment".

In Brief

Hinayana has been used by both past and present Mahayanists as a name to refer variously to one or more *doctrines, traditions, practitioners* or *thoughts* that are generally concerned with the achievement of Nirvana as an Arahant or a Pratyeka-Buddha, as opposed to the achievement of liberation as a Samyaksambuddha, wherein the Samyaksambuddha (according to Mahayana lore) is deemed to operate from a basis of vowing to effect the spiritual liberation of all beings and creatures from the suffering of samsara (not just himself or a small number of others). Hinayana is sometimes said to be corresponding solely to the Early Buddhist Schools, and not to the current Theravada school, while sometimes it is held to be also cognate with the modern Theravada tradition. Many hold that the term was coined to be purposely pejorative, while others do not.

Scholar Isabelle Onians asserts that although "the Mahayana... very occasionally referred contemptuously to earlier Buddhism as the Hinayana, the Inferior Way," "the preponderance of this name in the secondary literature is far out of proportion to occurrences in the Indian texts." She notes that the term Uravakayana was "the more politically correct and much more usual" term used by Mahayanists.

- Hinayana as *doctrine* would (from a Mahayana perspective) include the Sutras taught by Buddha that admonish the practitioner to follow the Sravaka path or strive for Paccekabuddha hood. In such teachings there is no emphasis on pledging to emancipate the totality of sentient beings from the pain and bondage of samsara-the focus is more on practice for individual liberation. However, the Buddha did not teach in this manner according to the Pail Canon. In the Pail Canon the Buddha never admonishes his disciples to strive to become a Paccekabuddha, and 'sravaka' just translates as follower or disciple: *any* disciple of Buddha would be a savaka. There is thus no mention of a 'Savakapath' as 'savaka' refers to *all* disciples, not to a limited class of disciples.
- Hinayana as a *tradition* in general would include those schools who solely follow the sutras of the Pail Canon or the Agamas (being, Pre-sectarian Buddhism and the Early Buddhist Schools). Some recent Mahayanist scholars have also used the name Nikaya Buddhism to refer to these schools. Some of these schools actively rejected the Mahayana sutras during the time of the rise of the Mahayana, around 2,000 years ago.
- Hinayana as *practitioner* would be an individual of any school (including Mahayana) who practices to eliminate suffering according to basic Buddhist teachings; if successful, he is called an Arahant. (Similarly, a follower of a bodhisattva path in any school would be Mahayana

in this sense.) As a follower of what Mahayana terms "Hinayana", he or she will not strive to become a Buddha, nor will he or she take the Mahayana Bodhisattva-vow of pledging to come back into samsara countless times in the future in order to liberate all other sentient beings from suffering. Also, the 'Pratyeka-Buddha' is regarded by Mahayana as being Hinayanist. Mahayana only considers the ideal of a Samyaksambuddha 'Great'; the other enlightened ideals are considered by Mahayana orthodoxy to be (depending on the translation) either 'inferior', 'degrading', 'base' or 'low'.

Within Buddhism the differing interpretations of Hinayana have consequences that are sometimes quite far-reaching. It is primarily the interpretation of Hinayana as a tradition that has led to the most concern, especially as many people have seen the term as a slur against Pre-sectarian Buddhism, Theravada and the other Early Buddhist schools (the Nikaya Buddhism–schools). These schools solely follow the sutras that are included in the Pail Canon, and which are aimed at helping to achieve the extinction of suffering, as attained by the Arahants.

Jonathan Silk has argued that the term "Hinayana" was used to refer to whomever one wanted to criticize on any given occasion, and did not refer to any definite grouping of Buddhists.

In the Vajrayana practice tradition of Buddhism the Hinayana is seen as one of the three major yanas (or 'vehicles') of Buddhism, alongside the Mahayana and Vajrayana. According to this view, there were three 'turnings of the wheel of dharma'. In the first turning, Shakyamuni Buddha taught the dharma as the Four Noble Truths at Varanasi which led to the Hinayana schools, of which only the Theravada remain today (although they object to the term 'Hinayana'). In the second turning, the 'Perfection of Wisdom' sutras were taught at Vulture's Peak and led to the Mahayana schools. The teachings which constituted the third turning of the wheel of dharma were taught at Shravasti and expounded that all beings have Buddha Nature. This third turning is described as having led to the Vajrayana.

Origins of Hinayana: Vehicles and Paths

It appears that the distinction between vehicles and paths arises in early Mahayana sutras, such as the *Lotus Sutra*, where it is stated that there is one *path*-the path to Nirvana-, but there are different *vehicles*. The vehicles are described (by Mahayana) as representing the fruit of the two types of Buddha found in the Pail Canon, plus the path of the Arahants.

For instance, in Chapter three of the *Lotus Sutra*, there is a parable of a father promising three carts to lure sons out of a burning building, where the goat-cart represents the Sravaka-vehicle; the deer-cart, Pratyeka-Buddhahood; and the bullock-cart, Samyaksambuddha-hood. According to early Mahayana (as found in the Lotus sutra), it is the *vehicles* that are taught as a method for journeying on the path to enlightenment. It is here that we can see the basis for term being used to indicate differences of doctrine. The Lotus Sutra declares that the bullock-cart is "supremely restful", implying that the goat-cart and the deer-cart are inferior to the bullock-cart. This is where we begin to see the terminological origins for the term *Hinayana*: The Sravakayana and the Pratyekabuddhayana as vehicles inferior to the superior bullock-cart of the *Mahayana*.

The Dharmakshema Mahaparinirvana Sutra also speaks of the inferior nature of the Hinayana when compared to the higher level of the Mahayana. In that sutra the Buddha states:

"Noble son, there are also two groups of people within this great congregation: those who seek the Inferior Way (*Hinayana*) and those who seek the Great Way (*Mahayana*). In past days I turned the lesser Wheel of the Dharma for the Ravages, but now here in Kuinagara I turn the great Wheel of the Dharma for Bodhisattvas."

The term first appeared in the Mahayana Prajnaparamita literature. Possibly the earliest instance appears in the *Perfection of Wisdom in 8,000 Lines* (*Acmasahasrika Prajnaparamita Sutra*), believed by scholars to have been composed some time between the 1st century BCE and the 1st century CE. Chapter 11 ("Mara's Deeds") depicts a conversation between Buddha and the Bodhisattva Subhuti, where in Buddha admonishes those Bodhisattvas who disavow this sutra in flavour of certain unnamed Buddhist sutras. In the following passage, the term *Hinayana* is translated as "inferior vehicle" (emphasis added). "*Subhuti, do these Bodhisattvas appear to be very intelligent who, having obtained and met with the irreversible, the great vehicle, and then again abandon this, turn away from this, and prefer an* inferior vehicle *[...] this is seen as being done to these Bodhisattvas by Mara."*

Substitute Terms for Hinayana

Mahayana Buddhists sometimes refer to all forms of non-Mahayana Buddhism, past and present, including the Theravada school, as members of the Hinayana grouping. This term, which literally means "the inferior vehicle", tends to relate to those Buddhists who were deemed by Mahayanists to have rather narrow aspirations: instead of vowing (as the Mahayanists ideally did) to strive for the liberation both of themselves and all other sentient beings from samsara, the "Hinayanists" were viewed as being excessively concerned with their own individual release into Nirvana.

The term, "Hinayana", is now widely regarded as derogatory and inaccurate (at least in reference to the Theravada, but also to the other, already non-existent, schools).

In the Mahayana tradition, the label Hinayana is attributed to the Buddha himself (e.g. in the Lotus Sutra). As it is a polemical term and represents a specifically Mahayana point of view, other terms have been suggested to describe the Buddhist schools which chose not to adopted the Mahayana sutras. As noted above, in India Hinayana was not the predominant term used in Mahayana texts for early Buddhist schools, Sravakayana being much more commonly used (with the former used only rarely). Among the terms that have been used as substitutes for "Hinayana" are the following:

- Uravakayana Buddhism – The term most often historically used Mahayana texts to refer to early Buddhist schools. This term refers to the "ravages," meaning disciples, followers, or hearers. They who followed the Buddha and sought solely to eliminate suffering, thus culminating in Arahantship. This term originates (like the term Hinayana) from within Mahayana Buddhism, and thus faces some of the same objections as "Hinayana", though it is less obviously derogatory. Uravakayana can also refer to a tendency or intention found in an individual; this is, one might be a member of a Mahayana school, but be personally following a Uravakayana path. Uravakayana is also contrasted with the term "Bodhisattvayana".

- Early Buddhism-refers to the variations within Buddhism (both Pre-sectarian Buddhism as the Early Buddhist schools) that were current before the Mahayana movement emerged.
- Early Buddhist schools – This term properly covers all the schools that existed before the emergence of the Mahayana. The arising of the Mahayana school of Buddhism (1st/2nd century CE) went together with the adoption of new (previously not-existing) sutras, and introduced new (or emphasized old but not very central) philosophies such as the Bodhisattva and having the intention of liberating all sentient beings. Since this constituted a serious break with the previous traditions and customs that the earlier schools had in common, the Mahayana is seen as a 'reformist' or revolutionary movement, and not included in any lists of the early schools. Thus, there is a large correlation between the earlier schools and the label 'Hinayana'. Also the Mahayana itself never groups itself with the previously existing schools. Some of the later 'early schools' might have arisen (meaning: split off) from another, older, early school, and might have come into existence at about the same time as the Mahayana. However, these schools kept to the larger framework and attitude of the earlier schools.
- Eighteen Schools (or Twenty Schools) – This term is historically oriented, based on the lists of the various Early Buddhist schools. However, the list itself is numerically inexact since the exact number and the names of the schools differ between the various lists. These were the schools that the emerging Mahayana-movement was familiar with because they were existing at that time. Subsequently, these eighteen schools split up further into a larger number, and the Hinayana label could have also been applied to those later split-offs. Also, the Mahayana writer Bhavya (Bhavaviveka) says in the Tarkajvala that Mahayana is oncluded in the eighteen schools.
- Southern Buddhism – This frequently used geographical designation is appropriately applied to the Theravada, whose centres in Sri Lanka and Southeast Asia are located south of the centres of Mahayana (China, Tibet, Japan). In

its early period, however, there was significant overlap between the geographical regions of Mahayana and the early schools.

- Pail Buddhism – This term only applies to the Theravada, whose scriptures (the Pail canon) are in the Pail language. The other "Hinayana" schools wrote either in Sanskrit, in other Prakrits (notably Gander) or in Buddhist Hybrid Sanskrit, a mixed language with both Sanskrit and Prakrit elements.
- Nikaya Buddhism –

The term Nikaya Buddhism was invented by Mahayanist scholars, in order to find a more acceptable (less derogatory) term than Hinayana to refer to the Early Buddhist schools.

The Early Buddhist schools are those schools of Buddhism which accept only the scriptures which correspond to the Suttapitaka, Vinayapitaka and (possibly) an Abhidhammapitaka. These schools of Buddhism do not recognize or accept the Mahayana Sutras as the word of Buddha. Examples of these schools are pre-sectarian Buddhism, the early Buddhist schools, and any possible other schools or views in which the historical Tipitaka represents the scripture with the highest authority. Some scholars use the term as excluding pre-sectarian Buddhism.

The most famous example of these historical Tipitaka texts is the Pail Canon. Other scriptures which correspond to these are the agamas and some of the Gandharan Buddhist Texts. Hinayana or Nikaya Buddhism is distinguished from the Buddhism of the various Mahayana and Vajrayana schools, which accept the authenticity of a range of other scriptures as spoken by Buddha (mainly the Mahayana Sutras). Many of the sutras corresponding to those of the Pail Canon are accepted by every school.

Historically, there were many 'Nikaya schools', but only one still exists today in (close to) its original form: the Theravada. Mahayana and Vajrayana Buddhism use the ordination lineages of these schools. There were once at least eighteen Nikaya schools.

Hinayana and Nikaya Buddhism

Many commentors on Buddhism have used the term Hinayana to refer to Nikaya Buddhism. However, that term is now generally seen as flawed:

- Hinayana, (literally "inferior vehicle"), is often regarded as an offensive or pejorative term.
- Hinayana was coined by the Mahayana, and has never been used by Nikaya Buddhists to refer to themselves.
- Hinayana as a technical term, indicated the vehicles of both the Savakabuddha and the Pratyekabuddha, whereas as a division of Buddhism, it refers solely to the individuals who follow the former vehicle, towards the achievement of Savakabuddhahood, while the Mahayana in the sense of the Bodhisattva path existed within the early schools already.
- It is sensible to use a terms for a division of population which is ideally used by themselves, and failing that, at least not offensive to them.

According to Robert Thurman, the term "Nikaya Buddhism" was coined by Professor Masatoshi Nagatomi of Harvard University, as a way to avoid the usage of the term Hinayana. "Nikaya Buddhism" is thus an attempt to find a more neutral way of referring to Buddhists who follow one of the early Buddhist schools, and their practice. The term Uravakayana (literally, "hearer vehicle" or "disciples' vehicle") is also sometimes used for the same purpose. Other terms that have been used in similar senses include sectarian Buddhism, conservative Buddhism and mainstream Buddhism (this last might be considered derogatory by Mahayanists, as implying that they are fringe). Note that *Nikaya* is also a term used in Theravada Buddhism to refer to a subschool or subsect within Theravada.

Like the term Hinayana Buddhism, the term Nikaya Buddhism focuses on the presumed commonality between the schools, and not on the actual schools themselves. This commonality is thought to be found in a certain attitude. The difference is that in 'Hinayana Buddhism' the common attitude was stated to be a certain 'selfishness', while the term 'Nikaya Buddhism' tries to shift the attention to the more neutral issue of attitude concerning the authenticity of scriptures.

Some Disadvantages of the Term Nikaya Buddhism

Some disadvantages of the term Nikaya Buddhism are:

- The term is not well known.

- The term Nikaya Buddhism isn't very clear: it's not obvious from the term what is meant by it.
- Neither possible literal interpretation fits the coverage of the term "Hinayana":
  * If the term refers to the nikayas into which the Buddhist sangha divided, it excludes the period before these divisions (pre-sectarian Buddhism).
  * If it refers to the scriptures known as nikayas or agamas, it has just the opposite effect, excluding the schools that use Abhidhamma: such as the Theravada, Sarvastivada, Dharmaguptaka, etcetera.
- When used, it is used by scholars only, and hasn't found adoption by any of the existing schools of Buddhism.
- The term 'Nikaya Buddhism' is just a replacement of the term Hinayana, which keeps in place the tendency to regard the separate early schools (and their differing ideologies) as one form or type of Buddhism. The early Buddhist schools themselves never used a term to refer to all the early schools together as one type of Buddhism.
- Conflating all the early schools as one 'type of Buddhism' originated with some proponents of Mahayana, who introduced the name "Hinayana" to distinguish their concept of the Dharma from the already existing schools. So, in some ways, the usage of the term 'Nikaya Buddhism', although neutral in import, points to a Mahayana (or Vajrayana) view of Buddhism.
- If Nikaya is used in its proper sense of monastic grouping, then Chinese and Tibetan Buddhism are included in it, belonging to the Dharmaguptaka and Mula-Sarvastivada Nikayas respectively.
- Theravada – This term properly refers to only one school among many non-Mahayana schools that once existed, many of which espoused philosophical notions contrary to those of the Theravadins. It would be altogether inaccurate to refer to such Buddhists as the Sarvastivadins as Theravadins. Some scholars, such as Dr. Walpola Rahula, have pointed out that there was small contact between early Mahayanists and Theravadins, and have suggested that the term "Hinayana" was never intended to include

the Theravada. Judging by the content of Mahayana polemic, it seems certain that other sects of northern India were the primary targets of the "Hinayana" critique.

- Conservative Buddhism
- Mainstream Buddhism: this term might be considered derogatory by Mahayanists, as it seems to suggest they are fringe (when in fact they are the majority)
- Sectarian Buddhism
- Non-Mahayana Buddhism.

Hinayana as a Pejorative

There remains an open and active debate regarding the issue of whether Hinayana was coined to be pejorative or merely classification. The arguments for the term as being pejorative largely depends upon the etymological roots of the prefix 'Hina': Hina-is defined as such: "inferior, less, low, base, mean, incomplete, deficient, wanting and so on." Since the meaning of 'Hina' covers both a pejorative and non-pejorative meaning, it is difficult to come to a definite conclusion. The term could have been chosen because it provided both meanings.

Those who assert the idea of Hinayana as a pejorative logically also are among those who subscribe the idea of an early (historical) Mahayana schism, and who believe that there was a history of polemics between the early Mahayana and other early Buddhist schools. An argument used by those who consider Hinayana to be pejorative is based on the fact that if the term was to mean *only* 'Small or Lesser vehicle', then the term chosen would have been, "Culla" or in Sanskrit "Ksulla-ksudra" giving us Ksudrayana-though 'ksudra' has also had a history of being used in a somewhat pejorative manner.

Those who assert that the term was coined in a merely classification manner (denying the historical Mahayana schism and a history of polemics) believe that the usage of 'Hina-' as a prefix represents those "inferior": inferior because they do not lead to the attainment of full Buddhahood (*Samyaksambuddha*).

We can find Mahayana Sutras and traditions which repeatedly admonish the trainee Bodhisattva not to criticise any of the Buddhist schools. The mere fact that there is such a strong admonishment against criticising the Hinayana indicates that it was either a common attitude, or that there was a degree of defensiveness within Mahayana regarding this issue. By the 3rd Century CE, in the ethics chapter of Asanga's Bodhisattvabhumi, we find an explicit injunction not to criticise or reject the Hinayana texts or traditions, where Trainee Bodhisattvas are instructed not to "disparage the Hinayana, or over-encourage others to learn Mahayana". Candragomin wrote a very influential twenty verse summary of Asanga's Ethics, written or summarised as a set of vows to be taken by a trainee Bodhisattve.

The 15th Verse (derived from Asanga's chapter on ethics) cites "rejecting the Sravakayana" as a root downfall. Candragomin's vows were adopted by the Indo-Tibetan Mahayana tradition via Atisha, and are still used today by the Gelugpa and Kagyupa schools.

Hinayana and Theravada

Most western scholars regard the Theravada school to be one of the Hinayana schools referred to in Mahayana literature, or regard Hinayana as a synonym for Theravada. These scholars understand the term to refer to schools of Buddhism that did not accept the teachings of the Mahayana Sutras as authentic teachings of the Buddha. At the same time, scholars have objected to the prejorative connotation of the term Hinayana and some scholars do not use it for any school.

Some Theravada Buddhists have opposed the identification of Theravada with Hinayana. As Walpola Rahula noted in his *Gems of Buddhist Wisdom*:

We must not confuse Hinayana with Theravada because the terms are not synonymous. Theravàda Buddhism went to Šri Lanka during the 3rd Century B.C. when there was no Mahayana at all. Hinayana sects developed in India and had an existence independent from the form of Buddhism existing in Sri Lanka. Today there is no Hinayana sect in existence anywhere in the world. Therefore, in 1950 the World Fellowship of Buddhists inaugurated in Colombo unanimously decided that the term Hinayana should be dropped when referring to Buddhism existing today in Sri Lanka, Thailand, Burma, Cambodia, Laos, etc. This is the brief history of Theravada, Mahayana and Hinayana.

The argument that the Theravada should not be considered a "Hinayana" school from the Mahayana perspective is based on a different understanding of the concept "Hinayana". The proponents of this view argue that unlike the now-extinct Sarvastivada school, the primary object of Mahayana criticism, the Theravada school does not claim the existence of independent dharmas; in this it maintains the attitude of early Buddhism. Some contemporary Theravadin figures have thus indicated a sympathetic stance toward the Mahayana philosophy found in the Heart Sutra and the Fundamental Stanzas on the Middle Way.

The Mahayanists were bothered by the substantialist thought of the Sarvastivadins and Sautrantikas, and in emphasizing the doctrine of emptiness, Kalupahana holds that they endeavored to preserve the early teaching. The Theravadins too refuted the Sarvastivadins and Sautrantikas (and other schools) on the grounds that their theories were in conflict with the non-substantialism of the canon. The Theravada arguments are preserved in the Kathavatthu.

9

Mahayana

Mahayana is one of the two main existing branches of Buddhism and a term for classification of Buddhist philosophies and practice. It was founded in India. The name Mahayana is used in three main senses:

1. As a living tradition, Mahayana is the larger of the two major traditions of Buddhism existing today, the other being Theravada. This classification is largely undisputed by all Buddhist schools.
2. According to the Mahayana method of classification of Buddhist philosophies, Mahayana refers to a level of spiritual motivation (also known as Bodhisattvayana). According to this classification, the alternative approach is called Hinayana, or Shravakayana. It is also recognized by Theravada Buddhism, but is not considered very relevant for practice.
3. According to the Vajrayana scheme of classification of practice paths, Mahayana refers to one of the three routes to enlightenment, the other two being Hinayana and Vajrayana. This classification is the teachings of Vajrayana Buddhism, and is not recognized by Mahayana and Theravada Buddhism.

Although the Mahayana movement traces its origin to Gautama Buddha, scholars believe that it originated in India in the 1st century CE, or the 1st century BCE. Scholars think that Mahayana only became a mainstream movement in India in the fifth century CE, since that is when Mahayanic inscriptions started to appear in epigraphic records in India. Before the 11th century CE (while

Mahayana was still present in India), the Mahayana Sutras were still in the process of being revised. Thus, several different versions may have survived of the same sutra. These different versions are invaluable to scholars attempting to reconstruct the history of Mahayana.

In the course of its history, Mahayana spread throughout East Asia. The main countries in which it is practiced today are China, Japan, Korea, and Vietnam. The main schools of Mahayaṇa Buddhism today are Pure Land, Zen (Chan), Nichiren Buddhism, Shingon, Tibetan Buddhism and Tendai. The latter three schools have both Mahayana and Vajrayana practice traditions.

Origin of the Name

The historical source of the name Mahayana is polemical, having its origin in a debate about what the real teachings of the Buddha are. As such, its use in any context except as that pertaining to a living tradition is controversial amongst Theravadin practitioners and some scholars.

The earliest known mention of "Mahayana" occurs in the Lotus Sutra between the first century BCE and the first century CE. However, some scholars such as Seishi Karashima suggest the term first used in an earlier Gander Prakrit version of the Lotus Sutra was not "*Mahayana*" but the Prakrit word "*mahajana*" in the sense of "*mahajnana*" (great knowing). At a later stage when the early Prakrit word was converted into Sanskrit, this "*mahajana*", being phonetically ambivalent, was mistakenly converted into "*Mahayana*", possibly by contamination arising through proximity to the famous Parable of the Burning House which talks of carts (Skt: *yana*).

History

Mahayana Buddhism in India can be divided into two periods: early Mahayana Buddhism and late Mahayana Buddhism

Early Mahayana Buddhism

The period of Early Mahayana Buddhism concerns the origins of Mahayana and the contents of early Mahayana Sutras.

Origins of Mahayana

The origins of Mahayana are still not completely understood.

Although the Mahayana movement traces its origin to Gautama Buddha, scholars believe that it originated in South India in the 1st century CE, or the 1st century BCE. Alternatively, some scholars say there is some evidence that Mahayana originated in North-west India in the 1st century CE. Some scholars say that Mahayana could have initially developed in the south-east of India as a non-monastic tradition, and that later it underwent a process of monasticization and emerged in the north-west of India as a monastic movement. Mahayana was first propagated into China by Lokaksema, the first translator of Mahayana sutras into Chinese during the second century CE.

Three sources appear to have made significant contributions to the rise of Mahayana Buddhism:

1. The Early Buddhist Schools. Some important Mahayana texts such as the Prajnaparamita often refer to doctrines associated with the Sarvastivada, which were mentioned or incorporated into Mahayana texts. In terms of content, however, the Mahasanghika doctrine is closer to Mahayana thought, particularly those of the sub-schools such as the Lokottaravadins.
2. Biographical literature of the Buddha composed by people said to have belonged to 'the vehicle that praised the Buddha'. This literature (comprising the Jatakas, Avadanas and other texts describing the life of Buddha) may have had its origins in the various Early Schools, but developed in ways that transcended the existing sectarian lines and contributed to the rise of Mahayana Buddhism. Buddhist poets wrote their work with purposes different from those of scholars who were concerned with doctrinal issues, and they used literary expressions which transcended doctrinal lines between the schools.
3. Stupa worship. Stupas — which were initially mere monuments to Gautama Buddha — increasingly became the place of devotion and of spreading Buddhism to the masses, the majority of whom were illiterate laymen. On the inside wall of the stupa, pictures were drawn or sculpted depicting the life of Buddha and his previous lives as a bodhisattva. This has given rise to devotion to the Buddha and the bodhisattvas, distinct from the purely

monastic sangha of the Early Buddhist schools. However, this theory has been rejected by a number of scholars. Early Mahayanists may well have used the stupas that were not affiliated with the Early Buddhist Schools as the basis for proselytizing.

The commonly expressed misconception that Mahayana started as a lay-inspired movement is based on a selective reading of a very tiny sample of extant Mahayana Sutra literature. Currently scholars have moved away from this limited corpus of literature, and have started to open up early Mahayana literature which is very ascetic and expounds the ideal of the monks' life in the forest. A scholarly consensus about the origin of the Mahayana has not yet been reached, but it has been suggested that by the time Mahayana in India became mainstream in the 5th century CE, it had become what it originally most strongly objected to: a fully landed, sedentary, lay-oriented monastic institution. Before that, the Mahayana movement may well have been either a marginalized ascetic group of monks living in the forest, or a group of conservatives embedded in mainstream, socially engaged early Buddhist monasteries. Most scholars conclude that Mahayana remained a marginal movement until the 5th century CE.

Earliest Mahayana Sutras

The earliest sutras which show some Mahayana influence are called the Proto-Mahayana Sutras such as the Ajitasena Sutra. These sutras contains a mixture of Mahayana and pre-Mahayana ideas, and occur in a world where monasticism is the norm, which is typical of the Pail Suttas; there is none of the antagonism towards the ravages or the notion of Arahantship, which is typical of many later Mahayana Sutras such as the Lotus Sutra, or Vimalakirti Nirdesha. However, the sutra also has an Arahant seeing all the Buddha fields, it is said that reciting the name of the sutra will save beings from suffering and the hell realms, and a meditative practice is described which allows the practitioner to see with the eyes of a Buddha, and to receive teachings from them that are very much typical of Mahayana Sutras.

The earliest proper Mahayana Sutras were the very first versions of the Perfection of Wisdom series and texts concerning Aksobhya Buddha, which were probably composed in the first century BCE in the south of India. Some slightly *later* early

Mahayana Sutras are the Chinese translations made by the Kushan monk Lokaksema in the Chinese capital of Luoyang, between 178 and 189 CE He translated the following sutras: Astasahasrika, Aksobhyatathagatasyavyuha, Suramgamasamadhi sutra, an early version of a sutra connected to the Avatamsakasutra, Druma-kinnararajapariprccha, Bhadrapalasutra, Ajatasatrukaukrtya-vinodana, and the Kasyapaparivarta, which were probably composed in the north of India in the first century CE. Thus scholars generally think that the earliest Mahayana sutras were mainly composed in the south of India, and later the activity of writing additional scriptures was continued in the north.

But, to equate evidence for the presence of an evolving body of Mahayana scriptures with the existence at the time of Mahayana as a distinct religious movement, has been described as being an assumption which may be a serious misstep.

Earliest Inscription Related to Mahayana

The earliest stone inscription containing a recognizably Mahayana formulation and a mention of the Buddha Amitabha was found in the Indian subcontinent in Mathura, and dated to around 180 CE. Remains of a statue of a Buddha bear the Brahmi inscription:

Made in the year 28 of the reign of king Huvishka,... for the Buddha Amitabha" (Mathura Museum).

However, this image was in itself extremely marginal and isolated in the overall context of Buddhism in India at the time, and had no lasting or long-term consequences

The epigraphical evidence for Mahayana in the period before the 5th century is very limited in comparison to the multiplicity of Mahayana writings transmitted from Central Asia to China at that time.

Late Mahayana Buddhism

During the period of Late Mahayana Buddhism, four major types of thought developed: Madhyamaka, Yogacara, Tathagatagarbha, and Buddhist Logic as the last and most recent. In India, the two main philosophical schools of the Mahayana were the Madhyamaka and the later Yogacara. There were no great Indian teachers associated with tathagatagarbha thought.

From the 5th century CE onwards, Mahayana was a strong movement in India, possibly owing to support by the Gupta dynasty. It spread from India to South-East Asia, and towards the north to Central Asia and Far East. The influence of Mahayana in China seems to have been reached at an earlier time than in India, where Mahayan remained an obscure group until the 5th century.

The late stage of Mahayana Buddhism in India are largely Vajrayana schools, and was replaced in India and Central Asia after the early milliennium by Islam (Sufism etc) and Hinduism, and in South-East Asia by Theravada Buddhism from Sri Lanka and Islam, and maintain to exist in certain regions of the Himalayas. The earlier stage forms such as Pure land Buddhism are still popular in East Asia, where many new religious movements and syncretisms have also been formed with Mahayana elements.

Madhyamaka

Madhyamaka is a Buddhist Mahayana tradition systematized by Nagarjuna. Nagarjuna may have arrived at his positions from a desire to achieve a consistent exegesis of the Buddha's doctrine as recorded in the Agamas. In the eyes of Nagarjuna the Buddha was not merely a forerunner, but the very founder of the Madhyamaka system. The tradition and its subsidiaries are called "Madhyamaka"; those who follow it are called "Madhyamikas."

According to the Madhyamikas, all phenomena are empty of "self nature" or "essence" (Sanskrit: Svabhva), meaning that they have no intrinsic, independent reality apart from the causes and conditions from which they arise.

Madhyamaka is the rejection of two extreme philosophies, and therefore represents the "middle way" between eternalism—the view that something is eternal and unchanging—and nihilism. Nihilism here means the assertion that all things are intrinsically already destroyed or rendered nonexistent. This is nihilism in the sense of Indian philosophy, and may differ somewhat from Western philosophical nihilism.

Prajnaparamita

Madhyamaka is a source of methods for approaching Prajnaparamita, or "perfection of wisdom", the sixth of the Six Perfections of the bodhisattva path. The term is used as the collective title of key Mahayana sutras. This is also often explained in

Mahayana hagiography as the teaching on shunyata that occurred at Vulture Peak, Raj Gir, and has been categorized as the Second Turning of the Wheel of Dharma.

Modern Adherents

Not all Mahayana Schools necessarily adhere to the Madhyamaka view or approach, but Tibetan Buddhist and Zen traditions adhere to a form of Madhyamaka, though they have differences in method. The present day schools of Tendai, Sanron and the Maha-Madhyamaka are also heirs to the Madhyamaka tradition.

Tibetan Categories

There is currently no historical evidence that the Madhyamikas divided themselves into distinct schools, but later Tibetan scholars—in particular Tibetan translator Patsap Nyima Drak in the 11th century—categorized views into distinct "schools".

According to the Tibetan view, subdivisions of Madhyamaka are:

- PrsaEgika
- Svatantrika
- The later Yogacara and Madhyamaka synthesis, sometimes rendered Yogacara -Svatantrika-Madhyamaka.

It is important to note that while these different tenet systems were discussed, it is debated to what degree individual writers in Indian and Tibetan discussion held each of these views and if they held a view generally or only in particular instances.

Both Prasangikas and Svatantrikas cited material in the Agamas in support of their arguments.

Prasa Egika

In the philosophy of Mahayana Buddhism, specifically in the Madhyamaka view, Prasa Egika is a category of Madhyamaka viewpoints attributed primarily to Indian scholar Candrakirti, but based also on Buddhapalita's commentaries on Nagarjuna. Nagarjuna used the method of logical consequence (*prasanga* in Sanskrit) to refute flawed views. This type of reductio ad absurdum argument to establish ultimate truth within the two truths doctrine then featured prominently in Buddhapalita and Candrakirti's works. No historic evidence exists that Indian philosophers referred to themselves with the PrasaEgika term or categorized themselves in this way. It is more likely the work of Tibetan translator Patsap Nyima Drak in the 11th century who organized the different Madhyamaka viewpoints into specific categories.

History

The Madhyamaka views generally were expounded as commentaries upon the work of Nagarjuna, who wrote about the Prajnaparamita sutras. Buddhapalita was an early adopter of syllogistic methods in his teachings, although of a particularly limited form. He commented upon Nagarjuna using logical consequences. Bhavaviveka later commented upon and critiqued Buddhapalita. Then Candrakirti later responded to these criticism of Bhavaviveka and that response of Candrakirti's became identified as exemplary of the Prasangika approach and view.

When Buddhism was established in Tibet, however, the primary philosophic viewpoint established there was that of Shantarakshita – a synthesis of Yogacara and Madhyamaka – in the 9th century. Much later Je Tsongkhapa established Candrakirti's work as primary and it continues as the main approach to Madhyamaka in the Gelug school. Other lineages of Tibetan Buddhism also contemplate PrasaEgika views but there is disagreement concerning which approach is the most expeditious for students on a path.

Svatantrika Debate

Bhavaviveka was later categorized as presenting a Svatantrika view, in opposition to Candrakirti's. While this was a later Tibetan distinction, it was useful for students to study the viewpoints as a set of tenets that could be debated and discussed. This usage is sometimes referred to as the "PrasaEgika school" and the "Svatantrika school", even though no schools with those names existed.

The PrasaEgika-Svatantrika distinction included both a technical component and a set of metaphysical implications. On one level, the disagreement centered around the role of *prasanga* in formal debate. While the Prasangika view holds it to be the only valid method of demonstrating the two truths, the Svatantrika felt that assertions about the nature of the ultimate were also necessary as opposed to just negating mistaken views. Je Tsongkhapa's critique of the Svatantrika position was based on the belief that any Buddhist making positive assertions about the conventional world was committed to the existence of an illusion. The Svatantrika response was that there are different levels of existence, and that a conventional thing could self-exist, exist from its own side, and have inherent existence, but that it still would not exist absolutely, ultimately, or really.

The Padmakara Translation Group convey a critique of the Prasangika view of the Gelugpa (the critique holds that Gelugpa Prasangika is not an independent dharma but in effect is interpenetrated by the Svatantrika, its oppositional complement) in relation to the Two Truths and convey the view of these critics who perceive a concordance with aspects of the Gelugpa Prasangika with the view expounded by Bhavya:

The Gelugpa interpretation of Prasangika has often been described by its critics as a form of Svatantrika in disguise, since its presentation of "conventional," as distinct from "true," existence seems very close to the "existence according to characteristics" that Bhavya had ascribed to phenomena on the relative level.

Negation

One distinction in the PrasaEgika approach is the use of affirming and non-affirming negations. The PrasaEgika approach limits oneself to the use of non-affirming negations. That means that the predicate of a syllogism is negated but its opposite is not affirmed as a result. For example, the syllogism *"It follows that the subject, all things, are not produced because they are dependently arisen"* negates without making a claim about production of conventional appearances.

The Svatantrika, however, may use affirming negations when discussing the ultimate. They might instead say, *"It follows that the subject, all things, are not* ultimately *produced because they are dependently arisen"* which negates ultimate production but also implies that they may be produced in a conventional sense or view. The non-affirming negations used in PrasaEgika however do not imply any phenomenon in place of what is negated.

Tsongkhapa added a distinction to the Prasa Egika approach with respect to what is negated in a syllogism. In his presentation of Prasa Egika one takes care to choose an object of negation which does not imply that it is an established entity, instead one refutes the imputation of establishment itself. Ju Mipham critiqued that distinction as introducing side effects, therefore there are different interpretations of the approach depending upon which interpretation one uses.

Svatantrika

In the philosophy of Mahayana Buddhism, specifically in the Madhyamaka view, Svatantrika is a category of Madhyamaka viewpoints attributed primarily to Indian scholar Bhavaviveka. It is used in contrast with another such subcategory, Prasangika Madhyamaka.

The key distinction between these viewpoints is the degree to which one uses works with assertions about the ultimate nature of reality or if one refrains completely from doing so. If one works with assertions that is a Svatantrika approach and refraining from doing so is a Prasangika approach.

Besides the technical definitions, the styles of the different approaches are notable. Svatantrika style approaches have a more structured syllogistic form making assertions with argumentation, and the Prasangika approach may make assertions but with significantly less reasonings for assertions. Instead they mainly point out errors resulting from taking reasonings to logical extremes.

History

The Prasangika/Svatantrika distinction represents a native Tibetan interpretation of Indian disputes among Nagarjuna commentators

- Buddhapalita (whom Tibetan tradition credits as the founder of the Prasangika "school");
- Bhavaviveka (whose criticisms of Buddhapalita are retrospectively imagined as the foundation of the Svatantrika "school"); and
- Chandrakirti (who defended Buddhapalita against Bhavaviveka, and is therefore associated with Prasangika).

Note that none of these "schools" seem to have existed in ancient India, but were created after the fact by Tibetan doxographers. For that matter the very name "Svatantrika" represents a back-translation into Sanskrit, coined by modern scholars, for the Tibetan term *rang rgyud ba.*

The term refers to Bhavaviveka's criticism that Buddhapalita ought not to have relied solely on *reductio ad absurdum* arguments – hence the name "Prasangika," from *prasanga* ("consequence") – but ought to have set forth "autonomous" (*Svatantrika*) syllogisms of his own. (Whether a Madhyamaka viewpoint would allow the necessary factual claims, or statements of epistemological principles, for such an argument was the major point in dispute.) Dreyfus and McClintock observe:

"In this regard, Bhavaviveka should probably be seen as quite successful: apart from Candrakirti and Jayananda, nearly all other Indian Madhyamikas were to follow in his footsteps and embrace autonomous arguments as important tools in their endeavors to establish the supremacy of the Madhyamaka view."

The name of the inventor of the Prasangika/Svatantrika distinction is not known. One suspect is the 11th-century Tibetan translator of Candrakirti, Patsap Nyima Drak. The rise of Prasangika can be attributed to the influence of Tsongkhapa, the Gelugpa founder, who ironically sides with Svatantrika writers on several important points (including the necessity of proposing formal theses as part of a logical argument).

As interpreted by Tibetan writers such as Tsongkhapa, the Prasangika/Svatantrika distinction involved not only issues of logic, but also affected the two schools' respective understandings of *sunyata* ("emptiness"). However, mainstream Sakyas (following Rongtön and Gorampa) hold the position that the distinction between these two schools is merely of pedagogical nature. With regard to the view of the ultimate truth both have no difference.

Subdivisions

Before the Prasangika/Svatantrika distinction rose to prominence, other divisions of Madhyamaka were proposed. Yeshe De (Wylie: Ye shes sde; 8th-9th century) posited two alternative categories:

(1) Sautrantika Madhyamika, including Bhavaviveka; and

(2) Yogacara Madhyamaka, including Shantarakshita, Kamalasila, and Haribhadra.

Later Gelugpa scholars as well as Nyingmapas considered both of the above to constitute subdivisions of Svatantrika, however, under the names of

(1) Sautrantika Svatantrika Madhyamaka; and

(2) Yogacara Svatantrika Madhyamaka.

The preferred Gelugpa approach, Prasangika, was represented chiefly by Candrakirti. Classical Indian commenters did not acknowledge Candrakirti as an important Nagarjuna commentator, but the Tibetan tradition after the 14th century considers his commentary critical. Though lacking a formal categorization, there are key differences between the viewpoint of Tsongkhapa's interpretation of Prasangika and earlier forms of Prasangika.

Enumerated Ultimate

A further distinction exemplified between views by Shantarakshita was the process of using an enumerated or approximate ultimate as a contemplation, such as only negating existence but not yet relating to non-existence or other extremes, as a way to develop one's view before working with the final contemplations of going beyond all extremes concurrently. The approach of working with an enumerative ultimate first would fit within the Svatantrika view since it uses autonomous arguments whereas the final contemplations is in accord with and — according to Ju Mipham — as efficacious the Prasangika approach.

Scriptural Interpretation

Addressing the Three Turnings of the Wheel of Dharma, Ian Charles Harris reports that "Bhavaviveka held the third turning to reflect the teaching of the *Sandinirmocanasutra* [*Sutra of Unraveling the Thought*, the scripture which is the basis for the doctrine of the Three Turnings] while the third was in conformity with the *Prajnaparamita* corpus."

Debates

Je Tsongkhapa in the 14th century critiqued the Svatantrika viewpoint. He asserted that because the Svatantrika conventionally establish things by their own characteristics, that they do not arrive at a complete understanding of emptiness. So he asserted that not only were their methods different but also that students using Svatantrika do not achieve the same realization as those using the Prasangika approach. Sakya and Kagyu scholars argued against this interpretation. An ongoing debate about these points continues. As a result of Je Tsongkhapa's view, the Gelugpa lineage establishes a sort of ladder of progressively refined worldviews and identify the Svatantrika view as inferior to the Prasangika. His critics variously claim that there is no difference in the realization of those using the Svatantrika and Prasangika approaches and that the Svatantrika approach is better for students who are not able to understand the more direct approach of Prasangika but it nonetheless results in the same ultimate realization.

According to the Nyingma lineage, an amusing critique by Ju Mipham of Je Tsongkhapa's assertion was to argue that Je Tsongkhapa was also a Svatantrika because of the way he refutes true establishment instead of objects themselves. Further, Ju Mipham argues that Je Tsongkhapa's approach is an excellent Svatantrika approach that leads students further but will not lead to the true ultimate until they go further.

The debate is also not strictly along lineage lines, there are some non-Gelugpa's who prefer Je Tsongkhapa's points and a notable Gelugpa, Gendün Chöphel, preferred and wrote about Ju Mipham's interpretation.

The debate between proponents of Prasangika and Svatantrika somewhat resembles the debates of proponents of shentong (empty of other) and rangtong (empty of self) views but they are separate distinctions.

Yogacara -Svatantrika-Madhyamaka

A Yogacara and Madhyamaka synthesis was posited by Shantarakshita in the 8th century and may have been common at Nalanda University at that time. Like the PrasaEgika, this view approaches ultimate truth through the prasaEga method, yet when speaking of conventional reality they may make autonomous statements like the earlier Svatantrika and Yogacara approaches.

This was different from the earlier Svatantrika in that the conventional truth was described in terms of the theory of consciousness-only instead of the tenets of Svatantrika, though neither was used to analyse for ultimate truth.

For example, they may assert that all phenomena are nothing but the 'play of mind' and hence empty of concrete existence—

and that mind is in turn empty of defining characteristics. But in doing so, they're careful to point out that any such example would be an approximate ultimate and not the true ultimate. By making such autonomous statements, Yogacara -Svatantrika-Madhyamaka is often mistaken as a Svatantrika or Yogacara view, even though a PrasaEgika approach was used in analysis. This view is thus a synthesis of Madhyamaka and Yogacara .

Interdependence

The Madhyamaka concept of emptiness is often explained through the related concept of interdependence. This is in contrast to independence, that phenomena arise of their own accord, independent of causes and conditions. Although a common way to think about emptiness, it is a conceptual way of talking about it—to lead a student closer to the non-conceptual wisdom of the ultimate truth—and it would not withstand analysis as an ultimate view. In the first chapter of the *Mulmadhyamakakarika,* Nagarjuna provides arguments that even causes and conditions are empty of inherent existence or essence. This analogy, however, connects the conclusion of the Middle Way tenets with the codependent origination teachings of the first turning.

The analogy to interdependence is considered helpful for students, and is presented in the famous ninth chapter of Shantideva's Bodhicharyavatara, as well as by modern writers like Thich Nhat Hanh who, in *The Heart of Understanding,* discusses the Heart Sutra in terms of interdependence.

In this analogy, there is no first or ultimate cause for anything that occurs. Instead, all things are dependent on innumerable causes and conditions that are themselves dependent on innumerable causes and conditions. The interdependence of all phenomena, including the self, is a helpful way to undermine mistaken views about inherence, or that one's self is inherently existent. It is also a helpful way to discuss Mahayana teachings on motivation, compassion, and ethics. The comparison to interdependence has produced recent discussion comparing Mahayana ethics to environmental ethics.

Yogacara

Yogacara (Sanskrit: "yoga practice"; "one whose practice is yoga") is an influential school of Buddhist philosophy and psychology emphasizing phenomenology and (some argue) ontology through the interior lens of meditative and yogic practices. It developed within Indian Mahayana Buddhism circa the fourth century C.E. Yogacara discourse is founded on the existential truth of the human condition: there is nothing that humans experience that is not mediated by mind.

The orientation of the Yogacara school is largely consistent with the thinking of the Pail Nikayas. It frequently treats later developments in a way that realigns them with earlier versions of Buddhist doctrines. Lusthaus concludes that one of the agendas of the Yogacara school was to reorient later refinements, in all their complexity, so as to accord with the doctrines of earliest Buddhism.

Nomenclature, Orthography and Etymology

Sanskrit: *Yogacara, Vijnapti-mantra, Vijnapti-matrata,* or *Cittamâtra*

Tibetan: *sems tsam*

Chinese: *Weighs*/UX‹ ("Consciousness-Only"), *Fixing* Olive ("Dharma Characteristics"), *Yucca Zong* \test—[("Yoga School")

Japanese: *Yugagyo-ha, Yuishiki*

English: Way of Yoga School, Yoga Practice School, Knowledge Way, Consciousness-Only School, Subjective Realism

"Yogacara " may be orthographically rendered according to English convention as "yogachara", which also approximates the phonetic value. An alternate nomenclature for the school is "Vijnanavada" (Sanskrit: *vada* means "doctrine" and "way"; *vaginae* means "consciousness" and "discernment". Hence, "Vijnanavada" may be rendered as "Consciousness Doctrine" or "Discernment Way"; though it is commonly rendered as "Knowledge Way".

History

The Yogacara is, along with the Madhyamaka, one of the two principal schools of Indian Mahayana Buddhism.

Origination

Masaaki (2005) states that: "[a]ccording to the *SaCdhinirmocana Sutra,* the first Yogacara text, Buddha set the "wheel of the doctrine" (Dharmacakra) in motion three times." Hence, the *SaCdhinirmocana Sutra,* as the doctrinal trailblazer of Yogacara , inaugurated the endemic categorical triune of the Three Turnings of the Wheel of Dharma; establishing its tenets among the exegesis of the Dharmacakra's "Third Turning". The Yogacara texts are generally considered part of the Third Turning along with the relevant Sutra. Moreover, Yogacara discourse surveys and syncretically redacts *all* Three Turnings.

The origins of the scholarly Indian Yogacara tradition were rooted in the syncretic scholasticism of Nalanda University where the doctrine of Vijnapti-matra or Cittamatra was first extensively propagated. Doctrines, tenets and derivatives of this school have influenced and become well-established in China, Tibet, Japan and Mongolia and throughout the world via the dissemination and dialogue wrought by the Buddhist diaspora.

Yogacara , like all Indian schools of Buddhism, eventually became extinct within India.

Vasubandhu, As a Ega and Maitreya-Natha

Yogacara , which had its genesis in the aforementioned sutra, was largely formulated by the brahmin born half-brothers Vasubandhu and Assuage (who was said to be inspired by the quasi-historical Maitreya-Natha or the divine Maitreya). This school held a prominent position in the Indian scholastic tradition for several centuries due to its lauded pedigree and propagation at Nalanda.

Yogacara and Madhyamaka

Notably, this school was in protracted dialectic with the Madhyamaka; there is disagreement among contemporary Western and traditional Buddhist scholars about the degree to which they were opposed, if at all. In short (and though rather simplistic and not entirely true), while the Madhyamaka held that asserting the existence or non-existence of any ultimately real thing was inappropriate, some exponents of Yogacara asserted that the mind (or in the more sophisticated variations, primordial wisdom) and only the mind is ultimately real. Not all Yogacarins asserted that mind was truly existent, according to some interpretations Vasubandhu and Assuage in particular did not.

Later Yogacara views synthesized the two, particularly Uantarakcita, whose view was later called "Yogacara -Svatantrika-Madhyamaka" by the Tibetan tradition. In his view the

Madhyamika position is ultimately true and at the same time the mind-only view is a useful way to relate to conventionalities and progress students more skillfully toward the ultimate. This synthesized view between the two positions – which also incorporated views of valid cognition from Dignaga and Dharmakirti – was one of the last developments of Indian Buddhism before it was extinguished in the eleventh century during the Muslim incursion.

This view was also expounded by Xuanzang, who after a suite of debates with exponents of the Madhyamaka School, composed in Sanskrit the no longer extant three-thousand verse treatise *The Non-difference of Madhyamaka and Yogacara* .

Later Yogacara teachings are especially important in Tantric Buddhism, which evolved within their development in India.

Yogacara in Tibet

Yogacara was transmitted to Tibet by Uantarakcita and later by Actaea; it was thereafter integral to Tibetan Buddhism although the prevailing Geluk-dominated view held that it was less definitive than Madhyamaka. Yogacara is primary to the Nyingmapa and its zenith, Dzogchen. Yogacara also became central to East Asian Buddhism. The teachings of Yogacara became the Chinese Wei Shi school of Buddhism.

Current debates among Tibetan schools between the "Shentong" (empty of other) versus "Rangtong" (empty of self) views appear similar to earlier debates between Yogacara and Madhyamaka, but the issues and distinctions have evolved further. Though the later Tibetan views could be said to have evolved from the earlier Indian positions, the distinctions between the views became increasingly subtle, especially after Yogacara incorporated the Madhyamika view of the ultimate. In the 19th century rime movement commenter Ju Mipham – in his commentary on Shantarakshita's synthesis – wrote that the ultimate view by both schools is the same and the result of each path also leads to the same ultimate state of abiding.

Divergence of the Yogacara of India and China

By the closure of the Sui Dynasty (589-618), Buddhism within China had developed many distinct schools and traditions. Xuanzang, in the words of Dan Lusthaus:

...came to the conclusion that the many disputes and interpretational conflicts permeating Chinese Buddhism were the result of the unavailability of crucial texts in Chinese translation. In particular, he [Xuanzang] thought that a complete version of the *Yogacara bhumi Uastra,* an encyclopedic description of the stages of the Yogacara path to Buddhahood written by Assuage, would resolve all the conflicts. In the sixth century an Indian missionary named Paramartha (another major translator) had made a partial translation of it. Xuanzang resolved to procure the full text in India and introduce it to China.

Moreover, Dan Lusthaus charts the different dialectic and divergent traditions of Buddhism within India and China discovered by Xuanzang and mentions the Buddha-nature, *Awakening of Faith,* and Tathagatagarbha:

Xuanzang also discovered that the intellectual context in which Buddhists disputed and interpreted texts was much vaster and more varied than the Chinese materials had indicated: Buddhist positions were forged in earnest debate with a range of Buddhist and non-Buddhist doctrines unknown in China, and the terminology of these debates drew their significance and connotations from this rich context. While in China Yogacara thought and Tathagatagarbha thought were becoming inseparable, in India orthodox Yogacara seemed to ignore if not outright reject Tathagatagarbha thought. Many of the pivotal notions in Chinese Buddhism (e.g., Buddha-nature) and their cardinal texts (e.g., *The Awakening of Faith*) were completely unknown in India.

Principal Exponents of Yogacara

Principal exponents of Yogacara categorized and alphabetized according to location:

- China: Xuanzang „SXY and Kuiji ZUW (K'uei-chi);
- India: the half-brothers Assuage and Vasubandhu; Sthiramati and Dharmapala
- Japan: Chits and Chidatsu ◎ (NB: both these people are mentioned in Kusha (Buddhism))
- Korea: Daehyeon, Sinhaeng, Weonchuk and Weonhyo
- Tibet: Dolpopa, Taranatha, Jamgon Kongtrul Lodro Thaye, Ju Mipham.

Yogacara Textual Corpus

Sutras

The *SaCdhinirmocana Sutra* ("Unravelling the Mystery of Thought Sutra, 2nd Century CE) was the seminal Yogacara sutra, which continued to be a primary referent for the tradition.

Also containing Yogacara elements were the *Pratyutpanna Samadhi Sutra* (1st Century CE) and *Dauabhumika Sutra.* The later *Laekavatara Sutra* ("Descent into Laeka Sutra", 4th century CE) also assumed considerable importance. Other prominent Yogacara sutras include the Urimaladevisi Chanada Sutra and the Ghanavyuha Sutra.

Five Treatises of Maitreya

Among the most important texts to the Yogacara tradition to be the "Five Treatises of Maitreya." These texts are said to have been related to Assuage by the Buddha Maitreya. They are as follows:

- *Ornament for Clear Realization* (*Abhisamaya-alaekara,* Tib. *mngon par rtogs pa'i rgyan*)
- *Ornament for the Mahayana Sutras* (*Mahayana-Sutra-alaekara,* Tib. *theg pa chen po'i mdo sde'i rgyan*)
- *Sublime Continuum of the Mahayana* (*Ratnagotravibhaga,* Tib. *theg pa chen po rgyud bla ma'i bstan*)
- *Distinguishing Phenomena and Pure Being* (*Dharma-dharmatvibhaga,* Tib. *chos dang chos nyid rnam par 'byed pa*)
- *Distinguishing the Middle and the Extremes* (*Madhyan-tavibhaga,* Tib. *dbus dang mtha' rnam par 'byed pa*).

A commentary on the *Ornament for Clear Realization* called "*Clarifying the Meaning*" by Haribhadra is often used, as is one by Vimuktisena.

Most of these texts were also incorporated into the Chinese tradition, which was established several centuries earlier than the Tibetan. However, the *Ornament for Clear Realization* is not mentioned by Chinese translators up to the 7th Century, including Xuanzang, who was an expert in this field, which suggests it may possibly have emerged from a later period than is generally ascribed.

Other Texts

Vasubandhu wrote three foundational texts of the Yogacara : the "Treatise on the Three Natures", the "Treatise in Twenty Stanzas" and the "Treatise in Thirty Stanzas". He also wrote an important commentary on the Madhyantavibhanga. According to Buddhist scholar Jay Garfield:

While the Trisvabhava-nirdeua is arguably the most philosophically detailed and comprehensive of the three short works on this topic composed by Vasubandu, as well as the clearest, it is almost never read or taught in contemporary traditional cultures or centres of learning. The reason may be simply that this is the only one of Vasubandhu's root texts for which no autocommmentary exists. For this reason, none of Vasubandhu's students composed commentaries on the text and hence there is no recognized lineage of transmission for the text. So nobody within the Tibetan tradition (the only extant Mahayana scholarly tradition) could consider him or herself authorized to teach the text. It is therefore simply not studied, a great pity. It is a beautiful and deep philosophical essay and an unparalleled introduction to the Cittamatra system.

Authorship of critical Yogacara texts is also ascribed to Assuage personally (in contrast to the Five Treatises of Maitreya). Among them are the *Mahayana-sacgraha* and the *Abhidharma-samuccaya*. He is sometimes ascribed authorship of the *Ycgacara bhûmi Uastra*, a massive encyclopedic work considered the definitive statement of Yogacara , but most scholars believe it was compiled in the 5th century CE.

Other important commentaries on various Yogacara texts were written by Sthiramati (6th century CE) and Dharmapala (7th century CE), and an influential Yogacara -Madhyamaka synthesis was formulated by Uantarakcita (8th century).

Yogacara Tenets

Muller (2005) charts two principal points of entry into the tenets of Yogacara soteriology: the first, employs an admixture of the "eight consciousnesses" (Sanskrit: *Acma Vaginae*), "four parts of cognition", "three natures", and the "anatman", etc.; the second, embraces the "two hindrances".

Muller (2005) furthermore states that:

There is no special need to try to assess whether one of these approaches is better than the other, for indeed, in the vast and complex system that is known as Yogacara , all of these different approaches and categories are ultimately tied into each other, and thus, starting with any one of them, one can eventually enter into all of the rest.

Hattori Masaaki (2005) states that Yogacara :

...attaches importance to the religious practice of yoga as a means for attaining final emancipation from the bondage of the phenomenal world. The stages of yoga are systematically set forth in the treatises associated with this tradition.

Keenan, *et al.* (2003) states that:

...the Yogacara thinkers did not simply comment on Madhyamika thought. They attempted to ground insight into emptiness in a critical understanding of the mind, articulated in a sophisticated theoretical discourse.

Yogacarins developed an Abhidharma literature set within a Mahayana framework.

Consciousness-only

One of the main features of Yogacara philosophy is "Consciousness-only" ("Cittamâtra" or "Vijnapti-matra"). That term was used in Tibet and East Asia interchangably with Yogacara , although modern scholars believe it is inaccurate to conflate the two terms.

The Three Natures

The Yogacarins defined three basic modes by which we perceive our world. These are referred to in Yogacara as the three natures of perception. They are:

- *Parikalpita,* literally "fully conceptualized", or Imaginary Nature, wherein things are incorrectly apprehended based on conceptual construction, through attachment and erroneous discrimination.
- *Paratantra,* literally "other dependent", or Dependent Nature, by which the correct understanding of the dependently originated nature of things is understood.
- *Parinispanna,* literally "fully accomplished", or Absolute Nature, through which one apprehends things as they are

in themselves, uninfluenced by any conceptualization at all.

Also, regarding perception, the Yogacarins emphasized that our everyday understanding of the existence of external objects is problematic, since in order to perceive any object (and thus, for all practical purposes for the object to "exist"), there must be a sensory organ as well as a correlative type of consciousness to allow the process of cognition to occur.

Eight Consciousnesses

Perhaps the best known teaching of the Yogacara system is that of the eight layers of consciousness (Sanskrit: *Acma Vaginae*). This theory of the consciousnesses attempted to explain all the phenomena of cyclic existence, including how rebirth occurs and precisely how karma functions on an individual basis. For example, if I carry out a good or evil act, why and how is it that the effects of that act do not appear immediately? If they do not appear immediately, where is this karma waiting for its opportunity to play out?

The answer given by the Yogacarins, those that hold to the tenets of Yogacara , was the store consciousness (also known as the basal, or eighth consciousness; Sanskrit: *Alayavijnana*) which simultaneously acts as a storage place for karma and as a fertile matrix that brings karma to a state of fruition. It may be ultimately traceable to the "luminous mind" of the agamas. The likeness of this process to the cultivation of plants led to the creation of the metaphor of seeds (Sanskrit: *bija*) to explain the way karma is stored in the eighth consciousness. The Alayavijnana houses the karmic bija that "seed" our experience of reality and "perfume" our worldview. The type, quantity, quality and strength of the seeds determine where and how a sentient being will be reborn: one's species, sex, social status, proclivities, bodily appearance and so forth. The Alayavijnana and the Tathagatagarbha doctrine developed and resolved into the Mindstream or the "consciousness-continuity" doctrine (Sanskrit: *citta Sanatana*) to avoid being denounced as running counter to the doctrine of *Unity* and the tenets of *Anatman*.

On the other hand, the karmic energies created in the current lifetime through repeated patterns of behaviour are called habit energies (Sanskrit: *vasana*). All the activities that mold our bodymind, for better or worse—eating, drinking, talking, studying, practicing the piano or whatever—can be understood to create habit energies. And of course, one's habit energies can penetrate the consciousnesses of others, and vice versa—what we call "influence" in everyday language. Habit energies can become seeds, and seeds can produce new habit energies.

According to Walpola Rahula, all the elements of the Yogacara storehouse-consciousness are already found in the Pail Canon. He writes that the three layers of the mind ("Citta", "Manas", and "Vaginae") as presented by Assuage are also used in the Pail Canon: "Thus we can see that 'Vaginae' represents the simple reaction or response of the sense organs when they come in contact with external objects. This is the uppermost or superficial aspect or layer of the 'Vaginae-skandha'. 'Manas' represents the aspect of its mental functioning, thinking, reasoning, conceiving ideas, etc. 'Citta' which is here called 'Alayavijnana', represents the deepest, finest and subtlest aspect or layer of the Aggregate of consciousness. It contains all the traces or impressions of the past actions and all good and bad future possibilities."

Unity in Yogacara

The doctrine of emptiness (Sanskrit: *Unity*) is central to Yogacara , as to any Mahayana school. Early Yogacara texts, such as the *SaCdhinirmocana Sutra* and the *Yogacara bhumi Uastra*, often act as explanations on *Prajnaparamita* Sutras. Keenan (2003) holds that Unity and Pratityasamutpada and the theme of "Two Truths" are central in Yogacara thought and meditation.

As one Buddhologist puts it, "Although meaning 'absence of inherent existence' in Madhyamaka, to the Yogacarins means 'absence of duality between perceiving subject and the perceived object.'"

This is not the full story however, as each of the three natures (above), has its corresponding "absence of nature". i.e.:

- parikalpita => laksana-nihsvabhavata, the "absence of inherent characteristic"
- paratantra => utpatti-nihsvabhavata, the "absence of inherent arising"
- parinispanna => paramartha-nihsvabhavata, the "absence of inherent ultimacy"

Each of these "absences" is a form of sunyata, i.e. the nature is "empty" of some particular qualified quality. Yogacara gave special significance to the agamas' "Lesser Discourse on Emptiness". A passage there (which the discourse itself emphasizes) is often quoted in later Yogachara texts as a true definition of emptiness.

Meditation in the Yogacara Tradition

As the name of the school suggests, meditation practice was central to the Yogacara tradition. Practice manuals perscribe the practice of mindfulness of body, feelings, thoughts and dharmas in oneself and others, out of which an understanding of the non-differentiation of self and other is said to arise. This process is referred to in the Yogacara tradition as "turning about in the basis", the basis being the Alayavijnana.

Contemporary Scholarship

Lusthaus (1999) holds that Etienne Lamotte, a famous student of Louis de La Vallee-Poussin, "...profoundly advanced Yogaacaara studies, and his efforts remain unrivaled among Western scholars."

Tathagatagarbha Doctrine

In Mahayana and Tantric Buddhism, the Tathgatagarbha doctrine (often essentially the same as the Buddha nature concept) teaches that each sentient being contains the intrinsic, effulgent Buddhic element or indwelling potency for becoming a Buddha. There are conflicting interpretations of the idea in Mahayana thought. The idea may be traced to Abhidharmic thought, and ultimately to statements of the Buddha in the Nikayas. *Buddha-nature* and *sugatagarbha* are synonyms for tathagatagarbha.

Nomenclature and Etymology

The Sanskrit term "*tathagatagarbha*" may be parsed into *Tathagata* ("the one thus gone", referring to the Buddha) and *garbha* ("root/embryo"). where the latter has the meanings: "embryo", "essence"; whilst the former may be parsed into "tatha" ("[s]he who has there" and "agata" (semantic field: "come", "arrived", "not-gone") and/or "gata" ("gone").

Luminous Mind in the Nikayas

There is a clear reference in the Anguttara Nikaya to a

"luminous mind" present within all people, be they corrupt or pure, whether or not it itself is stained or pure. When it is "unstained," it is supremely poised for arahantship, and so could be conceived as the "womb" of the arahant, for which a synonym is tathagata. The Lankavatara Sutra describes the tathagatagarbha ("arahant womb") as "by nature brightly shining and pure," and "originally pure," though "enveloped in the garments of the skhandhas, dhatus and ayatanas and soiled with the dirt of attachment, hatred, delusion and false imagining." It is said to be "naturally pure," but it appears impure as it is stained by adventitious defilements. Thus the Lankavatara Sutra identifies the luminous mind of the Canon with the tathagatagarbha. It also the equates the tathagatagarbha with nirvana, though this is concerned with the actual attainment of nirvana as opposed to nirvana as a timeless phenomenon. The Canon does not support the identification of the "luminous mind" with nirvanic consciousness, though it plays a role in the realization of nirvana. Upon the destruction of the fetters, according to one scholar, "the shining nibbanic consciousness flashes out of the womb of arahantship, being without object or support, so transcending all limitations."

Central Notions of Tathagatagarbha

The Tathagatagarbha Sutra presents the Tathagatagarbha as a virtual Buddha-homunculus, a fully wisdom-endowed Buddha, "a most victorious body... great and indestructible", inviolate, seated majestically in the lotus posture within the body of each being, clearly visible only to a perfect Buddha with his supernatural vision. This is the most "personalist" depiction of the Tathagatagarbha encountered in any of the chief Tathagatagarbha sutras and is imagistically reminiscent of Mahayana descriptions of the Buddha himself sitting in the lotus posture within his own mother's womb prior to birth: "luminous, glorious, gracious, beautiful to see, seated with his legs crossed" and shining "like pure gold..." (*Lalita Vistara Sutra,* "Voice of Buddha", Dharma Publishing, 1983.

Other Tathagatagarbha sutras (notably the *Mahaparinirvana Sutra*) view the Buddha-garbha in a more abstract, less explicitly personalist manner. But all are agreed that the Tathagatagarbha is an immortal, inherent transcendental essence or potency and that it resides in a concealed state (concealed by mental and behavioural negativities) in every single being (even the worst-the icchantika).

Although attempts are made in the Buddhist sutras to explain the Tathagatagarbha, it remains ultimately mysterious and allegedly unfathomable to the ordinary, unawakend person, being only fully knowable by perfect Buddhas themselves. As the Srimala Sutra states: "the Tathagatagarbha is the sphere of experience of the Tathagatas [Buddhas]...". It cannot even be seen clearly by 10th-level (i.e. highest level) Bodhisattvas-although they vaguely perceive its presence. Yet once it is fully "seen and known", on that morning the Bodhisattva "attains the sovereign Self" (*aishvarya-atman*) and Buddhahood is achieved (*The Mahayana Mahaparinirvana Sutra in 12 Volumes*, tr. by Kosho Yamamoto, ed. by Dr. Tony Page, Nirvana Publications, London, 2000, Vol. 8). The Nirvana Sutra, which presents itself as the final teachings of the Buddha on the Tathagatagarbha, makes clear that there are two kinds of self of which he speaks: one mundane and mutable, the other Buddhic and eternal. The first is denied as truly real, while the second is affirmed as the only true Reality (*The Mahaparinirvana Sutra in 12 Volumes*, tr. by Kosho Yamamoto, ed. by Dr. Tony Page, Nirvana Publications, London, 2000, Vol. 3, and *passim*). In this same sutra the Buddha explains that he proclaims all beings to have Buddha-nature (which is used synonymously with tathagatagarbha in this sutra) in the sense that they will in the future become Buddhas. In the later Lankavatara Sutra it is said that the tathagatagarbha might be mistaken for a Self, which it is not. In fact, it states that it is identical to the teaching of no-self.

In some sutras the Tathagatagarbha is presented as being possessed of two elements, one essential, immutable, changeless and still, the other active and salvational. As Professor Robert E. Buswell Jr. writes in connection with the Vajrasamadhi-sutra: "This 'dharma of the one mind', which is the 'original tathagatagarbha', is said to be 'calm and motionless'...

The *Vajrasamadhi*'s analysis of tathagatagarbha also recalls a distinction the Awakening of Faith makes between the calm, unchanging essence of the mind and its active, adaptable function... the tathagatagarbha is equated with the 'original edge of reality' (*bhutakoti*) that is beyond all distinctions-the equivalent of original enlightenment, or the essence. But tathagatagarbha is also the active functioning of that original enlightenment-'the inspirational power of that fundamental faculty'.... The tathagatagarbha is thus both the 'original edge of reality' that is beyond cultivation (= essence) as well as the specific types of wisdom and mystical talents that are the byproducts of enlightenment (= function)....." The Tathagatagarbha itself thus needs no cultivation, only uncovering or discovery, as it is already present and perfect within each being.

Professor of Tibetan Buddhism, Jeffrey Hopkins, also explicates this idea of the Tathagatagarbha by elucidating: 'An unknown treasure exists under the home of a poor person that must be uncovered through removing obstructive dirt, yielding the treasure that always was there. Just as the treasure already exists and thus requires no further fashioning, so the matrix-of-one-gone-thus [i.e. the Tathagatagarbha], endowed with ultimate buddha qualities, already dwells within each sentient being and needs only to be freed from defilements.'

The Tathagatagarbha doctrine later became linked (in syncretic form-e.g. in the Lankavatara Sutra) with doctrines of Citta-matra ("just-the-mind") or Yogacara studies. Yogacarins aimed to account for the possibility of the attainment of Buddhahood by ignorant sentient beings (the "Tathagatagarbha" is the indwelling bodhi-Awakening-in the very heart of Samsara). There is also a tendency in the Tathagatagarbha sutras to support vegetarianism, as all persons and creatures are compassionately viewed as possessing one and the same essential nature-the *Buddha-dhatu* or Buddha-nature.

Some of the most important early texts for the introduction and elaboration of the Tathagatagarbha doctrine are the Mahayana Mahaparinirvana Sutra, the Tathagatagarbha Sutra, the Uramila-Sutra, the Anunatva-Apurnatva-Nirdesa sutra, and the Angulimaliya Sutra; the later commentarial/exegetical-style texts, the Awakening of Faith in the Mahayana scripture and the Ratnagotravibhaga summation of the Tathagatagarbha idea had a significant influence on the understanding of "Tathagatagarbha" doctrine.

The concept of the Tathagatagarbha is closely related to that of the Buddha-nature; indeed, in the Angulimaliya Sutra and in the Mahayana Mahaparinirvana Sutra, which latter is the lengthiest sutra dealing with the immanent and transcendent presence of the Tathagatagarbha within all beings, the terms "Buddha-nature" ("Buddha-dhatu") and "Tathagatagarbha" are employed as synonymous concepts.

Belief and faith in the true reality of the Tathagatagarbha is presented by the relevant scriptures as a positive mental act and is strongly urged; indeed, rejection of the Tathagatagarbha is linked with highly adverse karmic consequences. In the *Angulimaliya Sutra*, for instance, it is stated that teaching only non-Self and dismissing the reality of the Tathagatagarbha, karmically leads one into most unpleasant rebirths, whereas spreading the doctrine of the Tathagatagarbha will bring benefit both to oneself and to the world. We read:

"Those who were donkeys in previous lives and paid no attention to the Tathagatagarbha are now poor and eat coarse food as donkeys do. In future lives, too, apart from being poor, they will be born into lowly *kshatriya* [military] families. These are none other than the people who have no faith in the Tathagatagarbha and cultivate the notion of no-Self, for they will be like prostitutes, outcastes, birds and donkeys...

"People who lack learning and have wrong views get angry with those who teach the Tathagatagarbha to the world, and [those unlearned people] expound non-Self in place of the Self as their doctrine. He who teaches the Tathagatagarbha, even at the expense of his own life, knowing that such people are inexperienced with words and lacking in balance, has true patience and teaches for the benefit of the world."

Caution is required when discussing the doctrine of the Tathagatagarbha (as presented in the primary tathagatagarbha-sutric texts), so that the Tathagatagarbha does not become inaccurately denigrated or reduced to a "mere" tactical device or become dismissed as just a metaphor with no actual ontological reality behind it in the here and now (it is incorrect from the perspective of the Tathagatagarbha sutras to view the Tathagatagarbha solely as some future as yet non-existent potential or as a vacuous Emptiness; the Tathagatagarbha is not constrained by time, not subsumed within the past-present-future confines of temporality, but is changeless and eternal); conversely, it is erroneous to construe the Tathagatagarbha as a tangible, worldly, mutating, passion-dominated, desire-driven "ego" on a grand scale, similar to the "ego-lie" comprised of the five mundane skandhas (impermanent mental and physical constituents of the unawakened being).

The Tathagatagarbha is indicated by the relevant sutras to be one with the Buddha, just as the Buddha is the Tathagatagarbha at the core of his being. The Tathagatagarbha is the ultimate, pure, ungraspable, inconceivable, irreducible, unassailable, boundless, true and deathless Quintessence of the Buddha's emancipatory Reality, the very core of his sublime nature (Dharmakaya). The Tathagatagarbha is, according to the final sutric teaching of the Mahayana Nirvana Sutra, the hidden interior Buddhic Self (Atman), untouched by all impurity and grasping ego.

Because of its concealment, it is extremely difficult to perceive. Even the "eye of Prajna" (insight) is not adequate to the task of truly seeing this Tathagatagarbha (so the Nirvana Sutra): only the "eye of a Buddha" can discern it fully and clearly. For unawakened beings, there remains the springboard of faith in the Tathagatagarbha's mystical and liberative Reality.

It is possible to do a Madhyamaka interpretation of tathagatagarbha literature.

Tathagatagarbha in Zen

The role of the tathagatagarbha in Zen can not be discussed or understood without an understanding of how tathagatagarbha is taught in the Lankavatara Sutra. It is through the Lankavatara Sutra that the tathagatagarbha has been part of Zen (i.e., Chan) teaching since its beginning in China. Bodhidharma, the traditional founder of Chan-Zen in China, is traditionally known for carrying the Lankavatara Sutra with him when he came from India to China. The early Zen/Chan teachers in the lineage of Bodhidharma's school were known as the "Lankavatara Masters" The Lankavatara Sutra presents the Chan/Zen Buddhist view of the tathagatagarbha:

[The Buddha said,] Now, Mahamati, what is perfect knowledge? It is realised when one casts aside the discriminating notions of form, name, reality, and character; it is the inner realisation by noble wisdom. This perfect knowledge, Mahamati, is the essence of the Tathagatagarbha.

Because of the use of expedient means (upaya) by metaphors

(e.g., the hidden jewel) in the way that the tathagatagarbha was taught in some sutras, two fundamentally mistaken notions arose. First that the tathagatagarba was a teaching different from the teaching of emptiness (*sunyata*) and that it was a teaching that was somehow more definitive than emptiness, and second that tathagatagarbha was believed to be a substance of reality, a creator, or a substitute for the ego-substance or fundamental self (*atman*) of the Brahmans.

Responding to these two mistaken notions, in Section XXVIII of the Lankavatara, Mahamati asks Buddha, "Is not this Tathagatagarbha taught by the Blessed One the same as the ego-substance (*atman*) taught by the philosophers?"

The Blessed One replied: No, Mahamati, my Tathagatagarbha is not the same as the ego taught by the philosophers; for what the Tathagatas teach is the Tathagatagarbha in the sense, Mahamati, that it is emptiness, reality-limit, Nirvana, being unborn, unqualified, and devoid of will-effort; the reason why the Tathagatas who are Arhats and Fully-Enlightened Ones, teach the doctrine pointing to the Tathagatagarbha is to make the ignorant cast aside their fear when they listen to the teaching of egolessness and to have them realise the state of non-discrimination and imagelessness.

I also wish, Mahamati, that the Bodhisattva-Mahasattvas of the present and future would not attach themselves to the idea of an ego [imagining it to be a soul]. Mahamati, it is like a potter who manufactures various vessels out of a mass of clay of one sort by his own manual skill and labour combined with a rod, water, and thread, Mahamati, that the Tathagatas preach the egolessness of things which removes all the traces of discrimination by various skilful means issuing from their transcendental wisdom, that is, sometimes by the doctrine of the Tathagatagarbha, sometimes by that of egolessness, and, like a potter, by means of various terms, expressions, and synonyms.

For this reason, Mahamati, the philosophers' doctrine of an ego-substance is not the same as the teaching of the Tathagatagarbha. Thus, Mahamati, the doctrine of the Tathagatagarbha is disclosed in order to awaken the philosophers from their clinging to the idea of the ego, so that those minds that have fallen into the views imagining the non-existent ego as real, and also into the notion that the triple emancipation is final, may rapidly be awakened to the state of supreme enlightenment. Accordingly, Mahamati, the Tathagatas who are Arhats and Fully-Enlightened Ones disclose the doctrine of the Tathagatagarbha which is thus not to be known as identical with the philosopher's notion of an ego-substance.

Therefore. Mahamati, in order to abandon the misconception cherished by the philosophers, you must strive after the teaching of egolessness and the Tathagatagarbha. Also as described in the Lankavatara, in Chan/Zen the tathagatagarba is identical to the *Alayavijnana* known prior to awakening as the storehouse-consciousness or 8th consciousness. Chan/Zen masters from Honing in 7th century China to Hakuin in 18th century Japan to Hsu Yun in 20th century China, have all taught that the process of awakening begins with the light of the mind turning around within the 8th consciousness, so that the *Alayavijnana,* also known as the tathagatagarbha, is transformed into the "Bright Mirror Wisdom".

When this active transformation takes place to completion the other seven consciousnesses are also transformed. The 7th consciousness of delusive discrimination becomes transformed into the "Equality Wisdom". The 6th consciousness of thinking sense becomes transformed into the "Profound Observing Wisdom", and the 1st to 5th consciousnessses of the five sensory senses become transformed into the "All-performing Wisdom".

As D.T. Suzuki wrote in his introduction to his translation of the Lankavatara Sutra, "Let there be, however, an intuitive penetration into the primitive purity (*prakritiparisuddhi*) of the Tathagatagarbha, and the whole system of the Vijnanas goes through a revolution."

This revolution in the system of consciousness (*vaginae*) is what Chan/Zen calls awakening or "*kensho*", seeing into one's own nature.

Therefore, in modern-Western manifestations of the Zen Buddhist tradition, it is considered insufficient simply to understand Buddha-nature intellectually. Rather tathagatagarbha must be experienced directly, in one's entire bodymind. Enlightenment in a certain sense consists of a direct experience (*gata*) of the essence or womb (*garbha*) of thusness (*tatha*) and this is the tathagatagarbha of one's own mind, which is traditionally described and designated as unity (emptiness).

The Zen tradition often uses koan to evoke the revolution in consciousness of the turning of the light back to the tathagatagarbha or Buddha-nature. According to one of the most famous koans, a monk once approached the Zen master Chao-chou and asked him, "Does a dog possess Buddha-nature or not?" Chao-chou replied with the one-word answer "Wú" (pronounced "mu" in Japanese), literally meaning "no" or "without." Through an inquiring contemplation of the question and response, one may come to detach from the phenomena of externals in which the six sense conscoiusnesses are usually enthralled and realize the turning around of the light of the mind to gain a direct insight into the tathagatagarba of Buddha-nature.

Buddha-Bots

Buddha-nature (Awakened-nature) has been connected in recent decades with the developments of robotics and the possible eventual creation of artificial intelligence. In the 1970s, the Japanese roboticist Masahiro Mori popularized the idea that robots, under certain conditions, may possess Buddha-nature. Mori has since founded an institute to study the metaphysical implications of such technology.

Texts

Key texts associated with this doctrine are the Tathagatagarbha Sutra, which contains a series of very striking, concrete images for what the Tathagatagarbha is, *The Lion's Roar Discourse of Queen Srimala* (Srimala Sutra), which states that this doctrine is ultimate (not provisional or "tactical"), and perhaps most importantly the "Mahayana Mahaparinirvana Sutra", which likewise insists that the tathagatagarbha teaching is "uttarottara"-absolutely supreme-the "final culmination" and "all-fulfilling conclusion" of the entirety of Mahayana Dharma. The later Lankavatara Sutra presents the tathagatagarbha as being a teaching completely consistent with and identical to emptiness and synthesizes tathagatagarbha with the sunyata of the Prajnaparamita sutras. And sunyata is the thought-transcending realm of non-duality and unconditionedness: complete freedom from all constriction and limitation.

10

Buddhist Logic

'Buddhist Logic', the categorical nomenclature modern Western discourse has extended to Buddhadharma traditions of 'Hetuvidya' (Sanskrit) and 'Pramanavada' (Sanskrit), which arose circa 500CE, is a particular development, application and lineage of continuity of 'Indian Logic', from which it seceded. Indian logic, and Buddhist Logic—in main heralded by Dignaga (c 480-540 CE)—are both primarily studies of 'inference'-patterns, where 'inference' is a gloss of anumana (Sanskrit).

Sadhukhan, *et al.* (1994) frames the centrality of 'syllogism' to Buddhist Logic and foregrounds its indivisibility as an investigative, authenticating and proofing tool instituted to establish the valid cognitive insights of the Buddhadharma:

Buddhist logic obviously contains the forms and nature of syllogism, the essence of judgement, etc. for which it deserves the name of logic. But that logic is not only logic it also establishes the doctrines of the Buddhists. Thus the philosophical tenets were the fulcrum and the logic developed as tools to establish those.

Following the work of Tucci (1929) and the critique of Anacker (2005, rev.ed.) upon the collation of Frauwallner (1957), it is now understood that Vasubandhu's *Vada-vidhi* ("A Method for Argumentation") refined the five argument logic of the *Nyaya-Sutra* to a three argument form and not his pupil Dignaga. In addition to pruning the two redundant arguments from the syllogism, Vasubandhu tendered a further qualification: he posited that a sound relationship, a 'logical pervasion' (vyapti) needs to be defined between the first and second arguments, a relationship between the 'Demonstrandum' (pratijna) and the 'Justification' (hetu) that is assumed in the *Nyaya-Sutra* and other literature of the Nyaya school. This logical pervasion is required to fashion sound arguments. Vasubandhu's *Vada-vidhi* was reconstructed by Frauwallner from embedded quotations harvested from the works of Dignaga, amongst others. Dignaga, oft-cited as the wellspring of the logical triune in the Buddhadharma, is now invalidated.

Qualifications of what is Signified by the Lexical Signifier 'Logic' in the Dharmic Context

'Indian Logic' should not be understood as logic in the sense of 'Aristotelian syllogistic' (Greek or Classical Logic) or 'modern predicate calculus' (modern Western Logic), but as *anumana*-theory, a system in its own right. 'Indian Logic' was influenced by the study of grammar, whereas Greek or Classical Logic which principally informed modern Western Logic was influenced by the study of mathematics.

Nomenclature, Orthography and Etymology

'Buddhist Logic' (English)

Vidyabhusana (1921), Randle (1930) and Stcherbatsky (1930) employed terms such as "Indian Logic" and "Buddhist Logic" which established this terminology, though a key difference between Western Logic and Indian Logic is that certain epistemological issues are included within Indian Logic; whereas, in modern Western Logic they are deliberately excluded. Indian Logic includes general questions regarding the 'nature of the derivation of knowledge', epistemology, from information supplied by evidence, evidence which in turn may be another item of knowledge.

'Anumana' (Sanskrit)

Etymology: 'anu' subsequent + manas 'perception, mind') is identified as a 'source of knowledge', a *pramagac*. Though not the founders of 'Indian logic', the Nyaya school first codified and established a 'system of logic'. The Nyaya recognized four 'sources of knowledge' (pramana): perception, inference, comparison and testimony.

Antecedents and Secession

'Nyaya', (Sanskrit: "recursion", with the semantic amplification of 'syllogism, inference') is the name given to one of the six 'orthodox' (astika) schools of Sanatana Dharma, which may be understood as the "the school of logic". They Nyaya is founded in the Nyaya Sutras, attributed to Gotama (2nd century CE). Buddhist logic inherited much of the architecture of Nyaya's methodology, but where the Nyaya recognised a set of four pramanas: perception, inference, comparison and testimony, the logic of Buddhadharma only recognized two, perception and inference.

Syllogism

A syllogism is a form of inference. Ames (1993), holds that Bhavaviveka (c.500-c.578) appears to be the first Buddhist logician to employ the 'formal syllogism' of Indian Logic in expounding the Madhyamaka which he employed to considerable effect in his commentary to Nagarjuna's *Mulamadhyamakakarika,* entitled the *Prajnapradipa.* Though due to the work of Anacker (2005, rev.ed.) and those upon whom his work is founded, we know that the first Buddhist to refine the syllogism to its three line form is Vasubhandu.

Dharmic Logic in Western Discourse & Literature Review

Vidyabhusana (1921), Randle (1930) and Stcherbatsky (1930).

Lineage

Dr S.C. Vidyabhusana, Rahula Sankrityayana, Dr M. K. Ganguli, A. Vostrikov, Prof. Giuseppe Tucci, B. Baradiin, V. Vassiliev (1818—1900), E. E. Obermiller (1901-1935), Prof. Gerhard Oberhammer, Prof. E. Franwallner, F. Th. Stcherbatsky, E. Steikellner.

Robinson (1957) holds that Nakamura (1954), (building upon the methodology of Schayer [1933]):

...presents the case for the superiority of modern scientific, notational logic as an instrument for investigating Indian logic. Notational statement avoids the pitfalls and awkwardness of linguistic statement and rhetorical logic. It does not necessitate conversion of Indian forms into the standard forms of traditional Western logic, but clarifies the traditional Indian structure without requiring reformulation. To Nakamura's points I may add that modern logic asks a greater range of questions and hence sharpens the observation of the investigator.

Japanese Discourse

A number of excellent Japanese scholars...

Pramana Sets as Determining Traditions of Dharma

Decisive in distinguishing Buddhadharma from what is generally understood as Sanatana Dharma is the issue of epistemological justification. All schools of Indian logic recognize various sets of 'valid justifications for knowledge', or *pramana* – the Buddhadharma recognizes a pramana set that is smaller than the other Dharmic Traditions. Most pramanavada of Dharmic Traditions accept 'perception' (Sanskrit: pratyakca) and 'inference' (Sanskrit: anumana), for example, but for some schools of Sanatana Dharma and Buddhadharma the 'received textual tradition' is an epistemological category equal to perception and inference (although this is not necessarily true for some other schools). The Buddhadharma accepts 'received textual tradition' or Agama%, including Buddhavacana, only if it accords with pratyakca and anumana. Historically, Shakyamuni Buddha was qualifying the unquestionable authority of the Vedas on grounds of ahimsa as according to the Vedic Tradition of Sanatana Dharma, the Vedas are *apauruceya* "not of human agency", are supposed to have been directly revealed, and thus are called *œruti* ("what is heard").. Vedic injunctions required sacrifices, Œrauta (an etymon of the English 'slaughter'), particularly 'animal sacrifices' (Pashu-Yajna, Ashvamedha) and which the compassionate Shakyamuni Buddha countered.

Thus, in the Sanatana Dharma traditions, if a claim was made that could not be substantiated by appeal to the textual canon, it would be considered as ridiculous as a claim that the sky was green and, conversely, a claim which could not be substantiated via conventional means might still be justified through textual reference, differentiating this from the epistemology of hard science. Whereas, some schools of Buddhadharma, on the other hand, rejected an inflexible reverence of accepted doctrine. As the Buddhavacana *Kalama Sutta* III.65 states:

> Do not accept anything by mere tradition... Do not accept anything just because it accords with your scriptures... Do not accept anything merely because it agrees with your pre-conceived notions... But when you know for yourselves – these things are moral, these things are blameless, these things are praised by the

wise, these things, when performed and undertaken, conduce to well-being and happiness – then do you live acting accordingly.

The Theravada commentary, ascribed to Dhammapala, on the Nettipakarana, says *"na hi patio annat pama Gatarac atthi* (quoted in Pail Text Society edition of the Nettipakarana, 1902) which Nanamoli translates as: "for there is no other criterion beyond a text".

Hetuvidya

Hetu = conditionality, causation (hetu and pratyaya), contending with Buddhist agency...karma.

Vidya = (Sanskrit: Vidya; Tibetan: Rigpa), Avidya.

Early Buddhism and the Arising of Nagarjuna

Early Buddhist philosophers and exegetes of one particular early school (as opposed to Mahayana), the Sarvastivadins, created a pluralist metaphysical and phenomenological system, in which all experiences of people, things and events can be broken down into smaller and smaller perceptual or perceptual-ontological units called *dharmas*. Other schools incorporated some parts of this theory and criticized others. The Sautrantikas, another early school, and the Theravadins, the only surviving early Buddhist school, criticized the realist standpoint of the Sarvastivadins.

The Mahayanist Nagarjuna, one of the most influential Buddhist thinkers, promoted classical Buddhist emphasis on phenomena and attacked Sarvastivada realism and Sautrantika nominalism in his magnum opus The Fundamental Verses on the Middle Way.

Robinson makes an opinion that builds upon the foundation of Stcherbatsky (1927):

The Madhyamaka denies the validity of logic, i.e., of discursive conceptual thought, to establish ultimate truth. On the charge that in doing so he himself resorts to some logic, he replies that the logic of common life is sufficient for showing that all systems contradict one another that and our fundamental conceptions do not resist scrutiny.

Catuskoti

Catuskoti (Sanskrit), had antecedents in the Vedas and is also evident in a mutually iterating form known by the Greek term, 'Tetralemma' where 'tetra' holds the semantic field of "four" + 'lemma' hold the semantic field "auxiliary proposition".

Indian Transmission Lineages to Tibet and Concomitant Translations

Tom Tillemans, in discussing the Tibetan translation and assimilation of the Buddhadharma logico-epistemological traditions embodied by the legacy of Dignaga (c 480-540 CE) and Dharmakîrti (ca. 7th century), identifies two currents and transmission streams:

- first current, principally geographical located at Sangpu Neutok and grounded in the works of Ngok Lodzawa Loden Shayrap (1059–1109) and Chapa Chogyi Sengge (1109–69) and their disciples.. Chapa's *Tshad ma'i bsdus pa* (English: 'Summaries of Epistemology and Logic') became the groundwork for the 'Collected Topics' (Tibetan: Ḍura; Wylie: bsdus grwa) literature, which, in large, furnished Gelugpa base logical architecture and epistemology.
- second current of Sakya Pandita (1182–1251) who revealed the terma *Tsod-ma rigs-gter* (English: "Treasury of Logic on Valid Cognition"), who vehemently redressed the logical architecture of the Gangpu Neutok positions.

Sangpu Neutok (Wylie: sang-phu Ne'u-thog)

Dudjom (1904-87), *et al.* hold that 'Sangpu Neutok', a seminary founded 1073 by the 'translator' (Tibetan: lotsawa) Ngok Lekpei Sherap (1059-1109), was at the time of Longchenpa (1308 – 1364/ 1369) who studied there, "...the great academy for the study of logic in Tibet."

Gelugpa

The Vajrayana tradition of the Tibetan Buddhist Gelugpa with their penchant for dialectic and courtyard debate instituted, developed and perpetuated the systems of Indian Logic and Buddhist Logic they inherited, significantly contributing and extending the traditions of Hetuvidya and Pramanavada within the logico-epistemological traditions of the Buddhadharma. Particurly, post-Candrakirti (600–c. 650), the Gelugpa refined the Catuskoti and Shunyata into the Prasangika.

Vasubandhu: Avinâbhâva

Vasubandhu (fl. 4th c.)

Doctrine of Trairûpya

Dignaga's (c 480-540 CE) 'Three Modes' (Sanskrit: Trairûpya; Wylie: tshul-gsum)

Dharmakîrti: Death of the Trairûpya Doctrine

Later Developments

Dharmakirti's Theory of Inference

Dharmakirti (ca. 7th century), was an Indian 'scholar' (pandita) and Buddhist who contributed significantly to the Buddhist development and application of Indian philosophical logic. He was one of the primary theorists of Buddhist atomism, according to which the only items considered to exist are momentary Buddhist atoms and states of consciousness. The following exposition of Dharmakirti's Theory of Inference was drawn from Prasad (2002).

Doctrine of Anyapoha

Apoha is negative *abhavatmaka* in nature. Apohas are different due to the diversity in apohyas (things to be excluded). The word *apoha* which is the abridged form of anyapoha means the 'exclusion of negation of others (ataddvyavrtti)'. The word 'cow' gives its own meaning only by the exclusion of all those things which are other than cow. Dingnaga declares : word can express its own meaning only by repudiating opposite meanings, just as the words like 'krtaka' (i.e. that which has origin) designate their meanings only through the exclusion of their opposite like 'akraka' (i.e. that which does not have origin).

Dingnaga admits apoha can also possess some characteristics of the realists' universals such as oneness, enternity, complete subsistence in each individual etc. Dingnaga apprehends concept of universal through the negation of its non-self. He explains that if the non-self of a universal is absent in a locus, its presence in that locus can be inferred. For example, a cow is qualified by the deniability of the non-cow. This concept of Dingnaga similar to that Hegel, he also believes that universality of a concept is posited through its negativity. *Apoha* is not the object of sense perception (pratyaksa) Itis apprehensible only through word or inference.

In essence, Dingnaga uses *anyyapohaas* a substitute for universal. The concept of *apoha* depends upon the law of contradiction. The words blue and non-blue negate each other just because they are opposite to each other. According to Dingnaga, similar exclusion of others is due to the non-apprehension of the meaning of a particular word in other words. A particular word excludes the other particular words because its own meaning is not apprehends in the other ones. For example, the word *simsapa*-tree excludes the word *palasa*-tree because its own meaning is not available in the latter one.

Lexicon

- Apoha:
- Argument: vada, rtsod pa
- Characteristic: laksana, mtshan nid
- Condition: pratyaya, rkyen
- Demonstrandum: sadhya, bsgrub par bya ba
- Demonstrator: sadhaka, grub byed
- Dialectician: tartika, rtog ge ba
- Dialectics: tarka, rtog ge
- Direct perception: pratyaksa, mnon sum
- Event: dharma, chos
- Event-associate: dharmin, chos can
- Exemplification: drstanta, dpe
- Inference: anumana, rjes su dpag pa
- Interference: vyavakirana, hdres pa
- Invariable concomitance: avinabhava, med na mi hbyun ba
- Judgment: prajnanana, shes-cab
- Justification: hetu, gtan-tshigs
- Means of cognition: pramana, tshad pa
- Means of evidence: linga, rtags
- Pervading/pervasion/logical pervasion: vyapti, khyab pa.

Doctrine

Few things can be said with certainty about Mahayana

Buddhism, especially its early Indian form, other than that the Buddhism practiced in China, Vietnam, Korea, Tibet, and Japan is Mahayana Buddhism. Mahayana can be described as a loosely bound bundle of many teachings, which was thus able to contain the various contrasting ideas found between those differing teachings of whose elements it is comprised.

Mahayana is a large religious and philosophical structure. It constitutes an inclusive faith characterized by the adoption of new Mahayana sutras in addition to the earlier Agama texts, and a shift in the basic purpose and concepts of Buddhism. Mahayana sees itself as penetrating further and more profoundly into the Buddha's Dharma. There is a tendency in Mahayana sutras to regard adherence to Mahayana sutras as generating spiritual benefits greater than those which arise from being a follower of the non-Mahayana approaches to Dharma. Thus the Srimala Sutra claims that the Buddha said that devotion to Mahayana is inherently superior in its virtues to the following of the Sravaka or Pratyekabuddha path.

Mahayana Buddhist schools de-emphasize the ideal of the release from Suffering and the attainment of Nirvana, found in the Early Buddhist Schools. The fundamental principles of Mahayana doctrine were based around the possibility of universal liberation from suffering for all beings (hence "great vehicle") and the existence of Buddhas and Bodhisattva embodying Buddha-nature ([O'`). Some Mahayana schools simplify the expression of faith by allowing salvation to be alternatively obtained through the grace of the Buddha Amitabha by having faith and devoting oneself to chanting to Amitabha. This devotional lifestyle of Buddhism is most strongly emphasized by the Pure Land schools and has greatly contributed to the success of Mahayana in East Asia, where spiritual elements traditionally relied upon chanting of a Buddha's name, of mantras or dharanis; reading of Mahayana sutras and mysticism. In Chinese Buddhism, most monks, let alone lay people, practice Pure Land, some combining it with Chan (Zen).

Most Mahayana schools believe in a pantheon of quasi-divine Bodhisattvas that devote themselves to personal excellence, ultimate knowledge, and the salvation of humanity and all other sentient beings (animals, ghosts, demigods, etc.). Zen Buddhism is a school of Mahayana which often de-emphasizes the pantheon of Bodhisattvas and instead focuses on the meditative aspects of the religion. In Mahayana, the Buddha is seen as the ultimate, highest being, present in all times, in all beings, and in all places, and the Bodhisattvas come to represent the universal ideal of altruistic excellence.

Amitabha

Amitabha (wordstem), Hindi pronunciation: is a celestial buddha described in the scriptures of the Mahayana school of Buddhism. Amitabha is the principal buddha in the Pure Land sect, a branch of Buddhism practiced mainly in East Asia. According to these scriptures, Amitabha possesses infinite merits resulting from good deeds over countless past lives as a bodhisattva named Dharmakara. "Amitabha" is translatable as "Infinite Light," hence Amitabha is often called "The Buddha of Infinite Light."

Doctrine

According to the Larger Sutra of Immeasurable Life (Mahayana Amitayus Sutra) Amitabha was, in very ancient times and possibly in another realm, a monk named Dharmakara. In some versions of the Sutra, Dharmakara is described as a former king who, having come into contact with the Buddhist teachings through the buddha Lokesvararaja, renounced his throne. He then resolved to become a buddha and so to come into possession of a *buddhakcetra* ("buddha-field", a realm existing in the primordial universe outside of space time, produced by a buddha's merit) possessed of many perfections. These resolutions were expressed in his forty-eight vows, which set out the type of buddha-field Dharmakara aspired to create, the conditions under which beings might be born into that world, and what kind of beings they would be when reborn there.

In the versions of the sutra widely known in China, Vietnam, Korea and Japan, Dharmakara's eighteenth vow was that any being in any universe desiring to be born into Amitabha's Pure Land and calling upon his name even as few as ten times will be guaranteed rebirth there. His nineteenth vow promises that he, together with his bodhisattvas and other blessed Buddhists, will appear before those who call upon him at the moment of death. This openness and acceptance of all kinds of people has made the Pure Land belief one of the major influences in Mahayana Buddhism. Pure Land Buddhism seems to have first become popular in northwest

India/Pakistan and Afghanistan, from where it spread to Central Asia and China

The sutra goes on to explain that Amitabha, after accumulating great merit over countless lives, finally achieved buddhahood and is still alive in his land of Sukhavati, whose many virtues and joys are described.

The basic doctrines concerning Amitabha and his vows are found in three canonical Mahayana texts:

- The Larger Sukhavativyuha Sutra
- The Smaller Sukhavativyuha Sutra
- The Amitayurdhyana Sutra, or Vipassana Amitayus Sutra, (the Meditation on Amitayus).

Through his efforts, Amitabha created the "Pure Land". Sukhavati is situated in the uttermost west, beyond the bounds of our own world. By the power of his vows, Amitabha has made it possible for all who call upon him to be reborn into this land, there to undergo instruction by him in the dharma and ultimately become bodhisattvas and buddhas in their turn (the ultimate goal of Mahayana Buddhism). From there, these same bodhisattvas and buddhas return to our world to help yet more people.

Amitabha in Vajrayana Buddhism

Amitabha is also known in Tibet, Mongolia, and other regions where Tibetan Buddhism is practiced. In the Highest Yoga Tantra class of the Tibetan Vajrayana Amitabha is considered one of the Five Dhyani Buddhas (together with Akcobhya, Amoghasiddhi, Ratnasambhava, and Vairocana), who is associated with the western direction and the *skandha* of scan, the aggregate of distinguishing (recognition) and the deep awareness of individualities. His consort is PaG

aravasini. His realm is called either Sukhavati (Sanskrit) or Dewachen (Tibetan). As his two main disciples, similar as the Buddha Shakyamuni had two, are seen the Bodhisattvas Vajrapani and Avalokiteshvara, the former to his left and the latter to his right. In Tibetan Buddhism, there exists a number of famous prayers for taking rebirth in Sukhavati (Dewachen). One of these was written by Je Tsongkhapa on the request of Manjushri, who appeared to him in different visions.

The Tibetan Panchen Lamas and Shamarpas are considered to be incarnations of Amitabha.

He is frequently invoked in Tibet either as Buddha *Amitabha*-especially in the Phowa practices or as *Amitayus*-especially in practices relating to longevity and preventing an untimely death.

In Japanese Vajrayana, or Shingon Buddhism, Amitabha is seen as one of the thirteen Buddhist deities practitioners pay homage to Shingon, like Tibetan Buddhism, also uses special devotional mantras for Amitabha, though the mantras used differ. Amitabha is also one of the Buddhas featured in the Womb Realm Mandala used in Shingon practices, and sits to the west, which is where the Pure Land of Amitabha is said to dwell.

Mantras

Amitabha is the centre of a number of mantras in Buddhist Vajrayana practices. The Indic form of the mantra of Amitabha is (Devanagari: *oC amitbha hr+%*), which is pronounced in its Tibetan version as *Om ami dewa hri*. The Japanese Shingon Buddhist mantra is *On amirita teizei kara un* which represents the underlying Indic form *oC am[ta-teje hara hkC*.

Names in Various Languages

The proper form (wordstem) of Amitabha's name in Sanskrit is Amitbha, masculine, and the nominative singular is *Amitbha*. This is a compound of the Sanskrit words amita ("without bound, infinite") and abha ("light, splendor"). Consequently, the name is to be interpreted as "he who possesses light without bound, he whose splendor is infinite". The name *Amitayus* is also used. This is a compound of amita ("infinite") and ayus ("life"), and so means "he whose life is boundless".

In Chinese, his name is given as *Comity of*, where Comity is the Chinese representation of the first three syllables of either Amitabha *or* Amitayus, and Of is Chinese for Buddha (a very early borrowing of the first syllable of the Sanskrit word). The name Amitabha is given in Chinese as Wuliangguang, while the name Amitayus is given as Wuliangshou. These names are not, however, very commonly used.

In Vietnamese, Korean, and Japanese, the same Chinese characters used for Amitabha are used to represent his name, though they are pronounced slightly differently:

- Vietnamese: *A-di-a Ph-t*
- Korean: *Amit'a Bul*
- Japanese: *Amida Butsu.*

In Japanese, he is also called *Amida Nyorai,* meaning " the Tathagata Amitabha".

In Tibetan, Amitabha is called *'od.dpag.med* and, as Amitayus, *tshe.dpag.med.*

Iconography

It can be difficult to distinguish Amitabha from Uakyamuni, as both are portrayed as possessing all the attributes of a buddha but no distinguishing marks.

Amitabha can, however, often be distinguished by his mudra: Amitabha is often depicted, when shown seated, displaying the meditation mudra (thumbs touching and fingers together (as in the Kamakura statue of Amitabha) or the exposition mudra, while the earth-touching mudra (right hand pointed downward over the right leg, palm inward) is reserved for a seated Uakyamuni alone. He can also be seen holding a lotus in his hands while displaying the meditation mudra.

When standing, Amitabha is often shown with his left arm bare and extended downward with thumb and forefinger touching, with his right hand facing outward also with thumb and forefinger touching. The meaning of this mudra is that wisdom (symbolized by the raised hand) is accessible to even the lowest beings, while the outstretched hand shows that Amitabha's compassion is directed at the lowest beings, who cannot save themselves.

When not depicted alone, Amitabha is often portrayed with two assistants: Avalokitevara (Guânyîn) who appears on his right and Mahasthamaprapta (Da Shi Zhi) who appears on his left.

In Tibetan Buddhism, Amitabha is red in colour (red being the colour of love, compassion, and emotional energy). His direction is west and so he is envisioned as the (red) setting sun. He is seen as the supreme power and energy of nature, cast on an earthly plain, accessible to all sentient beings. For this reason he is considered one of the most popular of all Dhyani Buddhas.

His unique emblem is the lotus. He is thus associated with the attributes of the lotus: gentleness, openness, and purity.

Archeological Origins

The first known epigraphic evidence for Amitabha is the bottom part of a statue found in Govindnagar, Pakistan and now located at the Mathura Museum. The statue is dated to "the 28th year of the reign of Huvicka" (i.e., sometime in the latter half of the second century CE, during the period of the KucGa Empire), and was apparently dedicated to "Amitabha Buddha" by a family of merchants.

The first known sutra mentioning Amitabha is the translation into Chinese of the Pratyutpanna Sutra by the KucGa monk Lokakcema around 180 CE. This work is said to be at the origin of Pure Land practice in China.

The appearance of such literature and sculptural remains at the end of the 2nd century suggests that the doctrine of Amitabha probably developed during the 1st and 2nd centuries CE.

Mahayana Buddhism can in general be characterized by:

- Universalism, in that, in those schools of Mahayana that still have large followings, everyone will become a Buddha;
- Bodhicitta as the main focus of realization;
- Compassion through the transferral of merit;
- Transcendental immanence, in that the immortal Buddha Principle is present within all beings.

"Philosophical" Mahayana tends to focus on the first three characteristics (universalism, enlightened wisdom, compassion) and, in some schools, the Buddha-nature, without showing much interest in supernatural constructions, while "devotional" Mahayana focuses mainly on salvation towards other-worldly realms.

Universalism

Mahayana traditions generally consider that attainment of the level of an arhat is not final. This is based on a subtle doctrinal distinction between the Mahayana and some of the early Buddhist schools concerning the issues of *nirvana-with-remainder* and *nirvana-without-remainder*. The Mahayana position here is similar to that of the early school of the Mahasanghika.

Some of the early schools considered that nirvana-without-remainder always follows nirvana-with-remainder (buddhas first achieve enlightenment and then, at 'death', mahaparinirvana) and that nirvana-without-remainder is final; whereas the Mahayana traditions consider that nirvana-without-remainder is always followed by nirvana-with-remainder – the state of attainment of the Hinayana arhat is not final, and is eventually succeeded by the state of buddhahood, or total Awakening.

This distinction is most evident regarding doctrinal concerns about the capability of a Buddha after nirvana (which is identified by the early schools as being nirvana-without-remainder).

Most importantly, amongst the early schools, a Samyaksambuddha is not able to directly point the way to nirvana after death.

This is a major distinction between the early schools and some schools of the Mahayana, who conversely state that once a Samyaksambuddha arises, he or she continues to directly and actively point the way to nirvana until there are no beings left in samsara. Because the views of early schools and Mahayana differ in this respect, this is exactly why some Mahayana schools do not talk about a bodhisattva postponing nirvana, and exactly why the early schools do. However, some Mahayana schools do talk of a bodhisattva deliberately refraining from Buddhahood.

For example, the early schools held that Maitreya will not attain nirvana while Gautama Buddha's teachings still exist. In contrast, some Mahayana schools hold that Maitreya will be the next buddha manifest in this world and will introduce the dharma when it no longer exists; he is not postponing his nirvana to do so, and when he dies (or enters mahaparinirvana), he will likewise continue to teach the dharma for all time.

Moreover, some Mahayana schools argue that although it is true that for this world-system, Maitreya will be the next buddha to manifest, there are an infinite number of world-systems, many of which have currently active buddhas or buddhas-to-be manifesting.

Because the Mahayana traditions assert that eventually everyone will achieve samyaksam (buddhahood) or total enlightenment, the Mahayana is labelled universalist, whereas the stance of the early scriptures is that attaining Nibbana depends on effort and is not pre-determined.

Bodhisattva

Theravada Buddhism

The term *Bodhisatta* (Pail language) was used by the Buddha in the Pail Canon to refer to himself both in his previous lives and as a young man in his current life, prior to his enlightenment, in the period during which he was working towards his own liberation. When, during his discourses, he recounts his experiences as a young aspirant, he regularly uses the phrase "When I was an unenlightened Bodhisatta..." The term therefore connotes a being who is "bound for enlightenment," in other words, a person whose aim is to become fully enlightened. In the Pail Canon, the Bodhisatta is also described as someone who is still subject to birth, illness, death, sorrow, defilement and delusion. Some of the previous lives of the Buddha as a bodhisattva are featured in the Jataka Tales.

In the Pail Canon, the Bodhisatta Siddhartha Gotama is described as thus:

before my Awakening, when I was an unawakened bodhisatta, being subject myself to birth, sought what was likewise subject to birth. Being subject myself to aging... illness... death... sorrow... defilement, I sought [happiness in] what was likewise subject to illness... death... sorrow... defilement. —Ariyapariyesana Sutta

While Maitreya (Pail: Metteya) is mentioned in the Pail Canon, he is not referred to as a bodhisattva, but simply the next fully-awakened Buddha to come into existence long after the current teachings of the Buddha are lost.

In later Theravada literature, the term *bodhisatta* is used fairly frequently in the sense of someone on the path to liberation. The later tradition of commentary also recognizes the existence of two additional types of bodhisattas: the *paccekabodhisatta* who will attain Paccekabuddhahood, and the *savakabodhisatta* who will attain enlightenment as a disciple of a Buddha.

Mahayana Buddhism

Mahayana Buddhism, on the other hand, regards the Bodhisattva as a person who already has a considerable degree of enlightenment and seeks to use their wisdom to help other human beings to become liberated. In this understanding of the word the Bodhisattva is an already wise person who uses skillful means to lead others to see the benefits of virtue and the cultivation of wisdom.

The Mahayana encourages everyone to become bodhisattvas and to take the bodhisattva vows. With these vows, one makes the promise to work for the complete enlightenment of all sentient beings by practicing the six perfections. Indelibly entwined with the Bodhisattva Vow is *parinamana* (Sanskrit; which may be rendered in English as "merit transference").

In Mahayana Buddhism life in this world is compared to people living in a house that is on fire. They take this world as reality pursuing worldly projects and pleasures without realising that the house is on fire and will soon burn down (the inevitability of death). A Bodhisattva is the one who has determination to free sentient beings from samsara with the cycle of death, rebirth and suffering. This type of mind is known as bodhicitta; Sanskrit for mind of awakening. Bodhisattvas take bodhisattva vows in order to progress on the spiritual path towards buddhahood.

There are a variety of different conceptions of the nature of a bodhisattva in Mahayana. According to some Mahayana sources a bodhisattva is someone on the path to full Buddhahood. Others speak of bodhisattvas renouncing Buddhahood. According to the Kun-bzang bla-ma'i zhal-lung, a bodhisattva can choose either of three paths to help sentient beings in the process of achieving buddhahood. They are:

1. King-like Bodhisattva-one who aspires to become buddha as soon as possible and then help sentient beings in full fledge;
2. Boatman-like Bodhisattva-one who aspires to achieve buddhahood along with other sentient beings and
3. Shepherd-like Bodhisattva-one who aspires to delay buddhahood until all other sentient beings achieve buddhahood. Bodhisattvas like Avalokiteshvara, Shantideva among others are believed to fall in this category.

Tibetan doctrine (like Theravada, for different reasons) recognizes only the first of these, holding that Buddhas remain in the world, able to help others, so there is no point in delay.

Geshe Kelsang Gyatso notes: "In reality, the second two types of bodhichitta are wishes that are impossible to fulfil because it is only possible to lead others to enlightenment once we have attained enlightenment ourself. Therefore, only king-like bodhichitta is actual bodhichitta. Je Tsongkhapa says that although the other Bodhisattvas wish for that which is impossible, their attitude is sublime and unmistaken."

East Asian doctrinal traditions tend to emphasize the second and/or third, the idea of deliberately refraining from becoming a Buddha, perhaps forever.

According to many traditions within Mahayana Buddhism, on the way to becoming a Buddha, a bodhisattva proceeds through ten, or sometimes fourteen, grounds or *bhumi.* Below is the list of the ten bhumis and their descriptions from *The Jewel Ornament of Liberation,* a treatise by Gampopa (an influential teacher of the Tibetan Kagyu school) and the Avatamsaka Sutra. Other schools give slightly variant descriptions.

Before a bodhisattva arrives at the first ground, he or she first must travel the first two of the five paths:

1. the path of accumulation
2. the path of preparation

The ten grounds of the bodhisattva then can be grouped into the next three paths

1. Bhumi 1 the path of insight
2. Bhumi 2-7 the path of meditation
3. Bhumi 8-10 the path of no more learning.

The chapter of ten grounds in the Avatamsaka Sutra refers 52 stages, with the following 10 grounds.

1. Great Joy

* It is said that being close to enlightenment and seeing the benefit for all sentient beings, one achieves great joy, hence the name. In this bhumi the bodhisattvas practice all virtues (*paramita*), but especially emphasizing generosity (*dana*).

2. Stainless

* In accomplishing the second bhumi, the bodhisattva is free from the stains of immorality, therefore, this

bhumi is named 'Stainless'. The emphasized virtue is moral discipline (*œila*).

3. *Luminous*

   * The third bhumi is named 'Luminous', because, for a bodhisattva who accomplishes this bhumi, the light of Dharma is said to radiate from the bodhisattva for others. The emphasized virtue is patience (*kcanti*).

4. *Radiant*

   * This bhumi is called 'Radiant', because it is said to be like a radiating light that fully burns that which opposes enlightenment. The emphasized virtue is vigor (*virya*).

5. *Very difficult to train*

   * Bodhisattvas who attain this bhumi strive to help sentient beings attain maturity, and do not become emotionally involved when such beings respond negatively, both of which are difficult to do. The emphasized virtue is meditative concentration (*dhyâna*).

6. *Obviously Transcendent*

   * "By depending on the perfection of wisdom awareness, he [the bodhisattva] does not abide in either saCsra or Nirvga, so it is 'obviously transcendent'". The emphasized virtue is wisdom (*Prajna*).

7. *Gone afar*

   * Particular emphasis is on the perfection of skilful means, or upaya-kaushalya, to help others.

8. *Immovable*

   * The emphasized virtue is aspiration.
   * This, the 'Immovable' bhumi, is the bhumi at which one becomes able to choose his place of rebirth.

9. *Good Discriminating Wisdom*

   * The emphasized virtue is power.

10. *Cloud of dharma*

   * The emphasized virtue is the practice of primordial wisdom.

After the ten bhumis, according to Mahayana Buddhism, one attains complete enlightenment and becomes a Buddha.

With the 52 stages, the Shurangama Sutra in East Asia recognizes 57 stages. With the 10 grounds, various Vajrayana schools recognize 3-10 additional grounds, mostly 6 more grounds with variant descriptions.

Some sutras said a beginner would take 3-22 Maha AsaCkhyeya Kalpa to become a buddha. Pure Land Buddhism suggest buddhists to go to the pure lands to practise. Tiantai, Huayan, Zen and Vajrayana schools said they teach ways to attain buddhahood within one karmic cycle.

Various traditions within Buddhism believe in certain specific bodhisattvas. Some bodhisattvas appear across traditions, but due to language barriers may be seen as separate entities. For example, Tibetan Buddhists believe in various forms of Chenrezig, who is Avalokitesvara in Sanskrit, Guanyin (other spellings: Kwan-yin, Kuan-yin) in China and Korea, Quan Am in Vietnam, and Kannon (formerly spelled and pronounced: Kwannon) in Japan. Jizo or Ti Tsang is another popular bodhisattva in Japan and China (Ksitigarbha in Sanskrit). Jizo is known for aiding those who are lost. His greatest compassionate Vow being: "If I do not go to the hell to help the suffering beings there, who else will go?... if the hells are not empty I will not become a Buddha. Only when all living beings have been saved, will I attain Bodhi."

Many followers of Tibetan Buddhism consider the 14th Dalai Lama and the Karmapa to be an incarnation of that same bodhisattva Chenrezig, the Bodhisattva of Compassion.

The bodhisattva is a popular subject in Buddhist art.

The place of a bodhisattva's earthly deeds, such as the achievement of enlightenment or the acts of dharma, is known as a bodhimanda, and may be a site of pilgrimage. Many temples and monasteries are famous as bodhimandas; for instance, the island of Putuoshan, located off the coast of Ningbo, is venerated by Chinese Buddhists as the bodhimanda of Avalokitesvara. Perhaps the most famous bodhimanda of all is the bodhi tree under which Shakyamuni achieved buddhahood.

11

Important Bodhisattvas

- Avalokitesvara
- Manjusri
- Samantabhadra
- Ksitigarbha
- Maitreya
- Vajrapani
- Sadaparibhuta.

Avalokitevara

Avalokitevara is a bodhisattva who embodies the compassion of all Buddhas. He is one of the more widely revered bodhisattvas in mainstream Mahayana Buddhism. In China and its sphere of cultural influence, Avalokitevara is often depicted in a female form known as Guan Yin. (However, in Taoist mythology, Guan Yin has other origination stories which are unrelated to Avalokitevara.)

Avalokitesvara is also referred to as Padmapâni ("Holder of the Lotus") also Thirumai (Tirupati) or Lokeœvara ("Lord of the World"). In Tibetan, Avalokitevara is known as Chenrezig, and is said to be incarnated in the Dalai Lama, the Karmapa and other high Lamas. In Mongolia, he is called Megjid Janraisig, Xongsim Bodisadv-a, or Nidüber Üjegèi.

Etymology

The name Avalokitevara is made of the following parts: the verbal prefix *ava,* which means "down"; *lokita,* a past participle of the verb *lok* ("to notice, behold, observe"), here used in an active sense (an occasional irregularity of Sanskrit grammar); and finally *iuvara*, "lord", "ruler", "sovereign" or "master". In accordance with the rules of sound combination, becomes *evara*. Combined, the parts mean "lord who gazes down (at the world)". The word *loka* ("world") is absent from the name, but the phrase is implied.

It was initially thought that the Chinese mis-transliterated the word *Avalokitevara* as *Avalokitasvara* which explained why Xuanzang translated it as *Guan Zizai* instead of *Guan Yin*. However, according to recent research, the original form was indeed *Avalokitasvara* with the ending *svara* ("sound, noise"), which means "sound perceiver", literally "he who has perceived sound" (i.e., the cries of sentient beings who need his help). This is the exact equivalent of the Chinese translation *Guan Yin*. This name was later supplanted by the form containing the ending-*iuvara*, which does not occur in Sanskrit before the seventh century. The original form *Avalokitasvara* already appears in Sanskrit fragments of the fifth century.

The original meaning of the name fits the Buddhist understanding of the role of a bodhisattva. The reinterpretation presenting him as an *iuvara* shows a strong influence of Shaivism, as the term *iuvara* was usually connected to the Hindu notion of a creator god and ruler of the world. Attributes of such a god were transmitted to the bodhisattva, but the mainstream of the Avalokitevara worshippers upheld the Buddhist rejection of the doctrine of any creator god.

An etymology of the Tibetan name Chenrezig is *chen* (eye), *re* (continuity) and *zig* (to look). This gives the meaning of one who always looks upon all beings (with the eye of compassion).

Origin

Mahayana Account

According to Mahayana doctrine, Avalokitevara is the bodhisattva who has made a great vow to listen to the prayers of all sentient beings in times of difficulty, and to postpone his own Buddhahood until he has assisted every being on Earth in achieving nirvana. Mahayana sutras associated with Avalokitevara include the Heart Sutra (as disciple of the historical Buddha Shakyamuni) and the Lotus Sutra, particularly the 25th chapter, which is sometimes referred to as the *Avalokitevara Sutra*. Six forms of Avalokitevara in Mahayana: 1. great compassion, 2. great loving-kindness, 3. lion-courage, 4. universal light, 5. leader amongst gods and men, 6. the great omnipresent Brahman. Each of this bodhisattva's six qualities of pity, etc., breaks the hindrances respectively of the (6 realms) hells, pretas (hungry ghost), animals, asuras (demi god), men, and devas.

Vajrayana Account

In the Tibetan tradition, Avalokitevara is seen as arising from two sources. One is the relative source, where in a previous eon (*kalpa*) a devoted, compassionate Buddhist monk became a bodhisattva, transformed in the present kalpa into Avalokitevara. That is not in conflict, however, with the ultimate source, which is Avalokitevara as the universal manifestation of compassion. The bodhisattva is viewed as the anthropomorphised vehicle for the actual deity, serving to bring about a better understanding of Avalokitevara to humankind.

Seven forms of Avalokiteuvara in esoteric Buddhism: 1. Amoghapâúa. not empty (or unerring) net, or lasso. 2. Vara-sahasrabhuja-locana/Sahasrabhujasahasranetra, 1000-hand and 1000-eye, 3. Hayagriva, horseheaded, 4. Ekadasamukha,11-faced, 5. Cundi, 6. Cintamani-cakra;wheel of sovereign power, 7. arya Lokiteúvara, the Holy sovereign beholder of the world (loka), a translation of iuvara, means "ruler" or "sovereign", holy one.

Theravada Account

Although mainstream Theravada does not worship any of the Mahayana bodhisattvas, Avalokitevara is popularly worshiped in Burma, where she is called Lokanat, and Thailand, where she is called Lokesvara.

Modern Scholarship

Western scholars have not reached a consensus on the origin of the reverence for Avalokitevara. Some have suggested that Avalokitevara, along with many other supernatural beings in Buddhism, was a borrowing or absorption by Mahayana Buddhism of one or more Hindu deities, in particular Shiva or Vishnu.

The Japanese scholar Shu Hikosaka on the basis of his study of Buddhist scriptures, ancient Tamil literary sources, as well as field survey, proposes the hypothesis that, the ancient mount Potalaka, the residence of Avalokitevara described in the Gandavyuha Sutra and Xuanzang's Records, is the real mountain Potikai or Potiyil situated at Ambasamudram in Tirunelveli district, Tamil Nadu.

Shu also says that mount Potiyil/Potalaka has been a sacred place for the people of South India from time immemorial. With the spread of Buddhism in the region beginning at the time of the great king Aœoka in the third century B.C.E., it became a holy place also for Buddhists who gradually became dominant as a number of their hermits settled there. The local people, though, mainly remained followers of the Hindu religion. The mixed Hindu-Buddhist cult culminated in the formation of the figure of Avalokitevara.

In Theravada, Lokeœvara, "the lord, ruler or sovereign beholder of the world", name of a Buddha; probably a development of the idea of Brahma, Vishnu or Úiva as lokanâtha, "lord of worlds". In Indo-China especially it refers to Avalokiteuvara, whose image or face, in masculine form, is frequently seen, *e.g.*, at Angkor. A Buddha under whom Amitabha, in a previous existence, entered into the ascetic life and made his forty-eight vows.

Mantras

Om Mani Padme Hum

Tibetan Buddhism relates Chenrezig to the six-syllable mantra *Om Mani Padme Hum*. Thus, Chenrezig is also called Shadakshari ("Lord of the Six Syllables"). The connection between this famous mantra and Avalokitevara already occurs in the Karandavyuha Sutra (probably late fourth or early fifth century), one of the first Buddhist works to have reached Tibet (before the end of the fifth century).

In Shingon Buddhism, the mantra used to praise Avalokitevara is *On Aro-rikya Sowaka,* in sanskrit: Om Arolik Svaha (Oh, Unstained One, Hail!).

The Great Compassion Mantra is an 82 syllable mantra spoken by Avalokitevara to the assembly of Buddhas and Bodhisattvas, and extolling the merits of chanting the mantra. This mantra is popular in China, Japan and Taiwan.

The Thousand Arms of Avalokitevara

One prominent Buddhist story tells of Avalokitevara vowing never to rest until he had freed all sentient beings from samsara. Despite strenuous effort, he realizes that still many unhappy beings were yet to be saved. After struggling to comprehend the needs of so many, his head splits into eleven pieces. Amitabha Buddha, seeing his plight, gives him eleven heads with which to hear the cries of the suffering. Upon hearing these cries and comprehending them, Avalokitevara attempts to reach out to all those who needed aid, but found that his two arms shattered into pieces. Once more, Amitabha comes to his aid and invests him with a thousand arms with which to aid the suffering multitudes.

Many Himalayan versions of the tale include eight arms with which Avalokitevara skillfully upholds the dharma, each possessing its own particular implement, while more Chinese-specific ones give varying accounts of this number.

The Bao'en Temple located in northwestern Sichuan province, China has an outstanding wooden image of the thousand armed Avalokitevara, an example of Ming Dynasty decorative sculpture.

Tibetan Buddhist Beliefs Concerning Chenrezig

Avalokitevara is an important deity in Tibetan Buddhism, and is regarded in the Vajrayana teachings as a Buddha. In the Mahayana teachings he is in general regarded as a high-level Bodhisattva. The Dalai Lama is considered by the Gelugpa sect and many other Tibetan Buddhists to be the primary earthly manifestation of Chenrezig. The Karmapa is considered by the Karma Kagyu sect to be Chenrezig's primary manifestation. It is said that Padmasambhava prophesied that Avalokitevara will manifest himself in the Tulku lineages of the Dalai Lamas and the Karmapas. Another Tibetan source explains that Buddha Amithaba gave to one of his two main disciples, Avalokitevara, the task to take upon himself the burden of caring for Tibet. That is why he has manifested himself not only as spiritual teachers in Tibet but also in the form of kings (like Trisong Detsen) or ministers.

Other manifestations popular in Tibet include *Sahasra-bhuja* (a form with a thousand arms) and *Ekâdaúamukha* (a form with eleven faces).

In Tibetan Buddhism, White Tara acts as the consort and

energizer of Avalokitevara/Chenrezig. According to popular belief, Tara came into existence from a single tear shed by Chenrezig. When the tear fell to the ground it created a lake, and a lotus opening in the lake revealed Tara. In another version of this story, Tara emerges from the heart of Chenrezig. In either version, it is Chenrezig's outpouring of compassion which manifests Tara as a being.

Manjusri

Manjusri is a bodhisattva (emanating enlightened being) in the Mahayana and Vajrayana traditions of Buddhism.

Manjusri is the *bodhisattva* associated with wisdom, doctrine and awareness and in Vajrayana Buddhism is the meditational deity *(yidam)*, who embodies enlightened wisdom. Historically, the Mahayana Buddhist scriptures assert that Manjusri was a disciple of Gautama Buddha, although there is no mention of him in the early Pail scriptures.

The Sanskrit term *Manjuri* can be translated as "Gentle Glory". Manjuri is also known by the fuller Sanskrit name of *Manjuri-kumara-bhuta.*

In the Buddhist Tradition

Scholars have identified Manjusri as "the oldest and most significant mythic bodhisattva in the Mahayana tradition." Manjusri is first referred to in early *Mahayana* texts such as the Prajna-paramita Sutras and through this association very early in the tradition he came to symbolize the embodiment of *Prajna* (wisdom). Manjusri later figures extensively in many texts associated with Tantric Buddhism such as the *Manjuri-mula-kalpa.* and the *Manjurinâmasacgiti.*

Together with the Buddha and fellow disciple Samantabhadra he forms the Shakyamuni trinity (Jp: Sanzon Shaka). In Tibetan Buddhism he sometimes is depicted in a trinity with Avalokiteshvara and Vajrapani. Manjusri is mentioned in a number of Mahayana Buddhist sutras, particularly the Prajnaparamita Sutras. The Lotus Sutra assigns him a paradise called *Vimala,* which according to the Avatamsaka Sutra is located in the east. His consort in some Vajrayana traditions is Saraswati. He is also sometimes called Manjughosha.

Within Tibetan Buddhism, Manjusri is a tantric meditational deity or Yidam, and considered a fully enlightened Buddha. In the Shingon school of esoteric Buddhism, he is one of the thirteen deities to whom disciples devote themselves.

Manjusri leads the dragon king's daughter to enlightenment in the Lotus Sutra and he gives the second to last summation on emptiness in the Vimalakirti sutra. Je Tsongkhapa who founded the Gelug sect of Tibetan Buddhism received his teachings from visions of Manjusri. He is one of the four great bodhisattvas of Chinese Buddhism, the four being: Kshitigarbha, Manjusri, Avalokiteshvara, and Samantabhadra. When he attains buddhahood his name will be Universal Sight. His pure land will be one of the two best pure lands in all of existence in all the past, present and future. Manjusri says in the "Manjusri Speaks on the Inconceivable State of Buddhahood" sutra that if Shakyamuni has attained buddhahood then he [Manjusri] has attained buddhahood. He is a dharmakaya bodhisattva, which means that unlike an ordinary 10th stage bodhisattva who still has a bit further to go before full enlightenment is attained, Manjusri has no further to go and can attain buddhahood at any time but has yet to achieve buddhahood because his Bodhisattva vows are not yet fulfilled.

It says in a sutra on Manjusri's attainment of Buddhahood that the benefits gained by keeping Manjusri's name in mind are superior to the benefits gained by keeping in mind the names of billions of Buddhas. This sutra can be found in "A Treasury of Mahayana Sutras".

Manjusri Mantra

Chanting the Manjusri mantra:

"Om A Ra Pa Cha Na Dhîh"

is believed to enhance wisdom and improve one's skills in debating, memory, writing, explaining etc. *"Dhih"* is the seed syllable of the mantra and is chanted with greater emphasis.

In Japanese Shingon Buddhism, this mantra is transliterated and recited as:

"On a raha-shanô".

Iconography

A male Bodhisattva, he is depicted wielding a sword tipped

with the flames of enlightenment in his right hand, representing his realization of wisdom, which severs the conflict of duality. The scripture supported by the flower held in his left hand is the Prajnaparamita, representing his attainment of ultimate realisation and Enlightenment. Manjusri is frequently depicted in Chinese traditions as riding on the back of a lion.

Variations upon his traditional form as Manjusri include Guhya-Manjusri, Guhya-Manjuvajra, and Manjuswari, most of which are Tantric forms associated with Tibetan Buddhism. The two former appearances are generally accompanied by a shakti deity embracing the main figure, symbolising union of form and spirit, matter and energy.

Yamantaka

Yamantaka is a Mahayana Buddhist icmadevat (tib. *yidam*) of the Highest Yoga Tantra class in Vajrayana, popular within the Geluk school of Tibetan Buddhism. Yamantaka is seen as a wrathful manifestation of Manjuri, the buddha of wisdom, and in other contexts functions as a dharmapala.

Yamantaka is a Sanskrit name that can be broken down into two primary elements: *Yama*, the name of the god of death; and *antaka*, or "terminator". Thus, Yamantaka's name literally means "the terminator of death".

Within Buddhism, "terminating death" is actually a quality of all buddhas as they have stopped the cycle of rebirth, samsara. In this context, Yamantaka represents the goal of the Mahayana practitioner's journey to enlightenment, or the journey itself: in awakening, one adopts the practice of Yamantaka – the practice of terminating death.

"Yamantaka" or "Shri Bhagavan Yamantaka" (Glorious Lord Making an End of Yama*) is another name for [Shri] Vajra[maha]bhairava, who is the highest emanation of Bodhisattva Manjushri. Bodhisattva Manjushri, Shri Vajrabhairava and Shri Bhagavan Yamantaka together represent the [Buddha]dharmakaya (Body of [Enlightened] Doctrine) which is also called Vajradhara (Holder of the Thunderbolt) because it holds to the pledge of the thunderbolt (vajrasamaya) which is the pledge to carry out the action of the Buddha.

* Yama is the name of the warden of hell.

How does Yamantaka Terminate Death?

This question depends upon the meaning ascribed to the term *death* – but one way in which this ability can be identified is through the enlightening activity of wisdom. The wisdom mind is able to perceive that death has no intrinsic, concrete existence: our understanding of death emerges solely from the conventions of the world. Also, when we achieve the same realisation of Yamantaka-who is a Buddha-then we have transcended death.

There are three types of death spoken of in the Yamantaka Tantra : Outer death is the regular end of life, which is embodied by Yama, Lord of Death, who resides in the south, seven stories under the earth. The inner death is ignorance of the true nature of non-dual reality. Instinctive habitual grasping and aversion to objectively "real" objects and subjects arises from this ignorance. The secret death is dualistic appearance on the subtlest level of clear light mind and illusory body. With the practice of Yamantaka one overcomes those types of death and gains immortality as a Buddha.

In Other Buddhist Cultures

Manchu

According to a legend, Nurhaci, a military leader of the Jurchen tribes in Northeast China and founder of what became the Chinese imperial Qing Dynasty, believed himself to be a reincarnation of Manjusri. He therefore is said to have renamed his tribe the Manchu.

In Nepalese Mythology

According to Swayambhu Purana, the Kathmandu Valley was once a lake. It is believed that Manjusri saw a lotus flower in the centre of the lake and cut a gorge at Chovar to allow the lake to drain. The place where the lotus flower settled became Swayambhunath Stupa and the valley thus became habitable.

The Newars of the Kathmandu Valley, who adhere to both Buddhism and Hinduism, revere him as the Bodhisattva of Wisdom.

In China

Wutai Shan in Shanxi, one of the Four Sacred Mountains of Buddhism in China, which also had strong associations for Taoists, was considered by Chinese Buddhists to be the earthly abode of Manjusri. Manjusri was said to bestow spectacular visionary experiences to those on selected mountain peaks and caves there. These made it a popular place of pilgrimage, but patriarchs including Linji and Yun-men declared the mountain off limits.

Being in the North of China and revered, Mount Wutai was also associated with the Northern lineages of Zen. In some Taoist schools, Manjusri was said to be an ancient Taoist Immortal.

Master Sheng-yen (1988) renders the 'Manjusri Sutra' or 'Prajna Sutra" spoken by Manjuœri as saying to:

...contemplate the five skandhas as originally empty and quiescent, non-arising, non-perishing, equal, without differentiation. Constantly thus practicing, day or night, whether sitting, walking, standing or lying down, finally one reaches an inconceivable state without any obstruction or form.

Samantabhadra

Samantabhadra is a Bodhisattva in Mahayana Buddhism associated with Buddhist practice and meditation. Together with Shakyamuni Buddha and fellow bodhisattva Manjusri he forms the *Shakyamuni trinity* in Buddhism. He is the patron of the Lotus Sutra and, according to the Avatamsaka Sutra, made the ten great vows which are the basis of a bodhisattva. In China he is associated with action, whereas the bodhisattva Manjusri is associated with wisdom. In Japan this bodhisattva is often worshipped by the Tendai and Shingon sects, and as the protector of the Lotus Sutra by the Nichiren sect.

In the Nyingma school of Tibetan Buddhist Vajrayana, Samantabhadra is considered a primordial Buddha in indivisible yab-yum union with his consort Samantabhadri.

Samantabhadra/Kuntuzangpo is usually presented with colour black. The *Dorje Zahorma hat,* that is a special form of the Dorje Zahorma hat which is particular to Chatral Rinpoches tradition, is emblazoned with an image of Kuntuzangpo.

Origins

Samantabhadra is a key figure in the Flower Garland Sutra, particularly the last chapter, the Gandhavyuha Sutra. In the climax of the Gandhavyuha Sutra, the student Sudhana meets the

Bodhisattva Samantabhadra, who teaches him that wisdom only exists for the sake of putting it into practice; that it is only good insofar as it benefits all living beings.

In the Lotus Sutra, he is described at length in the epilogue, *The Sutra of Meditation on the Bodhisattva Universal Worthy*, with special detail given to visualization of the bodhisattva, and the virtues of devotion to him.

The Ten Vows of Samantabhadra

In the Flower Garland Sutra, the Buddha states that Bodhisattva Samantabhadra made ten great vows in his path to full Buddhahood:

1. To pay homage and respect to all Buddhas.
2. To praise all the Buddhas.
3. To make abundant offerings. (i.e. give generously)
4. To repent misdeeds and evil karmas.
5. To rejoice in others' merits and virtues.
6. To request the Buddhas to continue teaching.
7. To request the Buddhas to remain in the world.
8. To follow the teachings of the Buddhas at all times.
9. To accommodate and benefit all living beings.
10. To transfer all merits and virtues to benefit all beings.

The ten vows have become a common practice in East Asian Buddhism, particularly the tenth vow, with many Buddhists traditionally dedicating their merit and good works to all beings during Buddhist liturgies.

Iconography

Unlike his more popular counterpart Manjusri, Samantabhadra is only rarely depicted alone and is usually found in a trinity on the right side of Shakyamuni, mounted on a white elephant. In those traditions that accept the Avatamsaka Sutra as its root instruction, Samantabhadra and Manjusri flank Vairocana Buddha, the central Buddha of this particular sutra.

Known as Poxian in Chinese, he is sometimes shown in Chinese art with feminine characteristics, riding an elephant with six pairs of tusks while carrying a lotus leaf 'parasol' (Sanskrit: *chhatra*), bearing similar dress and features to some feminine depictions of Kuan Yin. It is in this guise that Samantabhadra is revered as the patron bodhisattva of the monasteries associated with Mount Emei in western China.

Among those esoteric traditions that treat Samantabhadra as the 'Primordial' (Sanskrit: Dharmakaya) Buddha, he is often represented 'naked' ("sky clad"; Sanskrit: *digambara*), with a dark blue body, in union with his consort Samantabhadri.

In Esoteric Traditions

Samntabhadra is also known as Vajradhara and Viœvabhadra, the different names foreground different attributes and essence-qualities. Samantabhadra appears in the Vajrayana tantric text the Kunjed Gyalpo Tantra, as the Primordial Buddha, the 'embodiment' (Sanskrit: *kaya*) or 'field' (Sanskrit: *kcetra*) of 'timeless awareness, gnosis' awakened since before the very beginning. Therefore in Tibetan Buddhism the Nyingma, or 'Old Translation' school, the Sakya and the Bon schools view Samantabhadra as the Primordial Buddha. However, the Kagyu and Gelug schools use Vajradhara to represent the Primordial Buddha.

Ksitigarbha

Ksitigarbha is a bodhisattva primarily revered in East Asian Buddhism, usually depicted as a Buddhist monk in the Orient. The name may be translated as "Earth Treasury", "Earth Store", "Earth Matrix", or "Earth Womb." Ksitigarbha is known for his vow not to achieve Buddhahood until all hells are emptied; therefore, he is regarded as the bodhisattva of hell beings. Usually depicted as a monk with a nimbus around his shaved head, he carries a staff to force open the gates of hell and a wish-fulfilling jewel to light up the darkness.

Overview

Ksitigarbha is one of the four principal bodhisattvas in East Asian Mahayana Buddhism. The others are Samantabhadra, Manjusri, and Avalokitesvara.

At the pre-Tang Dynasty grottos in Dunhuang and Longmen, he is depicted in classical bodhisattva shape. After the Tang Dynasty, he became increasingly depicted as a monk, carrying rosaries and a staff.

His full name in Chinese script is, or the Bodhisattva King *Dizang* of the Great Vow, pronounced as *Dayuan Dizang Pusa* in Mandarin Chinese, Daigan Jizo Bosatsu in Japanese, Chijang Posal in Korean.

This is a reference to his pledge, as recorded in the sutras, to take responsibility for the instruction of all beings in six worlds, in the era between the death of Gautama Buddha and the rise of Maitreya Buddha. Because of this important role, shrines to Ksitigarbha often occupy a central role in any Oriental Mahayana temples.

In China

Jiuhua Mountain in Anhui is regarded as Ksitigarbha's seat. It is one of the four great Buddhist mountains of China, and at one time housed more than 300 temples. Today, 95 of these are open to the public. The mountain is a popular destination for pilgrims offering dedications to Ksitigarbha.

In some areas, the admixture of traditional religions has led to Ksitigarbha being also regarded as a Taoist deity, albeit his duties differ to what Ksitigarbha does. For example, in Hong Kong and among Overseas Chinese communities, his images are usually found in the memorial halls of Buddhist and Taoist temples.

In Japan

In Japan, Ksitigarbha, known as *Jizo*, or *Ojizo-sama* as he is respectfully known, is one of the most loved of all Japanese divinities. His statues are a common sight, especially by roadsides and in graveyards. Traditionally, he is seen as the guardian of children, particularly children who died before their parents. Since the 1980s, he has been worshipped as the guardian of the souls of *mizuko*, the souls of stillborn, miscarried or aborted fetuses, in the ritual of mizuko kuyo In Japanese mythology, it is said that the souls of children who die before their parents are unable to cross the mythical Sanzu River on their way to the afterlife because they have not had the chance to accumulate enough good deeds and because they have made the parents suffer.

It is believed that *Jizo* saves these souls from having to pile stones eternally on the bank of the river as penance, by hiding them from demons in his robe, and letting them hear mantras.

Jizo statues are sometimes accompanied by a little pile of stones and pebbles, put there by people in the hope that it would shorten the time children have to suffer in the underworld. (The act is derived from the tradition of building stupas as an act of merit-making.) The statues can sometimes be seen wearing tiny children's clothing or bibs, or with toys, put there by grieving parents to help their lost ones and hoping that *Jizo* would specially protect them. Sometimes the offerings are put there by parents to thank *Jizo* for saving their children from a serious illness. *Jizo*'s features are commonly made more babylike to resemble the children he protects.

As he is seen as the saviour of souls who have to suffer in the underworld, his statues are common in cemeteries. He is also believed to be the protective deity of travellers, and roadside statues of *Jizo* are a common sight in Japan. Firefighters are also believed to be under the protection of *Jizo*.

Source

The story of Ksitigarbha is described in the *Sutra of The Great Vows of Ksitigarbha Bodhisattva*, one of the most popular Mahayana Buddhist sutras. This sutra is said to have been spoken by the Buddha towards the end of his life to the beings of the Trayastrimsa Heaven as a mark of gratitude and remembrance for his beloved mother, Mayadevi. It stated that Ksitigarbha practiced filial piety as a mortal, which eventually led to making great vows to save all sentient beings.

As Sacred Girl

In the Ksitigarbha Sutra, the Buddha claimed that in the distant past aeons, Ksitigarbha was a Brahmin maiden by the name of *Sacred Girl*. She was deeply troubled when her mother died, because she had often been slanderous towards the Triple Gem.

To save her from the great tortures of hell, the girl sold whatever she had and used the money to buy offerings that she offered daily to the Buddha of her time, known as The Buddha of Flower of Meditation and Enlightenment. She prayed fervently that her mother be spared the pains of hell and appealed to the Buddha for help.

While she was pleading for help at the temple, she heard Buddha telling her to go home, sit down, and recite his name if she wanted to know where her mother was. She did as she was told and her consciousness was transported to a Hell Realm where she met a guardian who informed her that through her fervent prayers and pious offerings, her mother had accumulated much merit and had already ascended to heaven. Sacred Girl was greatly relieved and would have been extremely happy, but the sight of the suffering she had seen in Hell touched her heart. She vowed to do her best to relieve beings of their suffering in her future lives of kalpas.

As a Monk

There is another legend about how Ksitigarbha manifested in China, and chose his bodhimanda to be Mount Jiuhua, one of the Four Sacred Mountains of China in Buddhism.

In the Eastern Han dynasty, during the reign of Emperor Ming, Buddhism started to flourish, reaching its peak in the era of the Tang Dynasty, eventually spreading to Japan and Korea. At the time, monks and scholars arrived from those countries to seek the Dharma in China. One of these pilgrims was a former prince from Silla whose Korean romanization was Kim Kiaokak and became a monastic under the name of *Earth Store* (Also called *Jijang*, the Korean pronunciation of *Dizang*). He came to the region of Anhui to Mount Jiuhua. After ascending, he decided to build a hut in a deep mountain area so that he may be able to cultivate.

According to records, the monk was bitten by a poisonous snake, but did not move, thus letting the snake go. A woman happened to pass by and gave the monk medicines to cure him of the venom, as well as a spring on her son's behalf. For a few years, the monk continued to meditate in his hut, until one day, a scholar named Chu-Ke led a group of friends and family to visit the mountain. Noticing the monk meditating in the hut, they went and took a look at his condition. They had noticed that the monk's bowl did not contain any food, and that his hair had grown back.

Feeling pity on the monk, Scholar Chu decided to build a temple as an offering to the monk. The whole group descended the mountain immediately to discuss plans to build the temple. Mount Jiuhua was also property of a wealthy person named the elder Wen-Ke, who obliged to build a temple on his mountain. Therefore, Wen-Ke and the group ascended the mountain once more and asked the monk how much land he needed.

The monk replied that he needed a piece of land that could be covered fully by his kasaya. Bewildered that a piece of sash could not be enough land to build a temple, the monk surprised them as he threw the kasaya in the air, and the robe expanded in size, covering the entire mountain! Elder Wen-Ke had then decided to renounce the entire mountain to the monk, and became the monk's protector. Sometime later, Wen-Ke's son also left the home life to start his life as a monk.

The monk lived in Mount Jiuhua for seventy five years before passing away at the age of ninety-nine. Three years after his nirvana, his tomb was opened, only to reveal that the body had not decayed. Because the monk led his wayplace with much difficulty, most people had the intuition to believe that he was indeed the transformation body of Ksitigarbha.

Monk Jijang's well-preserved, dehydrated body may still be viewed today at the monastery he built on Mount Jiuhua.

Iconography

Traditional Iconography

In Buddhist iconography, Ksitigarbha is typically depicted with a shaven head, dressed in a monk's simple robes (unlike most other bodhisattvas, who are dressed like Indian royalty). In his left hand, Ksitigarbha holds a wish granting jewel; in his right hand, he holds a monk's staff called in Japanese a *shakujo* (jingle staff), which is used to alert insects and small animals of his approach, so that he will not accidentally harm them. Such a staff is traditionally carried by high ranking monks of Chinese Buddhist temples. Usually, Ksitigarbha will sometimes be seen wearing a crown depicting the Five Dhyani Buddhas, worn by Tibetan and Chinese monks in Tantric rituals.

Like other Bodhisattvas, Ksitigarbha usually is seen standing upon a lotus base, symbolizing his release from the karmic wheel of rebirth. Ksitigarbha's face and head are also idealized, featuring the third eye, elongated ears and the other standard attributes of an enlightened being.

Popular Iconography in Japan

The Narihira Santosen Temple in Katsushika, Tokyo contains the "Bound Jizo" of Ôoka Tadasuke fame, dating from the Edo

Period. When petitions are requested before the Jizo, the petitioner ties a rope about the statue. When the wish is granted, the petitioner unties the rope. At the new year, the ropes of the ungranted wishes are cut by the temple priest. The vandalism of a Jizo statue is the theme of the J-Horror movie Shibuya Kaidan. The anime series Hell Girl is also loosely based on the legend of the Jizou.

Akasagarbha

Ksitigarbha has a twin known as Akauagarbha, the "Void Store". While theologically equally important, Akauagarbha entirely lacks the popular cult of Ksitigarbha.

Phra Malai

In Theravada Buddhism, the story of a Buddhist monk called Phra Malai, who has the similar qualities of Ksitigarbha, is well known throughout Southeast Asia, especially in Thailand and Laos. Legend has it that he was an arhat from Sri Lanka, who achieved great supernormal powers through his own merits and meditation. He is also honoured as a successor to Maudgalyayana, the Buddha's disciple foremost for his supernormal attainments. In the story this pious and compassionate monk descends to Hell to give teachings & comfort the suffering hell-beings there. He also learns how the hell-beings are punished according to their sins in the different hells.

Maitreya

Maitreya (Sanskrit) or Metteyya (Pail) is a future Buddha of this world in Buddhist eschatology. In some Buddhist literature, such as the Amitabha Sutra and the Lotus Sutra, he is referred to as *Ajita* Bodhisattva. Maitreya is a bodhisattva who in the Buddhist tradition is to appear on Earth, achieve complete enlightenment, and teach the pure dharma. According to scriptures, Maitreya will be a successor of the historic Uakyamuni Buddha, the founder of Buddhism. The prophecy of the arrival of Maitreya is found in the canonical literature of all Buddhist sects (Theravada, Mahayana, Vajrayana) and is accepted by most Buddhists as a statement about an actual event that will take place in the distant future.

Characteristics

One mention of the prophecy of Maitreya is in the Sanskrit text, the MaitreyavykaraGa (The Prophecy of Maitreya), it implies that he is a teacher of meditative trance sadhana and states that gods, men, and other beings:

"will lose their doubts, and the torrents of their cravings will be cut off: free from all misery they will manage to cross the ocean of becoming; and, as a result of Maitreya's teachings, they will lead a holy life. No longer will they regard anything as their own, they will have no possession, no gold or silver, no home, no relatives! But they will lead the holy life of chastity under Maitreya's guidance. They will have torn the net of the passions, they will manage to enter into trances, and theirs will be an abundance of joy and happiness, for they will lead a holy life under Maitreya's guidance." (Trans. in Conze 1959:241)

General Description

Maitreya is typically pictured seated, with either both feet on the ground or crossed at the ankles, on a throne, waiting for his time. He is dressed in the clothes of either a Bhiksu or Indian royalty. As a bodhisattva, he would usually be standing and dressed in jewels. Usually he wears a small stupa in his headdress that represents the stupa of the Buddha Sakyamuni's relics to help him identify it when his turn comes to lay claim to his succession, and can be holding a dharmachakra resting on a lotus. A khata is always tied around his waist as a girdle.

In the Greco-Buddhist art of Gandhara, in the first centuries CE in northern India, Maitreya is represented as a Central Asian or northern Indian nobleman, holding a "water phial" (Sanskrit: *Kumbha*) in his left hand. Sometimes this is a "wisdom urn" (Sanskrit: *Bumpa*). He is flanked by his two acolytes, the brothers Asanga and Vasubandhu.

Maitreya's Tucita Heaven

Maitreya currently resides in the Tucita Heaven (Pail: Tusita), said to be reachable through meditation. Uakyamuni Buddha also lived here before he was born into the world as all bodhisattvas live in the Tucita Heaven before they descend to the human realm to become Buddhas. Although all bodhisattvas are destined to become Buddhas, the concept of a bodhisattva differs slightly in Theravada and Mahayana Buddhism. In Theravada Buddhism, a bodhisattva is one who is only destined to one day become a Buddha, whereas in Mahayana Buddhism, a bodhisattva is one who has already reached a very advanced state of grace or enlightenment but holds back from entering nirvana so that he may help others.

Once Maitreya becomes a Buddha, he will rule over the Ketumati Pure Land, an earthly paradise sometimes associated with the Indian city of Varanasi (also known as Benares) in Uttar Pradesh. (All Buddhas preside over a Pure Land; the Buddha Amitabha presides over the Sukhavati Pure Land, more popularly known as the Western Paradise.)

Activity of Maitreya in the Current Age

In Mahayana schools, Maitreya is traditionally said to have revealed the Five Treatises of Maitreya through Asanga. These important texts are the basis of the Yogachara tradition and constitute the majority of the Third Turning of the Wheel of Dharma.

The Future Coming of Maitreya

Maitreya's coming will occur after the teachings of the current Gautama Buddha, the Dharma, are no longer taught and are completely forgotten. Maitreya is predicted to attain Bodhi in seven days (which is the minimum period), by virtue of his many lives of preparation for Buddha-hood (similar to those reported in the Jataka stories of Shakyamuni Buddha).

Maitreya's coming is characterized by a number of physical events. The oceans are predicted to decrease in size, allowing Maitreya to traverse them freely. The event will also allow the unveiling of the "true" dharma to the people, in turn allowing the construction of a new world. The coming also signifies the end of the middle time in which humans currently reside (characterized as a low point of human existence between the Gautama Buddha and Maitreya.)

Origins

The name Maitreya or Metteyya is derived from the word maitri (Sanskrit) or metta (Pail) meaning "loving-kindness", which is in turn derived from the noun mitra (Pail: mitta) in the sense of "friend".

The earliest mention of Metteyya is in the Cakavatti (Sihanada) Sutta in the Digha Nikaya 26 of the Pail Canon. He occurs in no other sutta, and this casts doubt as to the sutta's authenticity. Most of the Buddha's sermons are presented as preached in answer to a question, or in some other appropriate context, but this one has a beginning and an ending in which the Buddha is talking to monks about something totally different. This leads Gombrich to conclude that either whole sutta is apocryphal, or it has at least been tampered with.

Maitreya is sometimes represented seated on a throne Western-style, and venerated both in Mahayana and non-Mahayana Buddhism. Some have speculated that inspiration for Maitreya may have come from the ancient Indo-Iranian deity Mithra. The primary comparison between the two characters appears to be the similarity of their names. According to a book entitled *The Religion of the Iranian Peoples*, "No one who has studied the Zoroastrian doctrine of the Saoshyants or the coming saviour-prophets can fail to see their resemblance to the future Maitreya.

Paul Williams claims that some Zoroastrian ideas like Saoshyant influenced the cult of Maitreya, such as "expectations of a heavenly helper, the need to opt for positive righteousness, the future millennium, and universal salvation". Possible objections are that these characteristics are not unique to Zoroastrianism, nor are they necessarily characteristic of the belief in Maitreya.

It is also possible that Maitreya Buddha originated with the Hindu Kalki, and that its similarities with the Iranian Mithra have to do with their common Indo-Iranian origin.

In the Greco-Buddhist art of Gandhara, in the first centuries CE in northern India, Maitreya was the most popular figure to be represented, together with the Buddha Uakyamuni. In China, in the 4th–6th Centuries "[Buddhist artisans] used the names Shakyamuni and Maitreya interchangeably... indicating both that the distinction between the two had not yet been drawn and that their respective iconographies had not yet been firmly set" An example is the stone sculpture found in the Qingzhou cache dedicated to Maitreya in 529 CE as recorded in the inscription (currently in the Qingzhou Museum, Shandong). The cult of Maitreya seems to have developed around the same time of that of Amitabha, as early as the 3rd century CE.

Maitreya Claimants

Since his death, the Chinese monk Budai (Hotei) has been popularly regarded as an incarnation of the bodhisattva Maitreya.

His depiction as the *Laughing Buddha* continues to be very popular in East Asian culture.

While a number of persons have proclaimed themselves to be Maitreya over the years following the Buddha's parinirvana, none have been officially recognized by the sangha and Buddhists. A particular difficulty faced by any would-be claimant to Maitreya's title is the fact that the Buddha is considered to have made a number of fairly specific predictions regarding the circumstances that would occur prior to Maitreya's coming; such as that the teachings of the Buddha would be completely forgotten, and all of the remaining relics of Sakyamuni Buddha would be gathered in Bodh Gaya and cremated.

Non-Buddhist Views

Since the growth of the theosophist movement in the 19th century, non-Buddhist religious and spiritual movements have adopted the name and selected characteristics of Maitreya for teachers in their traditions.

Share International, which equates Maitreya with the prophesied figures of multiple religious traditions, claims that he is already present in the world, but is preparing to make an open declaration of his presence in the near future. They claim that he is here to inspire mankind to create a new era based on sharing and justice.

Since the beginning of the 1930s, the Ascended Master Teachings have placed Maitreya in the "Office" of "World Teacher" until 1956, when he was described as moving on to the "Office" of "Planetary Buddha" and "Cosmic Christ" in their concept of a Spiritual Hierarchy.

Some Muslim scholars who studied Buddhist texts believe that Maitreya is "Rahmatu lil-'alameen" (Mercy for The Worlds), which is the name for the prophet Muhammad as it is said in the Qur'an. According to the research on the book *Antim Buddha-Maitreya* scholars have summarized that Maitreya Buddha is Muhammad. After examining the Buddhist texts researchers concluded that Muhammad had been the last and final awakened Buddha to come into existence long after the current teachings.

The 19th Century religious reformer, Mirza Ghulam Ahmad, is believed in by the members of the Ahmadiyya Muslim

Community (the faith he brought) as fulfilling expectations regarding the Maitreya Buddha.

Bahá'ís believe that Bahaullah is the fulfillment of the prophecy of appearance of Maitreya. Bahais believe that the prophecy that Maitreya will usher in a new society of tolerance and love has been fulfilled by Bahaullah's teachings on world peace. This view has been of some effect, for example in Vietnam Bahaullah was identified with the Maitreya. Before the Communist government, the Bahai Faith grew in part with the coversion of a number of Buddhist monks. see Bahai Faith in Vietnam. The Bahai Faith has recently been able to re-register as a religion and there are some signs of large scale growth from the 50s–60s resuming.

More Self-Proclaimed Maitreyas

The following people listed are just a small portion of the several people who claimed themselves to be Maitreya. Many have either used the Maitreya incarnation claim to form a new Buddhist sect or have used the name of Maitreya to form a new religious movement or cult.

- Gung Ye, a Korean warlord and king of short-lived state of Taebong during the 10th century, claimed himself as living incarnation of Maitreya and ordered his subjects to worship him. His claim was widely rejected by most Buddhist monks and later he was dethroned and killed by his own servants.
- In 613 the monk Xiang Haiming claimed himself Maitreya and adopted imperial title.
- In 690 *Empress Wu* inaugurated the Second Zhou dynasty, proclaimed herself an incarnation of the future Buddha Maitreya, and made Luoyang the "holy capital." In 693 she replaced the compulsory Dao De Jing in the curriculum temporarily with her own *Rules for Officials*.
- Lu Zhong Yi, the 17th patriarch of I-Kuan Tao, claimed to be an incarnation of Maitreya.
- L. Ron Hubbard, founder of Dianetics and Scientology, suggested he was "Metteya" (Maitreya) in the 1955 poem *Hymn of Asia*. His editors indicated, in the book's preface, specific physical characteristics said to be outlined—in unnamed Sanskrit sources—as properties of the coming

Maitreya; properties which Hubbard's appearance supposedly aligned with.

- A Korean man by the name of SamHan Lee claimed Supreme Enlightenment in 1984 and since started calling himself a Tathagata. He says that he does not call himself a Buddha but that the next generation will call him as Maitreya Buddha when they understand his life.
- Real's Maitreya claims centre on the content of the *Agama Sutra* (Japanese: *Agon Sutra*), supposedly a very ancient text written by Buddha himself, but which has been deemphasized or forgotten by the majority of Buddhist cultures. Real has claimed directly to people attending Asia Raëlian Church seminars, that someone born in France, a country which is often symbolized by the cock (or rooster), west of the Orient, meets the criteria of the Maitreya. Real himself claims to be this individual.

Maitreya Sects in China

Pre-Maitreyan Buddhist Messianic Rebellions Southern and Northern Dynasties

515

The *Mahayana Rebellion.* In the late summer of that year, the renegade monk Faqing married a nun and formed a sect in the Northern Wei province of Jizhou (in the southern part of today's Hebei province) with the assistance of a local aristocrat named Li Guibo. The sect was named the *Mahayana* ("The Great Vehicle", in reference to Mahayana Buddhism), and Li Guibo was given the titles of *Tenth-stage Bodhisattva, Commander of the Demon-vanquishing Army,* and *King who Pacifies the Land of Han by Faqing.*

Using drugs to send its members into a killing frenzy, and promoting them to Tenth-Stage Bodhisattva as soon as they killed ten enemies, the Mahayana sect seized a prefecture and murdered all the government officials in it. Their slogan was *"A new Buddha has entered the world; eradicate the demons of the former age"*, and they would kill all monks and nuns in the monasteries that they captured, also burning all the sutras and icons. After defeating a government army and growing to a size of over 50,000, the rebel army was finally crushed by another government army of 100,000. Faqing, his wife, and tens of thousands of his followers were beheaded, and Li Guibo was also captured later and publicly executed in the capital city Luoyang.

The Fozu Tongji (Comprehensive Records of the Buddha), a chronicle of Buddhist history written by the monk Zhipan in 1269, also contains an account of the Mahayana Rebellion, but with significant deviations from the original account, such as dating the rebellion to 528 rather than 515.

516

The *Moonlight Child Rebellion.* Toward the end of that year, another sect was discovered by local authorities in Yanling (a county or prefecture of Jizhou). A man named Fa Quan and his associates were claiming that an eight-year-old child named Liu Jinghui was a Bodhisattva called the *Moonlight Child,* and that he could transform into a snake or a pheasant. They were arrested and sentenced to death on suspicion of seditious intent, but Jinghui had his sentence commuted to banishment on account of his youth and ignorance.

517

Early in the spring of that year, surviving remnants of the Mahayana rebels regrouped and mounted a sudden attack on the capital of Yingzhou province, which lay just northwest of their original base in Bohai prefecture. They were repelled only after a pitched battle with an army of slaves and attendants led by Yuwen Yan, the son of the provincial governor, and nothing more is known of their fate.

Although a "new Buddha" was mentioned, these rebellions are not considered "Maitreyan" by modern scholars. However, they would be a later influence on the rebel religious leaders that made such claims. Therefore, it is important to mention these rebellions in this context.

Maitreyan Rebellions

610

On the first day of the Lunar New Year, several tens of rebels dressed in white, burning incense and holding flowers proclaimed their leader as Maitreya Buddha and charged into the imperial palace through one of its gates, killing all the guards before they were themselves killed by troops led by an imperial prince. A massive investigation in the capital (Chang'an) implicated over a thousand families.

613

A skilled magician named Song Zixian claimed to be Maitreya in Tang County (northwest of Yingzhou), and supposedly could transform into the form of a Buddha and make his room emit a glow every night. He hung a mirror in a hall that could display an image of what a devotee would be reincarnated as – a snake, a beast or a human being. Nearly a thousand "from near and far" joined his sect every day, and he plotted to first hold a Buddhist vegetarian banquet (wuzhe fohui) and then make an attack on the emperor who was then touring Yingzhou. The plot was leaked out, and Song was arrested and executed with over a thousand families of his followers.

613

The monk Xiang Haiming claimed to be Maitreya in Fufeng prefecture (western Shaanxi) and led a rebellion. The elite of the Chang'an area hailed him as a holy man (dasheng) because they had auspicious dreams after following him, and his army swelled to several tens of thousands before he was defeated by government troops.

Tang Dynasty

710

Wang Huaigu declared, *"The Shakyamuni Buddha has declined; a new Buddha is about to appear. The House of Li is ending, and the House of Liu is about to rise"*.

Song Dynasty

1047

Army officer Wang Ze led a revolt of Buddhists expecting Maitreya; they took over the city of Beizhou in Hebei before they were crushed. The Song Dynasty government declared Maitreya Sects to be "heresies and unsanctioned religions". Tens of thousands of Maitreya Sect followers were killed.

Yuan and Ming Dynasty

1351

The *Red Turban Rebellion* (a.ka. *The First White Lotus Rebellon*).

Han Shantong, leader of the White Lotus Society, and Army Commander Liu Futong rebelled against the Mongol masters of the Yuan Dynasty. Shantong's anti-Mongol slogan was *"The empire is in utter chaos. Maitreya Buddha has incarnated, and the Manichaean King of Light has appeared in this world."*

In 1355, Han Shantong's son, Han Lin'er, was proclaimed "Emperor of the Great [Latter] Song" (1355-1368?) by Liu Futong. Liu Futong claimed Han Lin'er was a direct descendent of the Zhao royal family who ruled the Song Dynasty. After Liu Futong's death, Zhu Yuanzhang took up command of the Red Turban Rebellion and later assassinated Han Lin'er to become Emperor Hongwu of the Ming Dynasty.

According to Beijing University, "The leader of White Lotus sect, Han Shantong called himself *Ming Wang,* while his son, Han Lin'er called himself *Xiao Ming Wang,* both names reflecting the sect's beliefs. Zhu Yuanzhang had been a member of the White lotus Sect, and admitted to have been a branch of the White Lotus rebel army (being at one time vice-marshal of Xiao Ming Wang). When Zhu Yuanzhang took power, he chose the dynastic name "Ming"."

This suggests that the Ming Dynasty was named after the White Lotus figures of the "Big and Little Bright Kings".

Post-Maitreyan Rebellions

Qing Dynasty

1796 : The *White Lotus Rebellion* (a.k.a. *The Second White Lotus Rebellion*). It broke out among impoverished settlers in the mountainous region that separates Sichuan province from Hubei and Shaanxi provinces. It apparently began as a White Lotus Society protest against heavy taxes imposed by Manchu rulers of the Qing Dynasty.

The Yi He Tuan, often called in English the "Society of Harmonious Fists" was a 19th century martial-sect inspired in part by the White Lotus Society. Members of the "Harmonious Fists" became known as "Boxers" in the west because they practiced Chinese martial arts.

1899 : The *Boxer Rebellion.* It was a Chinese rebellion from November 1899 to September 7, 1901 against foreign influence in such areas as trade, politics, religion and technology that occurred in China during the final years of the Qing Dynasty. By August 1900, over 230 foreigners, tens of thousands of Chinese Christians, an unknown number of rebels, their sympathizers and other innocent bystanders had been killed in the ensuing chaos. The uprising crumbled on August 14, 1900 when 20,000 foreign troops entered the Chinese capital, Peking (Beijing).

Albeit not in the name of Maitreya, both rebellions were perpetrated solely or in part by the White Lotus Society, a rebellious Maitreya sect.

Alternative Persona

There was a sage of the same name in the epic Mahabharata. His lineage is unknown. He came to the court of Hastinapura to advise Duryodhana to restore the kingdom of the Pandavas, a little while after the sons of Pandu had gone into exile, having been defeated at dice.

However, Duryodhana didn't even bother to listen to the sage, and showed his disrespect all too plainly. Incensed, the sage cursed him and said, "Fourteen years hence, you shall be destroyed in battle by the Pandavas, along with your kinsmen and all that you hold dear. Bheema shall despatch you to the abode of Yama, by breaking your thighs with the mace." Some hold that the curse of this sage played a major part in encompassing the destruction of the Kauravas.

Vajrapani

VajrapGi (from Sanskrit *vajra*, "thunderbolt" or "diamond" and *pGi*, lit. "in the hand") is one of the earliest bodhisattvas of Mahayana Buddhism. He is the protector and guide of the Buddha, and rose to symbolize the Buddha's power. Vajrapani was used extensively in Buddhist iconography as one of the three protective deities surrounding the Buddha. Each of them symbolizes one of the Buddha's virtues: Manjusri (the manifestation of all the Buddhas' wisdom), Avalokitesvara (the manifestation of all the Buddhas' compassion) and Vajrapani (the manifestation of all the Buddhas' power).

Names

In Sanskrit, Vajrapani is also known as *vajra-sattva* and, in

Tibetan, as *Phyag na rdorje* (*Channa Dorje*). In Bengali he is known as "(*Bojropani*). In Mongolian *Ochirvaani* or *Bazarvaani*. In East Asia, Vajrapani is known by several names including *Jîngâng shou pusa* in Mandarin Chinese, pronounced in Japanese as *Kongo shu bosatsu*; in Korean as *Geumgang su bosal*; and in Vietnamese as *Kim cion the B.O. tat*; *Heyiluohuanyuecha* in Mandarin Chinese, pronounced in Japanese as *Wairaoneisa*, in Korean as *Hwairawonyeolcha*, and in Vietnamese as *Hoà di la hoàn duct xoa*; or *Basheluobonì* in Mandarin Chinese, pronounced in Japanese as *Bajarahaji*; in Korean as *Balsarapani*, and in Vietnamese as *Bit a la ba ne*.

The *Sutra of Golden Light* entitles him "great general of the yakshas".

Doctrine

On the popular level, Vajrapani, Holder of the Thunderbolt Scepter (symbolizing the power of compassion), is the Bodhisattva who represents the power of all the Buddhas, just as Avalokitesvara represents their great compassion, Manjushri their wisdom, and Tara their miraculous deeds. For the yogi, Vajrapani is a means of accomplishing fierce determination and symbolizes unrelenting effectiveness in the conquest of negativity. His taut posture is the active warrior pose (pratayalidha), based on an archer's stance but resembling the *en garde* position in Western fencing. His outstretched right hand brandishes a vajra and his left hand deftly holds a lasso-with which he binds demons. He wears a skull crown with his hair standing on end. His expression is wrathful and he has a third eye. Around his neck is a serpent necklace and his loin cloth is made up of the skin of a tiger, whose head can be seen on his right knee.

The Pail Canon's *Ambattha Suttanta* tells of one instance of him protecting the Buddha's honour. A young Brahman named Ambatha visited the Buddha and insulted him by saying the Shaykya clan (the enlightened one's family) were abjects who should revere the Brahmins. In return, the Buddha asked the Brahmin if his family was descended from a "Shakya slave girl". However, Ambatha further insulted the Buddha by not answering his question. When he failed to answer the question for a second time, the Buddha warned him that his head would be smashed to bits if he failed to do so a third time. Ambatha was frightened when he saw

Vajrapani manifest above the Buddha's head ready to strike the Brahmin down with his thunderbolt. He quickly confirmed the truth.

According to the *Pancavimsatisahasrika* and *Astasahasrika Prajnaparamita* any Bodhisattva on the path to Buddhahood is eligible for Vajrapani's protection, making them invincible to any attacks "by either men or ghosts".

Mantras

The Mantra *oC vajrapGi hkC pham* is associated with Vajrapani. His Seed Syllable is *hkC*.

Patron Saint of the Shaolin Monastery

In his book *The Shaolin Monastery* (2008), Prof. Meir Shahar notes Vajrapani is the patron saint of the Shaolin Monastery. A short story appearing in Zhang Zhuo's (660-741) Tang anthology shows how the deity had been venerated in the Monastery from at least the eighth century. It is an anecdotal story of how the Shaolin monk Sengchou (480-560) gained supernatural strength and fighting ability by praying to the Vajrapani and being force-fed raw meat. Shaolin abbot Zuduan (1115-1167) erected a stele in his honour during the Song Dynasty. It reads:

According to the scripture [*Lotus Sutra*], this deity (Narayana) is a manifestation of Avaokitesvara (Guanyin). If a person who compassionately nourishes all living beings employs this [deity's] charm, it will increase his body's strength (*zengzhang shen li*).

It fulfills all vows, being most efficacious.... Therefore those who study Narayana's hand-symbolism (*mudra*), those who seek his spell (*mantra*), and those who search for his image are numerous. Thus we have erected this stele to spread this transmission. – Stele re-erected (chong shang) by Shaolin's abbot Zuduan.

Instead of being considered a stand alone deity, Shaolin believes Vajrapani to be an emanation of the Bodhisattva Guanyin. The Chinese scholar A'De noted this was because the *Lotus Sutra* says Guanyin takes on the visage of whatever being that would best help pervade the dharma. The exact *Lotus Sutra* passage reads: "To those who can be conveyed to deliverance by the body of the spirit who grasps the *vajra* (Vajrapani) he preaches Dharma by displaying the body of the spirit who grasps the *vajra*."

He was historically worshiped as the progenitor of their famous staff method by the monks themselves. A stele erected by Shaolin abbot Wenzai in 1517 shows the deity's vajra-club had by then been changed to a Chinese staff, which originally "served as the emblem of the monk". Vajrapani's Yaksha-like Narayana form was eventually equated with one of the four staff-wielding "Kimnara Kings" from the *Lotus Sutra* in 1575. His name was thus changed from Narayana to "Kimnara King". One of the many versions of a certain tale regarding his creation of the staff method takes place during the Yuan Dynasty's Red Turban Rebellion. Bandits lay siege to the monastery, but it is saved by a lowly kitchen worker wielding a long fire poker as a makeshift staff.

He leaps into the oven and emerges as a monstrous giant big enough to stand astride both Mount Song and the imperial fort atop Mount Shaoshi (which are five miles apart). The bandits flee when they behold this staff-wielding titan. The Shaolin monks later realize that the kitchen worker was none other than the Kimnara King in disguise. Shahar notes the part of the kitchen worker might have been based on the actual life of the monk Honing (638-713). In addition, he suggests the mythical elements of the tale were based on the fictional adventures of Sun Wukong from the Chinese epic *Journey to the West*. He compares the worker's transformation in the stove with Sun's time in Laozi's crucible, their use of the staff, and the fact that Sun and his weapon can both grow to gigantic proportions.

Statues and paintings of Kimnara were commissioned in various halls throughout Shaolin in honour of his defeat of the Red Turban army. A wicker statue woven by the monks and featured in the centre of the "Kimnara Hall" was mentioned in Cheng Zongyou's seventeenth century training manual *Shaolin Staff Method*. However, a century later, it was claimed that Kimnara had himself woven the statue. It was destroyed when the monastery was set aflame by the KMT General Shi Yousan in 1928. A "rejuvenated religious cult" arose around Kimnara in the late twentieth century. Shaolin re-erected the shrine to him in 1984 and improved it in 2004.

The Buddhist monk Bodhidharma erroneously came to be known as the creator of the monastery's arts. This occurred when a Taoist with the pen name "Purple Coagulation Man of the Way" wrote the *Sinews Changing Classic* in 1624, but claimed to have discovered it. The first of two prefaces of the manual traces this qigong style's succession from Bodhidharma to the Chinese general Li Jing via "a chain of Buddhist saints and martial heroes." Scholars damn the work as a forgery because of its numerous anachronistic mistakes and the fact that popular fictional characters from Chinese literature, including the "Bushy Bearded Hero", are listed as lineage masters. In fact, the Qing scholar Ling Tingkan (1757-1809) "dismissed the manual's author as an 'ignorant village master'."

Iconography

Just as Buddhaghosa associated Vajrapani with the Hindu god Indra, his first representations in India were identified with the thunder deity. As Buddhism expanded in Central Asia, and fused with Hellenistic influences into Greco-Buddhism, the Greek hero Hercules was adopted to represent Vajrapani. He was then typically depicted as a hairy, muscular athlete, wielding a short "diamond" club. Mahayana Buddhism then further spread to China, Korea and Japan from the 6th century.

In Japan, Vajrapani is known as *Shukongôshin,* and has been the inspiration for the *Nio* (Awns, lit. Benevolent kings), the wrath-filled and muscular guardian god of the Buddha, standing today at the entrance of many Buddhist temples under the appearance of frightening wrestler-like statues.

Some suggest that the war deity Kartikeya, who bears the title Skanda is also a manifestation of Vajrapani, who bears some resemblance to Skanda because they both wield vajras as weapons and are portrayed with flaming halos. He is also connected through Vajrapani through a theory to his connection to Greco-Buddhism, as Wei Tuo's image is reminiscent of the Heracles depiction of Vajrapani.

Compassion

Compassion, or Karuna, is the other key concept of Mahayana, and is a necessity to Bodhicitta. Compassion is important in all schools of Buddhism, but is particularly emphasized in Mahayana. It is also linked to the idea that acquired merit can be transmitted to others.

The bodhisattvas are the main actors of compassion, Avalokitesvara (known in East Asia as Guan Yin) being foremost among them. Although having reached enlightenment, bodhiśattvas usually make a vow to postpone entering into nirvana until all other beings have also been saved. They devote themselves to helping others reach enlightenment. This teaching may be a "skillful means" teaching; one strives to liberate all beings only as long as one is under the delusion that there are any actual "beings" to save.

The Mahayana idea that liberation is universal also allows for one to focus less on the release of personal suffering and more on humanity's salvation, and is consequently described to be more universally compassionate and caring for the welfare of others than other traditions of Buddhism.

A comparison between the Hinayana and Mahayana Buddhist philosophy approaches, made by the 10th century Tibetan author Jé Gampopa in *The Jewel Ornament of Liberation* follows:

'Clinging to the well-being of mere peace' signifies the lower capacity [Hinayana] attitude wherein the longing to transcend suffering is focused on oneself alone. This precludes the cherishing of others and hence there is little development of altruism. [...] When loving kindness and compassion become part of one, there is so much care for other conscious beings that one could not bear to liberate oneself alone. [...] Master Manjushriikiirti has said: 'A Mahayana follower should not be without loving kindness and compassion for even a single moment', and 'It is not anger and hatred but loving kindness and compassion that vouchsafe the welfare of others'.

Skillful Means

Upaya is a term in Mahayana Buddhism which comes from the word *upa"i* and refers to something which goes or brings you up to something (i.e., a goal). It is essentially the Buddhist term for dialectics. The term is often used with *kaushalya; upaya-kaushalya* means roughly "skill in means". Upaya-kaushalya is a concept which emphasizes that practitioners may use their own specific methods or techniques in order to cease suffering and introduce others to the dharma. The implication is that even if a technique, view, etc., is not ultimately "true" in the highest sense, it may still be an *expedient* practice to perform or view to hold; i.e., it may bring the practitioner closer to true realization anyway. The exercise of skill to which it refers, the ability to adapt one's message to the audience, is of enormous importance in the Pail Canon.

Role and Function of Upaya

One consequence of this is that it is possible to endorse a form of Buddhist practice as viable while simultaneously critiquing its premises or contrasting it unfavourably to another, higher practice. In some Mahayana texts, such as the Lotus Sutra, this is used as a polemic device against prior Buddhist traditions; it is said that the Buddha gave them various upayas rather than revealing the ultimate truth, for which they were not ready.

Gregory (1999 : unpaginated) frames the hermeneutical classification of Buddhist schools (Chinese *panjiao* $RYe "doctrinal classification") as an "expedient means":

The doctrine of expedient means provided the main hermeneutical device by which Chinese Buddhists systematically ordered the Buddha's teachings in their classification schemes. It enabled them to arrange the teachings in such a way that each teaching served as an expedient measure to overcome the particular shortcoming of the teaching that preceded it while, at the same time, pointing to the teaching that was to supersede it. In this fashion a hierarchical progression of teachings could be constructed, starting with the most elementary and leading to the most profound.

The most important concept in skill in means is the use, guided by wisdom and compassion, of a specific teaching (means) geared to the particular audience taught. Edward Conze, in *A Short History Of Buddhism*, says "'Skill in means' is the ability to bring out the spiritual potentialities of different people by statements or actions which are adjusted to their needs and adapted to their capacity for comprehension."

The concept of skillfulness is prominent in Mahayana Buddhism with regards to the actions of a bodhisattva. The idea is that a bodhisattva or practitioner may use any expedient methods in order to help ease the suffering of people, introduce them to the dharma, or help them on their road to nirvana. In chapter 25 of the Lotus Sutra, the Buddha describes how the Bodhisattva Avalokitesvara changes his form to meet the needs of the student. If a monk is needed, the Bodhisattva becomes a monk for example.

This doctrine is sometimes used to explain some of the otherwise strange or unorthodox behaviour or 'crazy wisdom' engaged in by Buddhist practitioners in certain extreme cases and exemplified in the conduct of the Mahasiddha. In employing skillful means, it becomes theoretically possible that many seemingly proscribed practices, such as violence, theft, and sexuality could be seen as use of skillful means. The use of harsh violence to one's disciples has occasionally been used as a way of opening their eyes to the nature of self and suffering; an example is the story of a Zen priest who ended a conversation with a disciple by slamming shut a door on the disciple's leg, fracturing the leg and, according to the story, causing a deep insight in the disciple. There are a number of other stories of Buddhist saints and bodhisattvas taking part in fairly eccentric and unusual behaviors in the practice of skillful means. The practices and rituals of Vajrayana Buddhism are also often interpreted as a process of skillful means. They are understood to be means whereby practitioners use the very misconceptions and properties of mundane existence to help themselves reach enlightenment.

Images and Examples

Buddhist texts metaphorically explain the *upaya* concept through illustrations such as a burning house and an empty fist.

Parable of the Burning House

The *Lotus Sutra* contains a famous *upaya* story about using the expedient means of white lies to rescue children from a burning building. Note that this parable describes three *yana* "vehicles; carts" drawn by goats, deer, and oxen, which is a Mahayanist wordplay upon classifying Schools of Buddhism into Mahayana "great vehicle", Hinayana "lesser vehicle", and Vajrayana "adamantine vehicle".

Gautama Buddha elucidates *upaya* to his disciple Shariputra.

"Shariputra, suppose that in a certain town in a certain country there was a very rich man. He was far along in years and his wealth was beyond measure. He had many fields, houses and menservants. His own house was big and rambling, but it had only one gate. A great many people—a hundred, two hundred, perhaps as many as five hundred—lived in the house. The halls and rooms were old and decaying, the walls crumbling, the pillars rotten at their base, and the beams and rafters crooked and aslant. At that time a fire suddenly broke out on all sides, spreading through the rooms of the house. The sons of the rich man, ten, twenty perhaps thirty, were inside the house. When the rich man saw the huge flames leaping up on every side, he was greatly alarmed and fearful and thought to himself, I can escape to safety through the flaming gate, but my sons are inside the burning house enjoying themselves and playing games, unaware, unknowing, without alarm or fear. The fire is closing in on them, suffering and pain threaten them, yet their minds have no sense of loathing or peril and they do not think of trying to escape!

"Shariputra, this rich man thought to himself, I have strength in my body and arms. I can wrap them in a robe or place them on a bench and carry them out of the house. And then again he thought, this house has only one gate, and moreover it is narrow and small. My sons are very young, they have no understanding, and they love their games, being so engrossed in them that they are likely to be burned in the fire. I must explain to them why I am fearful and alarmed. The house is already in flames and I must get them out quickly and not let them be burned up in the fire! Having thought in this way, he followed his plan and called to all his sons, saying, 'You must come out at once!" But though the father was moved by pity and gave good words of instruction, the sons were absorbed in their games and unwilling to heed them. They had no alarm, no fright, and in the end no mind to leave the house. Moreover, they did not understand what the fire was, what the house was, what the danger was. They merely raced about this way and that in play and looked at their father without heeding him.

"At that time the rich man had this thought: the house is already in flames from this huge fire. If I and my sons do not get out at once, we are certain to be burned. I must now invent some expedient means that will make it possible for the children to escape harm. The father understood his sons and knew what various toys and curious objects each child customarily liked and what would delight them. And so he said to them, 'The kind of playthings you like are rare and hard to find. If you do not take them when you can, you will surely regret it later. For example, things like these goat-carts, deer-carts and ox-carts. They are outside the gate now where you can play with them. So you must come out of this burning house at once. Then whatever ones you want, I will give them all to you!' "At that time, when the sons heard their father telling them about these rare playthings, because such things were just what they had wanted, each felt emboldened in heart and, pushing and shoving one another, they all came wildly dashing out of the burning house. The father subsequently presents each of his sons with a large bejewelled carriage drawn by a pure white ox. When the Buddha asks Shariputra whether the father was guilty of falsehood, he answers.

"No, World-Honoured One. This rich man simply made it possible for his sons to escape the peril of fire and preserve their lives. He did not commit a falsehood. Why do I say this? Because if they were able to preserve their lives, then they had already obtained a plaything of sorts. And how much more so when, through an expedient means, they are rescued from that burning house! The Buddha explains his similes of the father representing a compassionate Tathagata who is like "a father to all the world", and the sons representing humans who are "born into the threefold world, a burning house, rotten, and old."

"Shariputra, that rich man first used three types of carriages to entice his sons, but later he gave them just the large carriage adorned with jewels, the safest, most comfortable kind of all. Despite this, that rich man was not guilty of falsehood. The Tathagata does the same, and he is without falsehood. First he preaches the three vehicles to attract and guide living beings, but later he employs just the Great Vehicle to save them. Why? The Tathagata possesses measureless wisdom, power, freedom from fear, the storehouse of the Dharma. He is capable of giving to all living beings the Dharma of the Great Vehicle. But not all of them are capable of receiving it. Shariputra, for this reason you should understand that the Buddhas employ the power of expedient means. And because they do so, they make distinctions in the one Buddha vehicle and preach it as three."

Central Tenets of Buddha-Nature Doctrine

The Buddha-nature doctrine centres on the possession by sentient beings of the supposedly innate, immaculate buddha-mind or buddha-element (*Buddha-dhatu*), which is, prior to the attainment of complete buddhahood, said to be not clearly seen and known in its full radiance.

The Buddha Nature is equated in the Mahaparinirvana Sutra with the changeless and deathless True Self of the Buddha. In the Lankavatara Sutra, however, it is said that the tathagatagarbha might be mistaken for a Self, which according to this sutra, it is not.. This Buddha-nature is described in the Mahaparinirvana

Sutra to be incorruptible, uncreated, and indestructible. It is eternal bodhi ("Awake-ness") indwelling samsara, and thus opens up the immanent possibility of Liberation from all suffering and impermanence.

No being of any kind is without the *Buddha-dhatu* (Buddha-nature). It is indicated in the Angulimaliya Sutra that if the Buddhas themselves were to try to seek for any sentient being who lacked the Buddha-nature, not one such person would be found. In fact, it is stated in that sutra that it is impossible for Buddhas not to discern the presence of the everlasting Buddha-nature in each and every being: "Even though all Buddhas themselves were to search assiduously, they would not find a Tathagatagarbha (Buddha-nature) that is not eternal, for the eternal *dhatu*, the *buddha-dhatu* (Buddha Principle, Buddha Nature), the *dhatu* adorned with infinite major and minor attributes, is present in all beings".

The eternality, unshakeability and changelessness of the Buddha-nature (often referred to as "Tathagatagarbha") is also frequently stressed in the sutras which expound this Buddha Element. The Srimala Sutra, for example, says:

"The Tathagatagarbha is not born, does not die, does not transfer, does not arise. It is beyond the sphere of the characteristics of the compounded; it is permanent, stable and changeless."

The development of the Buddha-nature doctrine is closely related to that of tathagatagarbha (Sanskrit: "Buddha-matrix"). In the *Anunatva-Apurnatva-Nirdesa*, the Buddha links the tathagatagarbha to the Dharmadhatu (ultimate, all-equal, uncreated essence of all phenomena) and to essential being, stating:

"What I call 'be-ing' (*sattva*) is just a different name for this permanent, stable, pure and unchanging refuge that is free from arising and cessation, the inconceivable pure Dharmadhatu."

This eternal refuge of the *Dharmadhatu/Buddha-dhatu* (transcendentally empty of all that is conditioned, afflicted, defective, and productive of suffering) is equated in the *Nirvana Sutra* with Buddhic Knowledge (*jnana*). Such Knowledge perceives both non-Self and the Self, Emptiness (*sunyata*) and non-Emptiness, wherein *"the Empty is the totality of* samsara *[birth-and-death] and the non-Empty is Great Nirvana."*

It is a recurrent theme of the Mahayana *Mahaparinirvana Sutra* that the Buddha-nature is indestructible and forever untarnished.

Professor Jeffrey Hopkins translates several passages from the sutra in which the Buddha speaks of this topic and defines the Buddha-nature as pure, eternal, truly real Self:

'... that which has permanence, bliss, Self, and thorough purity is called the "meaning of pure truth"'.

'Permanent is the Self; the Self is thoroughly pure. The thoroughly pure is called "bliss". Permanent, blissful, Self, and thoroughly pure is the one-gone-thus [i.e. Buddha]';

'Self means the matrix-of-one-gone-thus [i.e. the tathagatagarbha/Buddha-nature]. The existence of the buddha-nature in all sentient beings is the meaning of "Self"'.

'The buddha-nature, by its own nature, cannot be made non-existent; it is not something that becomes non-existent. Just the inherent nature called "Self" is the secret matrix-of-one-gone-thus [i.e. tathagatagarbha/Buddha-nature]; in this way that secret matrix cannot be destroyed and made non-existent by anything.' (Professor Jeffrey Hopkins, *Mountain Doctrine*, Snow Lion Publications, New York, 2006).

In explaining what it means by sentient beings' having the Buddha nature, the 'Mahaparinirvana Sutra' distinguishes three different ways of understanding the term "to have":

Good son, there are three ways of having: first, to have in the future, Secondly, to have at present, and thirdly, to have in the past. All sentient beings will have in future ages the most perfect enlightenment, i.e., the Buddha nature. All sentient beings have at present bonds of defilements, and do not now possess the thirty-two marks and eighty noble characteristics of the Buddha. All sentient beings had in past ages deeds leading to the elimination of defilements and so can now perceive the Buddha nature as their future goal. For such reasons, I always proclaim that all sentient beings have the Buddha nature.

Thus according to Heng-Ching Shih, the teaching of the universal Buddha nature does not intend to assert the existence of substantial, entity-like self endowed with excellent features of a Buddha. Rather, Buddha nature simply represents the potentiality to be realized in the future.

This type of interpretation of the Buddha-nature is not, however, universally accepted by Buddhists or scholars. Dr. Shenpen Hookham, Oxford Buddhist scholar and Tibetan lama of the Shentong tradition, writes of the Buddha-nature or True Self as something real and permanent, and already present within the being as uncompounded Enlightenment. She calls it 'the Buddha within', and comments:

'In scriptural terms, there can be no real objection to referring to Buddha, Buddhajnana [Buddha Awareness/Buddha Knowledge], Nirvana and so forth as the True Self, unless the concept of Buddha and so forth being propounded can be shown to be impermanent, suffering, compounded, or imperfect in some way... in Shentong terms, the non-self is about what is *not* the case, and the Self of the Third Dharmachakra [i.e. the Buddha-nature doctrine] is about what truly IS.' (Dr. Shenpen Hookham, *The Buddha Within*, State University f New York Press, 1991).

Buddhist scholar and chronicler, Dr. Merv Fowler, writes that the Buddha-nature really is present as an essence within each being. Fowler comments:

'The teaching that Buddha-nature is the hidden essence within all sentient beings is the main message of the *tathagatagarbha* literature, the earliest of which is the *Tathagatagarbha Sutra*. This short sutra says that all living beings are in essence identical to the Buddha regardless of their defilements or their continuing transmigration from life to life... As in the earlier traditions, there is present the idea that enlightenment, or nirvana, is not something which has to be achieved, it is something which is already there... In a way, it means that everyone is really a Buddha now.' (Merv Fowler, *Buddhism: Beliefs and Practices*, Sussex Academic Press, 1999).

Writer on Zen Buddhism, Peter Haskel, likewise indicates this idea of already and ever-present enlightenment (the Buddha-nature) within all beings. In his book, *Bankei Zen*, he shows how the Zen master, Bankei, taught that the Buddha Nature or Buddha Mind is inherent in each being from birth, is uncreated, unborn, and is of the same 'one substance' of past Buddhas and present beings, without any difference-just like the one water of the vast ocean (Peter Haskel, *Bankei Zen*, Grove Weidenfeld, New York, 1984).

In the Tibetan Book of the Dead, it is taught that at death there is an encounter with this true inner nature, sugatagarbha or Dharmata, when the veils of egocentricity tend briefly to drop away, and shining, unobstructed Awareness is disclosed to us. In line with Tibetan Nyingma doctrine, Tibetan lama, Chokyi Nyima Rinpoche, equates this radiant essence with the Buddha Nature. He writes:

"... all sentient beings already possess an enlightened essence, the sugatagarbha [i.e. the Buddha Nature]. This essence is present and permeates anyone who has mind, just as oil completely permeates any sesame seed... The moment our ego-clinging falls apart, then our innate wisdom, the luminosity of dharmata, will vividly, nakedly appear. This ground luminosity is not just empty; it is also luminous-aware."

An important Sanskrit treatise, entitled the *Ratnagotravibhaga*, on the Buddha Nature sees the Tathagatagarbha (Buddha Nature) as "Suchness" or "Thusness"-the abiding Reality of all things-in a state of tarnished concealment within the being. The idea is that the ultimate consciousness of each being is spotless and pure, but surrounded by negative tendencies which are impure. Professor Paul Williams comments on how the impurity is actually not truly part of the Buddha Nature, but merely conceals the immanent true qualities of Buddha Mind (i.e. the Buddha Nature) from manifesting openly:

"The impurities that taint the mind and entail the state of unenlightenment (*samsara*) are completely adventitious... On the other hand from the point of view of the mind's pure radiant intrinsic nature, because it *is* like this [i.e. pure and Buddhic], it is possessed of all the many qualities of a Buddha's mind. These do not need actually to be brought about but merely need to be allowed to shine forth. Because they are intrinsic to the very nature of consciousness itself they, and the very state of Buddhahood, will never cease."

Buddha-nature is completely rejected by Theravada Buddhism due to the fact that the concept comes from later Mahayana sutras which it sees as inauthentic.

Though not explicitly denied in any form of Indian Mahayana, some scholars, especially those associated with Madhyamaka, did not have an active interest in this doctrine. Nevertheless, the Buddha-nature doctrine did become a cornerstone of East Asian Buddhist and Tibetan Buddhist soteriological thought and practice. Buddha-nature remains a widespread and important doctrine in much of Far Eastern Buddhism today.

Bibliography

Adikaram, E. W.: *Early History of Buddhism in Ceylon,* D. S. Puswella, Migoda, 1946.

Agrawala, V. S.: *Shiva Mahadeva: The Great God,* Veda Academy, Varanasi, 1966.

Ahmad, Imtiaz: *State and Foreign Policy: India's Role in South Asia,* Vikas, New Delhi, 1993.

Ahmad, Jamil-ud-din: *Some Recent Speeches and Writings of Mr. Jinnah,* Lahore, Ashraf, 1952.

Aiyar, R. Krishnaswami: *Outlines of Vedaanta,* Chetana, Bombay, 1978.

Archer, W. G.: *The Kama Sutra,* Unwin Hyman, London, 1990.

Ashton, S.R. : *British Policy Towards the Indian States, 1905-1939,* London, Curzon, 1982.

Aurobindo, Sri: *Vyasa and Valmiki,* Acharya Press, Pondicherry, 1956.

Avalon, Arthur and Ellen: *Hymns to the Goddess,* Ganesh and Co., Madras, 1964.

Aziz, Ashraf: *Light of the Universe: Essays on Hindustani Film Music,* Three Essays Collective, New Delhi, 2003.

Bagchi, P. C.: *Studies in Dharmashastra,* University of Calcutta Press, Calcutta, 1939.

Bahadur, K.P.: *The Wisdom of Vedaanta,* Sterling Publishers Private Limited, New Delhi, 1996.

Banerjea, J. N.: *Pauranic and Vedanta Religion,* University of Calcutta, Calcutta, 1996.

Bankimchandra, C.: *Essentials of Dharma,* Sanskrit Book Depot, Calcutta 1979.

Basu, Manoranjan: *Dharmashastra: A General Study,* Shrimati Mira Basu, Calcutta, 1976.

Beaumont, Roger : *Sword of the Raj: The British Army in India, 1747-1947*, Indianapolis, Bobbs-Merrill, 1977.

Benjamin, Joseph : *Scheduled Castes in Indian Politics and Society*, New Delhi, Ess Ess Publications, 1989.

Bhattacharyya, B.: *Nispannayogavali of Mahapandita Abhyakara Gupta*, Oriental Institute, Baroda, 1949.

Borchert, Bruno: *Mysticism: Its History and Challenge*, Samuel Wiser, York Beach, 1994.

Bose, D. N.: *Dharmashastra: Their Philosophy and Occult Secrets*, Kali Press, Calcutta, 1965.

Bowle, John: *The Imperial Achievement: The Rise and Transformation of the British Empire*, Little, Brown, 1974.

Brockington, J. L.: *Righteous Rama: The Evolution of an Epic*, Oxford, London, 1984.

Bromley, D.: *Krishna Consciousness in the West*, Bucknell University Press, Lewisburg, 1989.

Brooks, E.: *The Original Analects: Sayings of Confucius and His Successors*. Columbia University Press, New York, 1988.

Bruhn, Klaus: *The Jina-lmages of Deogarh*, MacMillan, Leiden, 1969.

Burke, Mary Louise: *Swami Vivekananda in America: New Discoveries*, Advaita Ashrama, Calcutta, 1966.

Chaudhary, M.: *Partition and the Curse of Rehabilitation*, Calcutta, Bengal Rehabilitation Organization, 1964.

Chaudhuri, Nirad: *Thy Hand, Great Anarch! India: 1921-1952*, London, Chatto & Windus, 1987.

Coomeraswamy, Ananda K.: *Buddha and the Gospel of Buddhism*, MacMillan, London, 1928.

Crawford, Cromwell S.: *Ram Mohan Roy: His Era and Ethics*, Acharya Press, New Delhi, 1984.

Dalton, Dennis : *Gandhi's Power : Nonviolence in Action*, New Delhi, OUP, 2001.

Danielou, Alain: *The Complete Kama Sutra*, Park Street Press, Rochester, 2000.

Dasgupta, Shahana: *Rani Lakshmibai: The Indian Heroine*, Rupa & Company, Calcutta, 2002.

Datta, V.N.: *Sati: Widow Burning in India*, Manohar, New Delhi, 1990.

David, M. D.: *John Wilson and his Institutions*, Mumbai, 1957.

De Bary: *Self and Society in Ming Thought*, Columbia University Press, New York, 1970.

De, Sushil Kumar: *Ancient Indian Erotics and Erotic Literature*, Firma K. L. Mukhopadhyay, Calcutta, 1959.

Deak, Istvan: *The Lawful Revolution: Louis Kossuth and the Hungarians 1848-1849*, Columbia University Press, 1979.

Dhar, Niranjan: *Vedanta and Bengal Renaissance*, Minerva Associates, Calcutta, 1977.

Dikshit, D.P. *Political History of the Chalukyas of Badami*. New Delhi: Abhinav, 1980.

Donat, K.: *Meditate the Tantric Yoga Way*, George Allen and Unwin, London, 1973.

Doniger, W.: *The Rig Veda: An Anthology*, Penguin, New York, 1981.

Duboi, Abbe: *Hindu Manners, Customs and Ceremonies*, Fifth Indian Impression, CUP, 1985.

Dwivedi, M.: *The Principal Upanishads*, Adyar Library, Madras, 1931.

Eaton, Richard M.: *Sufis of Bijapur, 1300-1700: Social Roles of Sufis in Medieval India*, Princeton University Press, Princeton, 1978.

Edwardes, Michael: *Battles of the Indian Mutiny*, London; B. T. Batsford Ltd., 1963.

Erickson, Erik H.: *Gandhi's Truth: On the Origins of Militant Nonviolence*, Norton, New York, 1970.

Farquhar, J.N.: *Modern Religious Movements in India*, Munshiram, New Delhi, 1967.

Fay, Peter Ward: *The Opium War, 1840-42*, University of North Carolina Press, 1975.

Fisher, Michael H.: *The Politics of British Annexation of India - 1757-1857*, Oxford, 1996.

Frauwallner, E..: *History of Indian Philosophy*, Motilal, Delhi, 1973.

Gambhirananda, S.: *Brahma Sutra Shamkar Bhasya*, Adavita Ashrama, Calcutta, 1977.

Gambhirananda, Swami: *Brahma Sutra Shamkar Bhasya*, Adavita Ashrama, Calcutta, 1977.

Gandhi, M. K.: *The Story of My Experiment With Trust*, Washington, Public Affairs Press, 1948.

Garbe, R.: *The Philosophy of Ancient India*, Chicago University Press, Chicago, 1899.

Goradia, Nayana: *Lord Curzon: The Last of the British Moghuls*, New Delhi, Oxford University Press, 1993.

Goudriaan, T.: *Ritual and Speculation in Early Tantrism*, State University of New York Press, New York, 1992.

Gough, A.E.: *The Philosophy of the Upanisads and Ancient Indian Metaphysics*, MacMillan, London, 1882.

Grant, G. P.: *Philosophy in the Mass Age*, Copp Clark, Toronto, 1959.

Grisenold, H.D.: *Insights into Modern Hinduism*, Oxford, New York, 1934.

Growse, F. S.: *The Ramayana of Tulasidasa*, Motilal Banarsidass, Delhi, 1995.

Gurumurthy, S. : *Hindu Heritage, Assimilative, Not Divisive*, Vigil, Madras 1993.

Haich, E.: *Sexual Energy and Yoga*, Aurora Press, New York, 1982.

Hasan, Murhirul: *Legacy of a Divided Nation: India's Muslims Since Independence*, New Delhi, Oxford, 1997.

Hasan, Mushirul: *India's Partition: Process, Strategy and Mobilization*, New Delhi, Oxford UP, 1993.

Heifetz, Hank: *The Origin of the Young God: Kalidasa's Kumarasambhava*, University of California Press, Berkeley, 1985.

Heimann, Betty: *Facets of Indian Thought*, Geroge Allen & Unwin, London, 1964.

Heinsath, Charles: *Indian Nationalism and Hindu Social Reform*, Princeton University Press, Princeton, 1964.

Heschel, J.: *God in Search of Man: A Philosophy of Judaism*, Noonday Press, New York, 1997.

Hirschman, Edwin: *White Mutiny: The Ilbert Bill Crisis in India and the Genesis of the Indian National Congress*, New Delhi, Heritage, 1980.

Hixon, L.: *Mother of the Universe: Visions of the Goddess, Tantric Hymns of Enlightenment*, Quest Books, Wheaton, 1994.

Hopkins, J.: *Kalachakra Tantra Rite of Initiation*, Wisdom Publications, Boston, 1982.

Hopkirk, Peter: *The Great Game: The Struggle for Empire in Central Asia*, Kodansha, 1992.

Hume, R.E.: *The Thirteen Principle Upanishads*, Oxford University Press, London, 1971.

Hutchins, Francis: *Spontaneous Revolution: The Quit India Movement*, New Delhi, Manohar, 1971.

Irene, S.: *Vedic Heritage Teaching Program*. Arsha Vidya Gurukulam, Coimbatore, 1994.

Iyar, K.: *Vedanta: The Science of Reality*, Ganesh and Co., Mardas, 1930.

Iyengar, B.K.S.: *Light on the Yoga Sutras of Patanjali*, Aquarian Press, London 1993.

Jacob, K.: *Religion and Ethics in Advaita*, C.M.S. Press, Kottayam, 1982.

Jafar, Malik Muhammad: *Jinnah as a Parliamentarian*, Lahore, Afzar Publications, 1977.

Jain, Kailash Chand, *Lord Mahavira and His Times*, Saraswati Press, Delhi, 1974.

James, Lawrence: *The Rise and Fall of the British Empire*, St. Martin's, 1997.

James, Robert Rhodes: *The British Revolution, 1880-1939*, New York, Knopf, 1976.

Jean, M.: *Tantrik Yoga*, The Aquarian Press, Wellingborough, 1970.

John, B.: *Mantras: Sacred Words of Power*, George Allen and Unwin, London, 1977.

John, Elsner: *Pilgrimage: Past and Present in the World Religions*, Harvard University Press, Cambridge, 1995.

John, K.: *The Origin and Development of the State Cult of Confucius*, Paragon Book, New York, 1966.

Karmarkar, D.: *Sankara's Advaita*, Karnatak University, Dharwar, 1976.

Kaushik, Asha : *Globalization, Democracy and Culture : Situating Gandhian Alternatives*, Jaipur, Pointer, 2002.

Kaviraj, G.: *Aspects of Indian Thought*, University of Burdwan, Calcutta, 1966.

Kavlekar, K.K. : *Non-Brahmin Movement in Southern India, 1873-1949*, Kolhapur, Shivaji University, 19790

Keith, A.B. : *Rigveda Brahmanas*, Harvard University Press, Cambridge, 1920.

Keith, Arthur Berriedale: *The Religion and Philosophy of the Veda and Upanishads*, MacMillan, Delhi, 1925.

Kishwar, Madhu : *Religion at the Service of Nationalism, and Other Essays*, OUP, Delhi, 1998.

Klaus, K.: *A Survey of Hinduism*, State University of New York Press, Albany, 1989.

Knipe, M.: *Hinduism: Experiments in the Sacred*, Harper, San Francisco, 1991.

Knott, K.: *Hinduism, A Very Short Introduction*, Oxford University Press, New York, 1998.

Kosambi, D. D. : *The Culture and Civilisation of Ancient India in Historical Outline*, London, Routledge and Kegan Paul, 1956.

Kottackal, Jacob: *Religion and Ethics in Advaita*, C.M.S. Press, Kottayam, 1982.

Kuiper, F.B.J. : *Aryans in the Rigveda*, Rodopi, Amsterdam, 1991.

Kuppuswamy, Sastri S.: *Compromises in the History of Advaitic Thought*, Kalyani Press, Madras, 1940.

Louis, Fischer: *Essential Gandhi: An Anthology of His Writings*, Vintage, New York, 1983.

Low, D. A. and Brasted, Howard: *Freedom, Trauma, Continuities: Northern India and Independence*, New Delhi, Sage Publications, 1998.

Maheshwari, Shriram: *Rural Development in India: A Public Policy Approach*, New Delhi, Sage, 1995.

Makhan, L.: *The Ramayana of Valmiki*, Munshiram Manoharlal, New Delhi, 1978.

Mathew, Arnold: *Culture and Anarchy*, The University Press, Cambridge, 1935.

Mayer, A. : *Caste in an Indian Village: Change and Continuity 1954-1992*, Delhi, OUP, 1996.

Mazumder, Sukhendu : *Politico-Economic Ideas of Mahatma Gandhi: Their Relevance in the Present Day*, New Delhi, Concept Pub., 2004.

Mearns, David J.: *Shiva's Other Children: Religion and Social Identity amongst Overseas Indians*, Sage, Walnut Creek, 1995.

Mearns, J.: *Shiva's Other Children: Religion and Social Identity amongst Overseas Indians*, Sage, Walnut Creek, 1995.

Mehra, Parshotam: *A Dictionary of Modern Indian History, 1707-1947*, New Delhi, Oxford University Press, 1985.

Metcalf, Thomas R.: *The Aftermath of the Revolt: India, 1857-1870*, Princeton, Princeton University, 1964.

Mohan, K.: *The Mahabharata*, Munshiram Manoharlal, Delhi 1997.

Mookerjee, Ajit: *Kali The Feminine Force*, Thames and Hudson, London, 1988.

Mookerji, Satkari: *Modern Polity and Vedanta*, Sanskrit College, Calcutta, 1972.

Moon, Penderel: *The British Conquest and Dominion of India*, London, Duckworth, 1989.

Morris-Jones, W.H.: *The Government and Politics of India*, London, Hutchinson, 1971.

Nanda, B. R. : *Gandhi and His Critics*, Oxford University Press, Delhi, 1993.

Neale, Walter C.: *Economic Change in Rural India: Land Tenure and Reform in the United Provinces, 1800-1955*, New Haven, 1962.

Nevile, P.: *Lahore: A Sentimental Journey*, New Delhi, Penguin, 1993.

Oddie, G.A. : *Hindu and Christian in South-East India*, London, Curzon Press, 1991.

Pathak, Dr S.P.: *Jhansi during the British Rule*, Ramanand Vidya Bhawan, Delhi, 1987.

Preston, Diana: *The Boxer Rebellion*, Berkley Books, 2000.

Raimundo Panikkar: *The Vedic Experience: Mantramanjari*, Longman Todd, London, 1977.

Raja, C. Kunhan : *The Taittiriya Sarvanukramani of Yaska*, Madras, 1931.

Ramamurti, A.: *Advaitic Mysticism of Sankara*, Visvabharati, Santiniketan, 1974.

Ranajit Guha: *A Construction of Humanism in Colonial India*, CASA, Amsterdam, 1993.

Renou, Louis: *The Nature of Dharmashastra*, Walker and Co., New York, 1997.

Robson, Brian: *Sir Hugh Rose and the Central India Campaign*, Sutton Publishing Ltd for the Army Records Society, UK, 2000.

Satyapal Verma: *Role of Reason in Sankara Vedanta*, Parimal Publication, Delhi, 1992.

Savarkar, Vinayak Damodar : *The Indian War of Independence* 1857 Rajdhani Granthagar, Delhi, 1988.

Scheftelowitz, Isidor : *Die Kasmirische Rezension von Katyayanas Sarvanukramani,* Zeitschrift fur Indologie und Iranistik, 1922.

Shukla, D. N.: *Vastu-Shastra,* Motilal Banarsidass, Delhi, 1966.

Singh, Birendra Kumar: *Early Chalukyas of Vatapi, circa A.D. 500 to 757,* Delhi, Eastern Book Linkers, 1991.

Smith, Col. J. T. : *Silver and the India Exchanges,* Effingham Wilson, London, 1876.

Strauss, L.: *Political Philosophy,* The Bobbs Merrill Co., New York, 1975.

Swami Vishnu Tirtha: *Devatma Shakti,* Swami Shivom Tirth, Rishikesh, 1962.

Talageri, Shrikant : *Aryan Invasion Theory and Indian Nationalism,* Voice of India, Delhi, 1993.

Tejomayananda, Swami: *Hindu Culture: An Introduction,* Chinmaya Publications, Piercy, 1993.

Thapar, Romila : *Ashoka and the Decline of the Mauryas,* London, Oxford University Press, 1961.

Thompson, Edward: *The Making of the Indian Princes,* Oxford University Press, London, 1943.

Trautmann, Thomas R.: *Kautilya and the Arthasastra: A Statistical Study,* Leiden, Brill, 1971.

Trimingham, J.: *Sufi Orders in Islam,* Oxford University Press, New York, 1998.

Utpat, V.N.: *Riddles of Buddha and Ambedkar,* Itihas Patrika Prakashan, Thane 1988.

Vable, D.: *The Arya Samaj. Hindu without Hinduism.* Vikas Publ., Delhi, 1983.

Vedalankar, Pandit Nardev : *Basic Teachings of Hinduism,* Veda Niketan, Durban, 1978.

Visvantha, K.: *Essentials of Hinduism,* Narosa Pub. House, New Delhi, 1989.

Wendy Doniger: *Siva: The Erotic Ascetic,* Oxford University Press, Delhi, 1998.

Zaidi, A. Moin: *Evolution of Muslim political Thought in India,* New Delhi: S. Chand, 1975-79

Index

N

O

P

Q

R

S

T

U

V

Y

□□□